To David

Happy Christmas
2006

IN WHERE IT HURTS
BRYAN GUNN
MY AUTOBIOGRAPHY

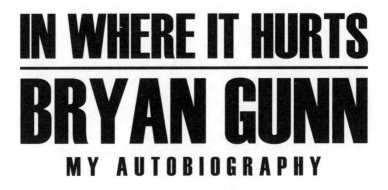

IN WHERE IT HURTS
BRYAN GUNN

MY AUTOBIOGRAPHY

WITH KEVIN PIPER
FOREWORD BY SIR ALEX FERGUSON

VSP

Vision Sports Publishing
2 Coombe Gardens,
London, SW20 0QU

www.visionsp.co.uk

This First Edition Published by
Vision Sports Publishing in 2006

Typeset by Palimpsest Book Production Limited,
Grangemouth, Stirlingshire
Printed and bound by Cromwell Press Ltd,
Trowbridge, Wiltshire

A CIP catalogue record for this book is
available from the British Library

ISBN 1–905326–00-9

Editor: Karen Buchanan
Cover design: Neal Cobourne
Proofreader: Rachel Lockhart
Photography: Roger Harris

Contents

Susan Ruth, Melissa Jayne and
Angus Fraser James Gunn . . . mine forever.

Francesca Ruth . . . we all miss you and treasure our memories.

Acknowledgements

BRYAN GUNN

I would like to thank everyone who has played a part in the last 42 years of my life. I have been so lucky to have met so many great, inspirational people in my lifetime that if I tried to put everyone down in writing I'm sure to miss out somebody really important. But here goes with the special ones:

- My dad – James, Jimmy, The Gunner – I miss him. He was a massive man who was my rock until 2002 when he sadly passed away. My mum, Jessie, made sure I wanted for nothing as a young person – boots, gloves and especially for washing my kit and waking me up in the mornings. My brother Alan for his competitive nature in everything as a youngster you'd expect from a brother.
- Ian 'Max' and Richard 'Dickie' Macleod – our good friends and neighbours and footballing buddies.
- Susan's dad John – we miss him. Susan's mum Ruth – I never met her but she must have been a great lady to bring Susan into the world. Susan's brother John – we miss him too. Allan, Kath and the rest of the Winward clan, all great people.

Acknowledgements

- Jock Mackay, Doug Lavin and Mike Morris for their support and help in preparing me for 'professional' football. Sadly Jock and Doug are no longer with us.
- Alex Ferguson, Archie Knox, Teddy Scott and Jim Leighton at Aberdeen for teaching me the skills and giving me the mentality to succeed in this great game.
- Ken Brown (for taking a big gamble on a young Scottish keeper), Dave Stringer, Mike Walker, John Deehan, Gary Megson and Martin O'Neill for all having faith in my ability at Norwich City – 477 times.
- Alex McLeish for his belief in me, my experience, my skills and for taking me to Hibs.
- Andy Roxburgh and Craig Brown for making my dreams come true by picking me for Scotland. Only six times though . . .
- David Hodgson – if it wasn't for you I would never had been through half of this . . .
- Robert and Jayne Fleck – thanks . . .
- My Testimonial Committee for all their hard work in 1996: Keith Colman, Gill Perks, Bev Spratt, Phil Grice, Gordon Irving, John Trafford, Henry Watt, Dave Chisnell, Trevor Burton, Dean Adams, John Garbutt and Susan.
- The Bryan Gunn Appeal – Keith Colman, Gill Perks, Becky Colman and Barbara Bryant. Also to everyone who has supported the Bryan Gunn appeal but if you want to support it now, visit – www.charitygiving.co.uk.
- The original Fandabidozi Club – all great friends: Henry, Tania, Roger, Rachel, Matthew, Vicki, John, Heidi, Darrell, Simone, Andy, Lou, Mehmet, Kathy, Jane and of course Robbie Williams. And the new members Nicky and Claire Louise . . .
- The Author – Kevin Piper – great job, great mate, great time doing this great, great book . . .
- The Piper family – Carolyn, Jack and Alice, you can have him back now!
- Vision Sports Publishing – Jim, Toby and Karen – 'bloody' good job!!
- All at Norwich City FC – especially Will, Peter and Joe . . . great proof readers . . . and Mike Davage our club historian.

- Roger Harris – what a photographer . . . 'Got it!'
- The Family – Susan (top artist, wife and mum), Melissa (top daughter and whatever you want to be) and Angus (top son and top (Scottish) goalkeeper or whatever you want to be).

Thanks for letting me do this. Love you all,
Bryan (Big Ben, Gunny, The Sheriff and The Ambassador).

KEVIN PIPER
Having recently declared my intention to write a book, learn the piano and become fluent in a foreign language, I guess it's a case of one down, two to go. For that I have to thank the living legend that is Mr Bryan Gunn. How could I possibly give Kevin Keelan the nod over you, mate? Not any more – you are Norwich City's all-time greatest number one! Thanks to Sir Alex Ferguson for a thoroughly entertaining chat about the big man's early days (you're lucky we didn't include everything he told me, Gunny). Susan, you were brilliant. Melissa and Angus – get to bed! Jim and Toby, your patience is much appreciated. Karen, you thoroughly deserve that b***** drink. Thanks also to Jerry Goss, Graham Dunbar, and to the *Eastern Daily Press* library. Last, but by no means least, massive thanks, love and appreciation to Carolyn, Jack and Alice – remember me? Now, where's that piano . . .

Foreword

By Sir Alex Ferguson

I first met Bryan when I signed him as a 14-year-old schoolboy at Aberdeen. He was a bit of a country boy in a way, coming down from the far north of Scotland and moving to the big city, but it didn't intimidate him at all. The first thing that hit me was his personality. It was abundantly clear from the beginning that he was a warm, outgoing and endearing character. You just couldn't help but like him.

We had a few scrapes in those early days at Pittodrie and I had to give him and some of his young team-mates, like Neale Cooper, John Hewitt and Eric Black, a rocket every now and then. But the next thing you knew Bryan, or Big Ben as we called him at Aberdeen, was walking through the door with a big smile on his face and he'd immediately make you laugh.

He became a brilliant babysitter for our sons, Mark, Darren and Jason, but only because my wife Cathy used to feed him so well! He'd come round and scoff three big platefuls of soup, a large dinner and then the lads' sandwiches. Talk about an appetite! He was great with the kids and they loved it when he took them over to a nearby pitch for a kickabout.

Bryan was great in training. He could strike a ball as well as anyone, so well in fact that I once played him at centre-forward in a reserve team match at Pittodrie. He scored a brilliant goal and set off on a complete lap of honour, running round the touchline slapping people's hands. It was a magnificent moment.

I'll never forget the night we won the Cup Winners' Cup with Aberdeen in Gothenburg. When the final whistle went, Big Ben leapt off the bench and flattened me as he ran onto the pitch to celebrate with the rest of the boys. I lay there in a puddle on the ground and he didn't even look round to see if I was all right!

Bryan was a tremendous young keeper, but Jim Leighton was the number one at Aberdeen. It must have been frustrating, but he never let it get him down. He was always totally professional and I could never fault his discipline, effort or commitment.

I tried hard to get him a decent move and was delighted when he signed for Norwich City. He went on to have a wonderful career and played a big part in a very successful period at Norwich, where he was a tremendous servant. I had no hesitation in taking Manchester United to Carrow Road for his testimonial. He thoroughly deserved it.

He sent me a Christmas card a couple of years ago signed 'The Sheriff' after he'd become Sheriff of Norwich. It didn't surprise me. In fact, I reckon he'd be disappointed if they didn't make him king one day! It was an inspired move to make him Ambassador at Norwich City. He's perfectly suited to the role; always cheerful and great with people. He'll do a brilliant job.

It's been a pleasure to work with Bryan as a player, to be part of his life, and to know him and Susan. We were honoured to be guests at their wedding and have valued their friendship ever since. They faced a massive challenge with the illness of their daughter Francesca. It says a lot about them and their relationship that they stayed strong and managed to come through it together.

It's a privilege to be asked to write the foreword to this book. I'm sure it will be a great read.

I wish Bryan, Susan, and his family every success.

Sir Alex Ferguson
Old Trafford, May 2006

Introduction

Earlier this year, as I was sitting at my desk in the sales and sponsorship department at Carrow Road, the phone rang. It was a television producer, inviting me to take part in ITV's charity football event *Soccer Aid*.

He explained the format: Robbie Williams was leading a star-studded England XI against a Rest of the World celebrity team led by Gordon Ramsay in a special match at Old Trafford. As part of the build-up there would be warm-up games for both teams. Would I like to play in a Scottish XI to take on the Rest of the World team at Fulham's Craven Cottage?

A few weeks later, I walked into the hotel foyer on the night before the game. One of the first people I spotted was Robbie. He recognised me immediately: "Hey, it's Bryan Gunn!" he said, coming over and giving me a big hug. "Good to see you again, Big Man."

It's a long time since we last met, but Robbie hadn't forgotten his regular trips to Norfolk where he came up to get away from the spotlight, all the fuss and attention, during his time with Take That. We had some laughs back then.

Robbie wasn't the only familiar face I bumped into at *Soccer Aid*, although it's probably stretching a point to say Lothar Matthaus was

Introduction

ever likely to be a bosom buddy. I saw him when I went to get my shirt signed in the Rest of the World dressing room after the game:

"You probably don't remember me," I said, "but we played against each other a long time ago. We had a big argument. Remember?" He didn't.

Great laughs with Robbie Williams, big rows with Lotthar Matthaus; just a couple of the many fond memories that have cropped up as I've spent the past year or so reflecting on my life for the purposes of this, my autobiography.

Much of my story is about football, of course. Hardly surprising; I was incredibly lucky to play more than 500 games as a professional, the vast majority in one of the best leagues in the world. I also fulfilled my childhood dream by being picked to play for my country, Scotland, and to go to a World Cup.

It hasn't all been fun and games, though. Far from it. There have been tough times, too, from career-threatening injuries to crushing defeats, late-night punch-ups and dressing room bust-ups.

None of that comes remotely close to the moment we discovered our daughter Francesca had been diagnosed with leukaemia. Susan and I were sure she would beat the disease but despite her brave battle we lost her when she was only two years old.

I'm proud to say Francesca's legacy lives on, through the *Bryan Gunn Leukaemia Appeal*. It began as a modest attempt to raise a few pounds over a couple of weeks. Thirteen years on it's still going strong, generating hundreds of thousands in the fight against childhood leukaemia.

With a pound from the sale of each copy this book going towards the appeal, we're hoping it won't be long before we're approaching the million pound mark. What we really yearn for, though, is to wipe out the disease once and for all.

Part of the reason I've decided to write my life story is to share some of the weird and wonderful experiences that come with being a professional footballer. Equally, it's a way of paying tribute to the many, many, people who've rallied to our cause after we lost Francesca. The response, from friends, family and total strangers alike, was – and continues to be – quite extraordinary.

On behalf of Susan, Melissa and Angus, I thank you all. Now, let's get in where it hurts . . .

Bryan Gunn

CHAPTER ONE

Son of a Gunn

I f I had been born much further north I might have ended up playing international football for the Faroe Islands. As it happened, I came into the world via Britain's most northerly mainland town, Thurso, a few miles from John O'Groats. It's more like a big village than a town, where everyone knows everyone else. The setting is stunning – the beach is a huge sweep of golden sand, facing the Pentland Firth and on a clear day you can see across the Firth to the Orkney Islands, a short ferry hop away. The Firth is the meeting point for seven currents and the sea is tumultuous, scything out stacks and craggy cliffs, while the wind decimates any flowers brave enough to try growing in the peaty soil. The very north of Scotland is a ruggedly beautiful wilderness and Thurso sits at the very edge of it, aloof from the rest of the British Isles.

Winters are tough but in summer it never gets properly dark, so we've probably got more in common with the Scandinavians. In fact I'm almost certainly descended from the Vikings. The town was the major gateway to the British mainland for the Vikings and became a key port for international trade between Scandinavia and the UK. Translated from Norse, Thurso means 'River of the God Thor' so a few hundred years ago my ancestors were probably the Gunnersonns rather than simply Gunns. Somewhere along the line we lost the 'sonn' part of the name after my distant relatives sailed over in their longships from Scandinavia to take up residence in ye olde Anglo-Saxon Britain. Having had such fearsome forefathers might explain the flowing blond hair that was my trademark in my younger days, and why I took up the crazy occupation of goalkeeping and spent 19 years earning a living by sticking my head in amongst the flying boots and elbows.

In fact, it's something of a miracle that I'm here at all. A few hundred years ago, the good old Gunns (clan motto 'Either at Peace or War') didn't exactly hit it off with the neighbours, especially the Sinclairs. The two clans were often at war, with things reaching a bloody head in 1585 when the Sinclairs launched a fierce attack against the Gunns. Legend has it my long-lost cousins were eventually defeated – and we've been bad losers ever since.

None of this would have been particularly significant, except for the fact that, in 1957, shortly after returning from two years' National Service as a tank driver with the Royal Artillery in Germany, my dad, James William Donald Gunn, met a young girl by the name of Jessie. She was a lovely lass, for sure, but her surname was . . . Sinclair! Family history wasn't on our side then, and from what Dad told me about his courting days he wasn't exactly the 'chosen one' for Jessie. It's fair to say there were one or two family barriers to break down before the in-laws finally accepted him. Thankfully, James and Jessie managed to put almost 500 years of unrest behind them and settle down. Well done, 'Jimmy' Gunn, as everyone used to call him, for breaking the mould.

At the time of their marriage on 21st October 1960 Dad was working as a long-distance lorry driver. Mum worked in the canteen at the Dounreay nuclear reprocessing plant, just a few miles up the road from Thurso. She was only there for a few months until I decided to come along.

I was born in Dunbar Hospital on Sunday 22nd December 1963. I reckon the Four Seasons' pop record was written in my honour! 'Oh What a Night' indeed.

A couple of years later my little brother Alan joined the clan. By now the four of us were living in a big farmhouse at Aimster, not far from Thurso, surrounded by fields full of cows and sheep. There was a long straight drive up to the house, with dykes on either side and old slate walls to keep the cows in. You could see the house from maybe a mile away.

Although I was only a toddler, I occasionally helped out by milking the cows, or at least trying to. The farmhands, all guys in their teens and early twenties, were like uncles to me. I would often grab a ball and pester them to play football with me. Sometimes we'd even use a turnip if we couldn't find a ball!

Maybe the seeds of wanting to be a goalkeeper were sown during those early kickabouts. I was only four and loved to dive on the ball when it came my way. I would do anything to get my hands on it just to make sure I got a kick. Maybe it was just the goalkeeper gene: when I first kicked the ball at my son Angus when he was a toddler his instinct was exactly the same – now he's a promising keeper with the Norwich City Academy.

I never worried about getting hurt. If I got hit with a hard shot, I'd just bounce up and ask for more. I used to love diving around a wet, muddy field getting filthy, the muddier the better. Mind you, being on a farm meant I often landed in a cowpat, with an almighty splat. I guess all this might explain why I grew much quicker than most other children my age: it must have been the fertilizer!

The weather can be pretty mean up in Thurso, but I never felt the cold (or the rain, or the hail, the snow, the sleet or even the bruises); I'd just enjoy a nice hot bath afterwards. With a little help from the fertilizer, I had inherited my mum and dad's tall, thin physique, and with my love of diving around in the mud in all weathers, I guess I was already marked out as a potential goalkeeper.

We left Thurso when I was about four and a half. My dad's lorry driving job had been taking him away from home two or three times a week, so he decided it was time for a change. We moved south to Invergordon, a small town in the mouth of the Cromarty Firth about 20 miles north of Inverness. Dad got a job at Taylor Woodrow helping to build a new aluminium smelter and we lived in a caravan for a year until our names came to the top of the council-house list.

You can do the journey from Invergordon to Thurso in about an hour and half these days, but back then it would take anything up to seven unbelievably tedious hours, depending on the severity of the blizzard. Every Hogmanay, at around 5pm, Dad would announce, "Right, that's it, we're off to Thurso to see Nana and the family." Incredibly, he always ensured we made it to his old house in time. If we arrived before midnight we would wait, freezing, in the car until entering the house just as the clock struck 12 to surprise Nana, although I think the 'surprise' wore off after the first few years.

Once we were inside it was always worth the drive. All my aunts, uncles and cousins would be there. There were loads of them. Jimmy Gunn had two sisters and five brothers. It was a similar story with the Sinclairs, only Mum was one of seven, with two brothers and four sisters. I absolutely loved those visits. It was great to see my cousins again, not least because it meant there were more people to play football with.

My dad's father, Grandad 'Ga-Ga', as we called him, always went crazy at us if the ball went onto his prized tatties. He would sit indoors near the front window keeping a watchful eye on us, and if the ball strayed onto his potato patch he would storm out of the house shouting: "Get off my f***ing tatties!", and give you a good kick up the backside if he caught you. I was the oldest of all the cousins, so I bravely used to make one of the others get the ball back, particularly my brother Alan.

We all adored Ga-Ga. I loved going up to see him, even though he scared the life out of us sometimes. His dog was like a mini version of him, a little Scottish terrier called Whisky that would bite your fingers when you went near it.

Grandad worked at Dounreay and died of a heart attack the day after he retired. For a few days before the funeral his body was laid out in the house, as is the tradition in Scotland. On the morning of the funeral my auntie asked me, "Do you want to go and see Ga-Ga?" I was only 12 and didn't really understand what being dead meant. I went into the next room fully expecting to see Ga-Ga sitting in his armchair. What I saw was him lying in a coffin, all pale and cold. It was horrible. I burst into tears and ran out of the room. It was a huge shock – although seeing him in a suit for the first time was pretty strange too!

Grandad hadn't been much of a sportsman but my dad was. He

played on the right wing for Invergordon Football Club in the North Reserve League, but was more of an athlete than a footballer. We often went to watch him competing in the various highland games in different towns, where he was always winning medals, mainly in events like sprinting, high jump and pole vault. The games were great fun and very much a community affair. There was Highland dancing, tossing the caber, tossing the hay bale over a high bar, sheep dog trials and all sorts.

I remember one year, Dad was about 36 and had given up competing, but the night before the Halkirk Highland Games, near Thurso, he suddenly decided he wanted to have a go again so he dug out his old spikes and off we all went. The old boy only ended up bringing home a winner's trophy for best overall athlete. He never did any training for these events, and he'd stopped competing a couple of years before, but he still scored more points in cycling, sprinting, pole-vaulting and the high and long jumps than anyone else. Incredible.

I enjoyed the games, but my sporting interests definitely lay elsewhere. If Dad was hoping I would uphold up the family tradition he didn't show it and I've never tossed a caber in my life. By now I was football crazy, playing at home, at school, in the street – wherever and whenever I could.

My love of diving around in the mud and covering myself from head to toe in filth didn't go down very well with Mum, however. Eventually she became so fed up with having to clean my clothes every day that she insisted I put a pair of shorts on under my trousers before I went off to school. I'd take my trousers off whenever I played football and dive around in my shorts, then put my them back on over my muddy legs before going back in for lessons. As soon as I got home Mum ordered me straight into the bath, but at least she didn't have to scrub my trousers clean every day.

The only problem for me and my mates was where to play after school as there wasn't a proper pitch near where we lived, so we had to improvise. Sometimes we would use the gable end of a house, until the residents got fed up with the thud, thud, thudding of the ball against the wall and came out to tell us to move on. But the town was developing quickly and there always seemed to be a building site on the go, so we'd often 'borrow' a couple of bits of wood, get a hammer and some nails and bang our own makeshift goalposts together. They didn't tend to stay in one piece for long though, especially if someone hit a particularly fierce shot against the woodwork. I was always worried I was going to get knocked out by a falling crossbar.

If all else failed there was always the 'danger box', the trusty old electricity substation – one of those huge power units you see on housing estates. Never mind the 'Danger, High Voltage' signs, the wall around it made a perfect goal. The only problem was that when the ball went over someone had to go and get it. The rules were simple: the last person to touch the ball had to get it back. I'll never forget the menacing buzz of the electricity whenever I leapt over the wall to retrieve the ball. It was terrifying. Mind you, we wanted to play so much that even if the sign had said "Hey, you eejuts, don't come in here because you could die", we still would have ignored it. Still, it was great for my goalkeeping technique. I soon stopped tipping shots over the bar and started catching them instead – at least until our furious mums found out what we were doing and banned us from playing there.

As long as I wasn't risking electrocution, my parents were always very encouraging about my football. My dad got me my very first pair of goalkeeping gloves (well, sort of). A few years after we moved to Invergordon he changed jobs again, becoming a welder, helping to build the oil rigs. He used to bring home lots of his work gloves and gave me a few pairs to try for size. They were big thick things with a coating of plastic on them, which gave me great grip in dry weather, but if I used them in the wet it was like trying to catch a bar of soap.

Dad also got me my first pair of boots. Thankfully these didn't come from his work, they were purchased on a special trip to Woolworths in nearby Dingwall when I was about ten years old. They were 'Emlyn Hughes' Gola boots with bright fluorescent orange stripes and they were brilliant. I was so proud.

As well as being my kit supplier, Dad coached my first proper team, Park Primary School in Invergordon. I wasn't first choice goalie though. Bobby Geddes was a couple of years older than me, which meant he got the nod for the school team. He was good: he later played for Dundee, Kilmarnock and Raith Rovers. To begin with I had to miss out, but I was desperately keen to play and it wasn't long before I got into the team as an outfield player. I used to mix being a centre-half with playing up front, which I really enjoyed. Over the years I became a decent striker and scored quite a few goals. Thankfully, Bobby eventually moved up to secondary school and I finally got my chance between the sticks.

Dad refereed our games, but certainly didn't show me any favouritism. I've only been sent off four times in my career and the very first time it was Dad who gave me my marching orders. I must have been about ten and we were playing a friendly against slightly older boys from the secondary school, Invergordon Academy. At least, it was meant to be friendly. I was playing in goal and went sliding out at the feet of one of their strikers, a boy called Grant Mackay. I got to the ball first and he followed through, catching me right in the goolies. It hurt. A lot. There were stud marks all up the inside of my leg. I thought it was a bad challenge and let rip with an almighty mouthful, something along the lines of, "You f***ing bastard!" Referee James Gunn, of Thurso, wasn't impressed. It was the first time he'd heard me swear and he promptly sent me off.

Our headmaster, Mr Macleod, was watching the match. He was a churchgoing man and Dad was sure he would discipline me for my outburst. At the end Mr Macleod came over.

"Why did you send Bryan off?" he asked.

"For swearing, did you not hear him?" Dad replied.

"No, because I was swearing so much myself. It was a terrible challenge."

Dad wasn't too impressed.

Park Primary played plenty of games against other schools in the area but the matches we really looked forward to were against our deadly local rivals, Alness. It was like Norwich City playing Ipswich Town; bags of local pride at stake and no holding back, even at that age. Alness had a handy young striker by the name of Eric Black. We had some good battles in those games and would get to know each other very well a few years later.

As a youngster I supported Celtic and Manchester United, mainly because of my best mate Ian 'Max' Macleod. He had a scarf with both

'Liverpool' and 'Rangers' on it. I supported Celtic and United just to be different from him. Our local team was Ross County, then a semi-professional club playing in the Highland League. Their ground was about 20 minutes away and we occasionally went to watch them, although not very often as I was usually playing on a Saturday afternoon. I also went to Hampden Park a few times to watch Scotland. Invergordon Football Club organised trips and we would all pile on a bus, scarves flapping as wildly as our trousers, and motor down to Glasgow. Games against England were always special. Saint and Greavsie – among many others – used to mercilessly take the mickey out of Scottish goalkeepers, but I was there in 1976 when Ray Clemence let the ball go through his legs and Kenny Dalglish scored the winner in Scotland's 2–1 victory. I think 'deliriously happy' best conveys my feelings at the time. I had my first 'Moscow Mule' that night, well, a couple maybe. Mmm, vodka, ginger beer and lime. Not sure I could drink that now.

I've always been a big fan of Ray Clemence, but one of my first heroes was Manchester United's Alex Stepney. He used to make goal-keeping look so easy. He wasn't a flash goalkeeper by any standards, but I don't think he could have been, given the state of the pitches and the way the old leather footballs would get wet and heavy and stick in the mud. Things like the shoulder charge were legal as well and goalkeepers generally had less protection. I admired people like him who just got on with the job. I wouldn't have fancied being a goal-keeper in that era, that's for sure.

When I was 13 Alex came up to Ross County with Manchester United for a pre-season friendly. I was so excited. I just had to get his autograph and legged it onto the pitch just before they kicked off the second half. The great man gave me his signature – on the back of one of my dad's blue Embassy Regal cigarette packets.

My budding football career continued to combine goalkeeping duties with regular stints as an outfield player. By the time I reached the second year of my secondary school, Invergordon Academy, I played in goal for my own under-14 year group, but was still eligible for the under-13s, where I played up front, scoring shed-loads of goals. I also played a lot of basketball and the teachers seemed to think I might have progressed to a high level in the sport if it wasn't for football. It certainly helped with my handling and general ball co-ordination.

I was starting to dream of becoming a professional footballer. In fact, it was all I used to think about. I even used my first job to work on my fitness. I used to earn a bit of pocket money (£4 to be precise) doing a paper round. I had to get up at 6am and cycle the couple of miles or so into Invergordon to pick up the papers. But when I got them I'd drop my bike off at home and run round the houses delivering them.

One Saturday morning, just after I'd returned home from my paper round, there was a knock on the door. It was a teacher, Mr Dunwoody. He was manager of the Invergordon Academy under-15s, the next year up from me. They were taking on a team from the Dingwall Academy and needed a goalkeeper. I was always up for a game and relished the chance to test myself alongside boys who were, at 14, a year older than me. We lost 9–0, the heaviest defeat of my entire career (both amateur and professional). It was a horrible day, but I did learn a valuable lesson. I let the ball through my legs for one of the goals, which taught me the importance of getting your body behind the ball. I decided then and there, "I bloody well won't do that again."

Despite the drubbing, they still told me I'd played well and it certainly didn't put me off. I wanted to be a professional goalkeeper, for sure.

CHAPTER TWO
The Naughty Choirboy

There is such a thing as a trendy maths teacher. Honestly. His name was Mike Morris and he managed our school team and really believed in me. With his encouragement, I began to really believe I could make it as a pro and started to make a name for myself as a goalkeeper outside the school gates.

Along with my dad, Mike encouraged me to play representative 'showcase' matches against the best players in my age group from Aberdeen, Glasgow and Edinburgh. I played trial games for Ross-shire and was then picked to play for the North of Scotland Schools FA against South of Scotland.

Mike used to drive us to games in his souped-up Ford Escort with flash alloy wheels. He was a huge Beach Boys fan and always had them playing on the car stereo. I still think of him every time I hear the Beach Boys, although I have to confess I was more of a Bay City Rollers fan myself. I never had posters on the wall or anything daft like that, but I did spend most of my paper-round money on ensuring I had all the gear, the shirts with tartan round the edge of the sleeve and pockets, the trousers with tartan down the seams. I was a bit of a fashion victim, right down to the Dr Martens with the obligatory yellow laces. Of course, I had long flowing locks in those days, which I treated to a feather cut. We all had them. There was only one local hairdresser and he knew only one style!

On our way home from these games Mike would assure me I had nothing to fear, saying, "You're as good as any of those other guys." Pitting yourself against the best keepers around and discovering you're as good, if not better, than most of them obviously boosts your confidence.

From the summer of 1978, things took off rather quickly. I made my debut for the Invergordon FC senior team. Their manager, Jock Mackay, got me my first trial with a professional team. He worked in the oil business with Bobby Watson, a former Rangers player who was the manager of Airdrie at the time. Jock recommended me to Bobby and also suggested he take a look at one of my team-mates at Invergordon, striker John Fraser. Bobby invited us both down for a trial in the school holidays, so my dad drove us the four hours to the outskirts of Glasgow.

We were there for a couple of days. It was a strange trial. We trained in the evenings because Airdrie were a part-time club and didn't train during the day. It was also fairly basic. John and me would jog around the track a few times, then he would go off to do some work with the rest of the team while I was put through some goalkeeping exercises and one-on-one sessions. That was about it, but they seemed happy with what they saw because at the end of the trial I went into the manager's office with my dad and they told me they wanted to sign me, there and then. In fact they suggested I move down right away and finish my schooling in Glasgow.

I was still only 14 and thought "Wow!", but I'd also been spotted by Aberdeen so I told them I'd enjoyed the trip but wanted to keep my options open.

I knew that Aberdeen had sent a scout called Lenny Taylor up to watch me play for Invergordon a few weeks earlier. We were playing Dingwall, again, and lost 6–0. Well, all I can say is I must have looked good in the warm-up because they still asked me to come down for a trial. I've always felt the warm-up is a very important part of a keeper's game, particularly if someone has come to take a look at you. It gives you the chance to show off skills you might not get a chance to use during the game, for one thing. More importantly, it settles you down and gets you up to speed to be able to handle anything the game throws at you right from the off. Nobody advised me to do it but I just invented my own warm-up routine which I would do religiously, right up until I hung up my boots, 20 years later.

Nowadays, there are substitute goalkeepers and goalkeeping coaches to warm up with, but back then you would have to beg the substitute striker to hit the ball at you. As part of my routine one of the lads would hit a dozen or so balls from close range to give me the feel of the ball and get me stretching, followed by a few shots from the edge of the 18-yard box and then some with pace from a bit further out, followed by some crossing and finally finishing off with ten saves in a row. If I let one in it was back to square one, it had to be ten in a row before I would allow myself back into the dressing room.

A couple of weeks later, Eric Black, the striker I often played against in those fierce school derbies, and I travelled down to Pittodrie together. I was really excited: the Dons were beginning to emerge as serious contenders to the Old Firm and while Airdrie held about 10,000 in a ground surrounded by terracing, Aberdeen's ground held more like 20,000 and at the time was one of the few all-seater stadiums in Britain. On top of that, Aberdeen was closer, only about two-and-a-half hours from home.

Eric and I were just two out of a big group of lads from all over the country who came together for a week that July. We got friendly with a couple of lads (Alan Lyons from Falkirk and Billy Muir from Kilmarnock) and we all used to hang around together. I remember we were terrified of this big, tough, Glaswegian centre-half called Mick Robertson, who used to go around collecting the dinner money from everyone, although we were pretty sure he never actually handed it in!

I was one of two goalkeepers on trial, the other being a lad called Nicky Walker who was a year older than me. We were put through our paces by Lenny Taylor and reserve team trainer Teddy Scott all week and then on the Friday we were finally taken to the stadium for a session with the club's professional keepers – Bobby Clark, Jim Leighton and John Gardiner. It was a dream come true. Bobby was a former Scotland goalkeeper and a real hero to me. Although he was getting past his best, it was fantastic to be able to watch him in action. He was a wonderful positional keeper who would make all his saves look 'easy'. They were easy because he was in the right position and he organised his defence so thoroughly. If you're in a good position you don't need to be spectacular. He had a great punch and used to practise it every Friday. It was scary just watching as the poor young defenders were sent in to try and put him off. I'm sure if he'd connected with them they would have been out for the count.

Bobby was still number one at Aberdeen, with Jim and John fighting it out for the number two slot. Jim was a fantastic shot-stopper and, watching him that morning, I could tell that he was soon going to beat John to the number two spot. After watching them for a bit, we were invited to join in. Bobby Clark took the session, on a patch of grass behind the Beach End goalmouth, and we practised crossing and shooting. I felt honoured to be training with the Aberdeen first-team squad. At one stage someone hit a hard shot that smacked me right on the nose. It caught me a real treat, so much so it knocked me over and brought tears to my eyes. John Gardiner came up to me and shouted, "Get up off the ground you big pansy." He was a bit rough and ready and I didn't take to him as much as Jim Leighton. Mind you, I could see what he meant.

That session was the first time I became aware of the manager, Alex Ferguson. Out of the corner of my eye I could see that he was half-watching us with his assistant, Pat Stanton. When we'd finished our drills, I was told he wanted to see me in his office. I tried not to run. I'd had a good session, pulled off a couple of decent saves, but would that be enough? Had I impressed Lenny and Teddy enough during the week? Was it a yes or a no? The short walk to Mr Ferguson's office seemed to take forever. I was a bag of nerves, but not because of the reputation the great man has acquired now. Back then, signing for Aberdeen was the big thing, not signing for Mr Ferguson, who was still an up-and-coming young manager. His office was a tiny room, about ten foot by ten foot, very drab and sparse – very brown as I remember. Mr Ferguson, still in his tracksuit, shook my hand and gave me a big smile.

"All right highlander," he said. "We'd like to sign you. Well done, Big Man."

I was ecstatic and almost didn't take it in when he said that they were going to pay me £7 a week, straight into my bank account. That was nearly twice as much as my paper round but, more to the point, my dream of becoming a professional footballer looked like it was about to come true. I don't remember what I said in response. I think I muttered, "Thank you very much, Boss", before backing out of the room and running across the corridor to the away dressing room, where us kids got changed. The second I saw Eric Black, our faces gave away that we'd both made it and we jumped around the dressing room together going absolutely mental.

My dad was delighted when he arrived to pick me up and we celebrated by going to the nearest sweetie shop and getting ¼lb of pineapple chunks and ¼lb of cola cubes for the drive back home. Sweets were my downfall. I loved them all: the penny chews, fruit salads, cola bottles, but I was a blackjack man and also particularly fond of the old-fashioned sweeties that came out of the big jars – working for the newsagent meant I got special rations when the jars were nearly empty.

I never got special treatment because of my football though. The nearest I came to that was getting extra helpings of mince and tatties from the school dinner lady – although I think that had more to do with the fact that she played bingo with my mum and dad.

Signing as an apprentice for Aberdeen meant staying in Invergordon for a couple of years to finish my education but coming back every school holiday for training. So Eric and I spent the summer of 1978 training at Pittodrie. It was great. We got the best digs, with Charles and Ruth Rettie. If you got in there, you knew you were probably doing all right, as it was really good accommodation and the Retties were very nice people, quite relaxed. Gordon Strachan and Alex McLeish had roomed there and, despite having become first-team regulars, they would still pop in for a cup of tea after pre-season training which was always a buzz. Gordon Strachan always called me 'Big Man' and I knew him as 'Wee Man' even though he was a good few years older than me. Eric, Billy, Alan and I would spend our free time down the amusement arcade on the beach and generally had a great summer hanging out together.

I finally signed the schoolboy forms proper a couple of months later, on 1st November 1978, seven weeks before my 15th birthday. Alex Ferguson invited Eric Black and me and our parents down to watch Aberdeen take on Fortuna Dusseldorf in the second round of the European Cup-Winners' Cup.

Alex Ferguson had built his reputation as an outstanding young manager partly on setting up the best scouting networks to secure the best of young Scottish talent and steal them away from under the Old Firm's noses. He was incredibly affable to our parents, real butter-wouldn't-melt. He let us take our mums and dads on a behind-the-scenes tour of the club before the game and then, following sandwiches and tea, we all settled down to watch the game from the directors' box. Aberdeen won 2–0 but were already trailing 3–0 from the away leg, so we were out of Europe. After the game, Alex Ferguson was all smiles as he took our parents into the oak-panelled boardroom reserved for important team meetings and got us to sign the contracts. He was charm itself, at pains to ensure that our parents understood they were entrusting us to his care and that he would make sure we were well looked after.

Despite the result, it was a great night. I could see my parents were extremely proud of me, although like many Scottish families we weren't given to making a song and dance about such successes – just a quick "Well done" and then back to normality. I took it all in my stride. I'd never have dreamt of boasting to my mates about it all, although I must admit I did like to sneak a look at the *Ross-shire Journal*, which came out every Thursday, to see if I was mentioned as Man of the Match or something. And as young players, we were secretly very pleased if we ever merited a mention in the bigger regional paper, *The Press and Journal*. I started to keep scrapbooks, which inevitably, fell to my mum to keep up – she's still got them now but there are pages and pages of cuttings that still need sticking in.

By now football had taken over my life; I would play four or five games every weekend. On Friday nights after school I played for

Invergordon FC's under-16s in the Ross-shire Youth League. On Saturday mornings I'd play for my school, Invergordon Academy. A quick change and then Saturday afternoons were spent in goal for the Invergordon FC men's team in the North Reserve League. Then on Sundays I'd be asked to play for a pub, usually The Marine or The Commercial Bar.

I also occasionally played outfield for the Academy on Saturday mornings because we had another talented young keeper called Duncan McDonald. He was a year younger than me and an excellent prospect, although sadly he was badly hurt in a car crash some years later which put an end to his playing days.

One Saturday I was playing in goal for the school on a playing field behind Ross County's Victoria Park stadium. There were two pitches, back to back, and County's goalkeeper Hamish Morrison was training in the goal just behind me. I kept looking round to watch him and was impressed by the gloves he was wearing and told him they were "quite cool". I was wearing a tatty green cotton pair with a bit of tape round them, yet another pair of my dad's old welding gloves. Hamish must have taken pity on me because he gave me his gloves there and then. What a top bloke. It was my first pair of proper goalkeeping gloves. I was made up. They were made by Uhlsport which, funnily enough, is the brand I went on to wear for most of my career.

On Saturday afternoons I played in goal for the Invergordon FC senior team along with Max Macleod in the North Reserve League. It was a good standard, just one level down from the Highland League. Max and me were very much the youngsters in the team, which also included Jimmy Dunwoody, our teacher at Invergordon Academy. It was funny; we called him 'Jimmy' on a Saturday, then 'Mr Dunwoody' when we were back at school on Monday morning.

The Sunday morning games for The Commercial, or 'The Comm' as we called it, weren't too serious, but there were quite a few pubs in Invergordon so there was plenty of healthy rivalry. Sometimes I would also have a cup match for the Invergordon FC under-16s on Sunday afternoons. I played as a striker in cup games and really enjoyed it, until I missed a crucial penalty kick in a final against Inverness Caledonian. I scored twice during normal time and it was 4–4 after 90 minutes. We were trailing by a goal in extra time when we were awarded a penalty. I don't know whether it was the fact I was on a hat-trick or the fact I could win it for my club that was weighing on my mind, but I didn't really connect with the ball properly and the keeper saved it.

The final whistle went soon afterwards. I was absolutely gutted. I came off the pitch and my dad said, "Never mind, it's only a game", which is the worst possible thing you can say to someone in a situation like that. I just stared and him and told him to "F*** off". To be fair, he didn't have a go at me. He could see I was really upset and probably realised what a daft thing it was to say. He just took it and let it go. We had a strong relationship and he knew how temperamental I was. If we lost I'd come home, chuck my bag in the corner, stomp up the stairs to my room and wait until hunger got the better of me. Of course, when we won, my poor parents would never hear the end of it – I'd be buzzing around.

By the end of the weekend I usually had cramp, which was hardly surprising. A budding young professional wouldn't get away with it nowadays because of the emphasis on proper fitness and strict training regimes in the modern game, but it didn't seem to do me any harm. In fact, you could say Invergordon FC helped to prepare me for life as a professional footballer. Some coach trips would be miles away to places like Wick, right up on the coast, not far from Thurso. As any footballer will tell you, long coach journeys can be really boring and you have to find something to help pass the time. The guys in the Invergordon team let me into their card schools, which was also good practice for the years ahead.

It was about this time I started experimenting with alcohol. One Friday evening after an under-16s game Max Macleod and me met up with a couple of older lads who played for the Invergordon FC senior team. We ended up in the high street where the older lads went into a pub and bought some cider and a couple of cans of Special Brew. One of them also had a potent strawberry wine homebrew. Big mistake!

It didn't take much to get us drunk and before long we were singing Bay City Rollers' songs, causing a lot of noise and generally making a nuisance of ourselves. Things got a little out of hand outside the cinema, where we hurled some abuse at the concierge. He decided to call the police. We were in the fish and chip shop when they turned up, by which time the older boys had made themselves scarce. Max and me were 'invited' to go to the police station because we had been drinking under age. To make matters worse, I knew the policeman, Sergeant McDonald. His son Brian was in the same class as me. Sergeant McDonald knew all about my football and the fact that I'd signed for Aberdeen. We were put into separate interview rooms where he gave me a severe telling-off and told me I had a lot to lose by mixing with the wrong people and behaving so badly. Then he took us home. I was really worried about what Mum and Dad would think, so when I got in I ran straight upstairs and locked myself in the bathroom. I knew Dad would be angry and disappointed. I spent most of the night apologising from the other side of the door. It was a sobering experience.

A few months later, in April 1979, I made my international debut, playing for Scotland under-15 schoolboys against West Germany at Chester. I was at school one day when Mike Morris pulled me to one side during break and told me the good news. Together with Paul McStay, Neale Cooper, David Bowman and Gary Mackay, I travelled down by coach a few days before the game. We were all really excited, but trying to appear dead cool and nonchalant, in that slightly cocky way you do when you're 15, talking ten to the dozen about absolute rubbish all the way down the motorway. We stayed in the halls of residence at Liverpool University and as a treat were taken to Goodison Park for the FA Cup semi-final replay between Liverpool and Manchester United a couple of nights before our game.

We all went to the match proudly dressed in our smart Scotland suits, complete with a silver, blue and red tie which had thistles on it. We were treated like VIPs, with good seats and hospitality in the lounges before and after the game. I got to watch my idol, Ray Clemence, in action and barely took my eyes off him the whole game. I met Ross Jack, an Everton player who went on to sign for Norwich. He made a point of coming over to us to say "Hello" which was a nice gesture and made us feel even more special. I know how important that kind of thing is when you're just starting out, so when local clubs ask me to present a Player of the Season award I always try to get along. One I made sure I got to recently was Loddon Grasshoppers, the team my son Angus was playing for. I was asked to present him with the Player of the Season award. I was beaming with pride, but he was so embarrassed.

Manchester United won the game 1–0 but unfortunately we lost 3–2 against West Germany. I can only remember two things about the game: first, their winner was a free kick, which went over the top of the wall and curled into the top corner; second, they had a chap called Raimond Aumann in goal for them.

The West Germany game was the only time I actually started for the Scotland under-15s. Hearts' Ian Westwater was the number one choice for the rest of the season. I was gutted, especially because we played Wales at Airdrie and Northern Ireland at Aberdeen. I still travelled with the squad, though, and had to take a couple of my O levels on the road. It didn't do me much good because I failed my French exam at Airdrie High School on the day of the match against Wales and didn't do much better in my physics, which I sat at Bankhead Academy in Aberdeen. It wouldn't have been so bad if I'd actually played in those games. That's the difficult thing about being a goalkeeper; you're either in, or you're out. Ian was the first choice, so he got picked and I didn't. Simple as that.

Anyway, I did all right in the subjects I actually liked, getting three A grades in maths, arithmetic and history. I wasn't very good at English, though, and got a C in that. I ended up with a B in chemistry, although I'm not sure how. I had my golf clubs with me on the day of the exam and did the multiple choice questions as quickly as possible so I could get to the course as soon as the test finished. I couldn't believe it when the results came back and I got a B.

I played quite a lot of golf by the time I was 15 and like a lot of kids we would take up tennis whenever Wimbledon was on or play snooker if there was a major tournament on the television. The only sport I didn't really take to was cricket. Max used to listen to cricket commentary on the radio and tell me about things like pigeons taking off after a shot was hit. I couldn't get into that. I always enjoyed the Olympics, particularly athletics. I did the high jump and hurdles and ran in the school relay team, but unlike my dad I never won anything or did anything special, so I always came back to football.

At the end of that 1978/79 season Aberdeen gave me permission to play in a couple of reserve team games for Ross County and a few weeks later they invited me to guest in a pre-season friendly against West Ham United. It was a great Hammers team, with players like Phil Parkes, Billy Bonds, Trevor Brooking, Frank Lampard (Snr) and David Cross. I started on the bench and we were 6–0 down at half-time when I came on for Hamish Morrison, the man who'd given me my first pair of Uhlsport gloves. Midway through the second half Trevor Brooking went on a mazy run and came all the way through, until I was facing him one-on-one. I dived at his feet and saved his shot with my goolies. The pain was unbelievable and I writhed around on the ground in agony. I had tears in my eyes. Trevor stood over me and said, "Good save, young man," in his typically polite and gentlemanly way. We ended up losing the match 8–2, or, to put it another way, we drew the second half 2–2. I was quite pleased about that.

It would have been great to play for Ross County on a more regular basis, given they were my local team, but by the time the 1979/80 season started I found myself playing against them in the Highland League. Nairn County manager Innes McDonald was looking for a couple of players and approached Alex Ferguson as Aberdeen is their nearest senior club. Fergie agreed to release me and Eric Black on loan for a season. The Highland League was a pretty good standard, and we'd often come up against ex-pros who'd dropped down a level towards the end of their careers. It was also a very physical league, which was good really because it toughened me up.

At this time I was dabbling in other interests, such as the Scouts, but football always came first which meant my interest usually waned after a few weeks. One time I decided I wanted to play the guitar. I have no idea why exactly but I was told I would need to learn the violin first, so we hired one and I went to lessons. My budding musical career soon hit the wrong note when I sat on the bow and broke it. I had to pay for it out of my paper-round money and it was quite expensive, so that was that.

I was also in the choir, usually in the back row, right from my primary school days through to secondary school. We used to rehearse at break time, which wasn't too much of a chore because there were a few nice young ladies in the group. And I must have had a half-decent voice because I was always in the school productions.

Late in 1979, our school choir was chosen to perform on *Songs of Praise* at St Giles Cathedral in Edinburgh, so one Saturday we all headed off to a guesthouse in the city. I must admit I wasn't having particularly religious thoughts that night as Alistair Jappy and me ended up in a room with a couple of the girls. We were just mucking about but suddenly there was a knock at the door. I dived under one of the girls' beds, but didn't realise my long legs were still poking out the end of it. Mike Morris, being a clever teacher-type, spotted them.

"What are you doing under there?" he roared.

I like to think I've never panicked under pressure, professionally or otherwise, so I thought quickly and innocently emerged from under the bed with a towel.

"Found it!"

Unfortunately, Mr Morris wasn't stupid and ordered us straight to our rooms.

We sang in the choir on the Sunday evening as arranged before returning to Invergordon where we were hauled up in front of the headmaster, Mr Bownes. He told us we were a disgrace to the school and said he would have to take disciplinary action. We were both suspended for two weeks and I never went back to school after that. It was near the end of the term, lessons were just about over and I was about to sit my exams. But I was worried that Aberdeen would find out about the episode, decide I was a troublemaker, and not take me on, so it was a very nervous few weeks.

That last year at school I sat my Highers exams, but knowing that I had a place at Aberdeen I didn't really study too hard. I improved my history O level from a C to an A grade, but failed English and maths Highers and managed a D in my O level in, er, secretarial studies. Goalkeepers don't really have the delicate touch required for 60wpm.

In between sitting my exams and going to Aberdeen I had about three months to kill so I took a part-time job at Jimmy Jack's dockyard at Evanton near Invergordon, where my dad also worked by now. My job was to clean the cranes, which were used to load and unload big oil pipes on and off the boats.

One lunchtime I was playing about in a forklift truck. I was close to the edge of the water and trying to get it to go forward but accidentally put it into reverse. The truck shot backwards towards the Cromarty Firth. Thank God I hit a bollard otherwise I would have gone over the edge and that would have been that!

Having survived the shipyard and the threat of dismissal before I'd even started, I finally drove down to Aberdeen with my mum and dad in the summer of 1980 to start my career with Aberdeen. Eric Black and his parents drove down with us in convoy.

Eric and I moved into digs together in a place called Bucksburn, on the outskirts of Aberdeen. Once we'd dropped off our bags, both families went for a farewell dinner at the local hotel, the Holiday Inn. While our parents ran through the obligatory speech about being proud of us, working hard and making the most of our opportunity, Eric and I noticed that the hotel had a happy hour *and* a nightclub.

Our folks said goodbye, and that was it; Blacko and me had left home and were about to start our new lives as full-time apprentices with Aberdeen Football Club.

CHAPTER THREE

Fergie's Babysitter

Mrs Welsh, or Margaret as we came to know her, was a lovely lady. She lived in a large first-floor flat on her own, having lost her husband a couple of years before we met her. She had two children – James and Margaret. They encouraged her to keep busy and to reply to an advert in the local paper which said Aberdeen Football Club were looking for digs for their young players.

Eric and I were Mrs Welsh's second batch of lodgers. Before us she'd looked after three lads from Glasgow: Dougie Bell, Tam McGuire and Mick Robertson, the lad who'd pulled the dinner money stunt when we were schoolboys. Margaret was a typically gentle Aberdonian lady, not used to the somewhat more rugged characteristics of folk from the west of Scotland, and I think that first experience was an eye-opener for her. But I think it's fair to say she'd lost her landlady 'L plates' by the time Eric and I arrived.

Fergie's Babysitter

For a few months Blacko and I were the only two lodgers at Bankhead Road. Then we were joined by a couple of other apprentices, Alan Lyons and Billy Muir, who we'd first met at our schoolboy trials a couple of years earlier. I shared the big bedroom with Alan and Billy, while Eric was in the single. It was a bit cramped, but I'm a sound sleeper so I never noticed the other two snoring, although a room of three teenage lads who constantly lived in trainers must have smelt pretty awful!

We were on £33 a week, plus our digs paid for, to start with. It was an enormous amount of money to us, but we were more concerned about becoming professional footballers – and what there was in the house to eat. We were still growing and all that training meant we had huge appetites. We'd sneak into the kitchen to raid the fridge for a cheese sandwich until Mrs Welsh decided she was in danger of being eaten out of house and home and started putting up signs, saying things like, 'Do Not Enter The Kitchen After 10pm'.

So, every Thursday, after we'd picked up our wages, I'd go to the local newsagents and buy a dozen bottles of orangeade and a box of 48 Golden Wonder cheese and onion crisps. I loved them then and I still love them now and will always buy a packet if I see them in the shop, just to see if they still taste the same. By Thursday evening I'd made a big hole in the box and they'd usually all be gone by the weekend. I shared one or two bags, but not many!

To be fair, Margaret fed us well. She cooked us dinner every night. One of her specialities was stovies, a popular but stodgy Aberdeen dish made from a mixture of beef, vegetables and potatoes with oatcakes. We eventually got used to them but because they were something of a local delicacy we'd often have them for lunch at the training ground as well, which got a bit much.

After a bowl of cereal in the morning, we'd get two buses to work, the second of which dropped us a short walk from Pittodrie. Unfortunately, this took us past a bakery and the smell of butterys (sort of flat croissants) was hard to resist. We nearly always ended up having two breakfasts.

Mind you, we soon burned them off. Like all football clubs, Aberdeen kept their apprentices busy all day. Our first job was to prepare the kit for the senior professionals for training each morning.

We all had designated players to look after. I couldn't believe my luck; not only did I get to take care of the goalkeepers, but I was also given club captain Willie Miller, Alex McLeish and Willie Garner to look after. In other words, the club's top defenders – what a privilege.

We had to polish their boots and make sure they were set out each morning, along with towels, each player's individually numbered training kit, that kind of stuff. Obviously Bobby and Jim also had their gloves, while Willie Miller insisted on wearing tie-ups for training. I also had to make sure he had a tube of cream for his piles each morning – thankfully he never asked me to apply it.

The older pros liked to test us out every now and then. Willie Garner was in and out of the team at the time but he'd played a number of games for Aberdeen and was a respected 'big voice' in the dressing room. He'd occasionally throw his boots back at me and say they weren't clean enough, or complain if I'd forgotten to leave his towel out. We soon caught on and learned not to be cheeky or answer back. It was all part of the learning curve.

The facilities at Aberdeen weren't exactly state-of-the-art back in the early 1980s. The club might have just won the Scottish League and qualified for the European Cup but the Dons' training ground was a couple of miles from Pittodrie at Seaton Park, on the university sports pitches. We didn't always train on a proper pitch, either. The groundsman would ask us not to use them if the goalmouths were tatty or the playing surface wasn't too clever, which meant we'd have to mark out a pitch on a surrounding grass area. In the winter, if it had been snowing or the weather was especially bad, we often trained on the beach. The only time we trained at Pittodrie was on a Friday morning, just as I had when I first went on trial. Even then we'd only use the grass area behind one of the goals.

So, most days we headed for Seaton Park. Teddy Scott drove the young players there in a minibus with the goalposts piled onto the roof so we could set them up while he drove back to Pittodrie to pick up the senior squad.

As a goalkeeper I frequently got called in to train with the first team, which was great because it meant working closely with experienced defenders like Willie Miller, Willie Garner, Alex McLeish and Stuart Kennedy. They certainly didn't go easy on me; training sessions were more like matches to them and if I made a mistake they'd really let me know about it, shouting that I was a "f***ing idiot". The criticism didn't faze me at all; I quickly learned to give as good as I got. "That was your fault; you should have cut the cross out," I would bark back. I think they respected the fact I stood up for myself now and then. I learned a lot and took that philosophy into my career; always trying to make sure team-mates knew when they made mistakes, even in training. If you're told what you've done wrong you can work on putting it right.

Early on in that 1980/81 season Pat Stanton left Aberdeen, rejoining Hibernian as manager and Alex Ferguson brought in the Forfar manager, Archie Knox, as his new assistant. Archie was fantastic. He was very enthusiastic and loved being on the training ground. He was really at home when he was shouting and screaming encouragement at players, although he was a good laugh too and got a lot out of us because we could relate to him and thoroughly enjoyed his sessions.

While Archie worked closely with players on technique and skills, Alex Ferguson focused more on tactics and preparation. He was a real student of the game and drove hundreds of miles to watch other clubs and study different players. He always knew the opposition inside out; from the systems they played, right down to the strengths and weaknesses of each individual player. He spent hours and hours meticulously preparing for each game.

Every now and then the gaffer took training, but he'd always ensure he was there to take part in the game at the end of the session. Being a tough old centre-forward, he loved giving defenders and goal-keepers a torrid time and he'd lost none of his desire over the years. He was a classic goal-hanger and always in the thick of the action, pouncing on rebounds and coming in for crosses with his elbows out (and seemingly specially sharpened). He'd get me in the ribs, then shoulder charge me – his charges were always a second late and would have been bookable offences in a real game – then he'd collapse on top of me the next time I went for the ball. He'd never apologise at the time; he'd maybe say sorry after the game if he'd won. Maybe. If he'd lost he'd call me a big softie. As a nuisance factor he scored ten out of ten. Or maybe eleven.

Jim Leighton and I loved to get him back though. The challenge when coming for a cross was to punch the ball clear while 'accidentally' punching Fergie's head at the same time. Or we'd dive at his feet to save a shot and accidentally catch him with our legs. If he was hurt, we never knew. If he'd lost we'd know about it all right.

Fergie hated losing. At the end of every day, once we'd finished all our chores and training, the younger players would play a game of 'tips' in the gym. It was similar to 'killer' in pool. There were six 'goals' painted on the walls of the gym and you each had a goal to protect, whilst at the same time trying to score against one of the other five players to cost them a life. Once you'd lost five lives you were knocked out, as was one of the goalmouths, and eventually the game boiled down to one v one. They were real blood and thunder affairs; very occasionally skill was involved, but the majority of the time it just involved hitting the ball as ferociously as possible. At what – or whom – didn't particularly matter. It was great fun. The only problem was the gym floor had been painted black a long, long time previously, which meant you ended up covered in black dust, like a miner, and had black snot for days.

Invariably, these games would be interrupted by Fergie, who would burst in through the gym doors and join in with us, before his end-of-week finale which was always a one v one game against Archie. He would demand to know who was going to be supporting him and who would be on Archie's side. I always had this slight sense of dread when those doors slammed open and Fergie appeared, for two very good reasons.

One: you couldn't sneak off down the corridor back to the changing rooms as they would expect you to stay there and cheer them on. If you decided to support Fergie, you'd get loads of grief from Archie, accusing you of sucking up to the boss. If you decided to support Archie and he won, Fergie would make you do a lap of the pitch and wouldn't speak to you for the rest of the day!

Two: these games always seemed to happen when we'd finished our chores and Fergie and Archie would always want to have a bath and a sauna after them. They only had showers in their changing room, which also doubled as the ref's changing room on matchdays, so they would use the facilities in the home dressing room. So, having spent half an hour ensuring the changing rooms were spotless, we then had to go back and spend another 20 minutes getting rid of all the soap suds!

Jim Leighton had become the regular first-team keeper by now, which didn't go down too well with John Gardiner. Once it became clear Jim was first choice for the number one shirt, John joined Dundee United, so I became Jim's number two and made my debut for the reserves while I was still only 16.

One of my first games was at home to Partick Thistle, a match I remember particularly well because I ended up in hospital. I came out for a corner and got a bang in the face from a big centre-forward called Doug Somner, an experienced and prolific striker who was coming back from injury. Dougie whacked me in the face, knocking me out and shattering my cheekbone in the process. I was taken to hospital where they made an incision in the side of my head and inserted a hook to pull the cheekbone back into place. The surgeon advised me to rest for a few weeks to make sure it settled down.

The following Saturday Aberdeen were playing Rangers at Pittodrie, with the two teams' reserves meeting at the same time at Ibrox Park. It goes without saying it's every Scottish schoolboy's dream to play at Ibrox or Parkhead and here was my opportunity. The only problem was I had a broken cheekbone and I'd been ordered to rest. I never even spoke to Alex Ferguson about it. I was desperate to play so I told Teddy Scott that the club needed me to play, I really wanted to play and I insisted I was fit enough to play. And that was it, as far as I was concerned.

Ibrox Park was a fantastic stadium, but making my debut there wasn't anything like it would be now. The ground was undergoing a process of transformation: the two end stands had already been redeveloped and another demolished, ready for rebuilding. The only original part of the ground was the old main stand. We ran out onto the three-sided pitch to a rousing reception from about 100 people. I'm not sure if there was a dog.

Rangers had some big names in their reserve team that day. Tommy McLean, Alex MacDonald, Alex Miller and goalkeeper Peter McCloy were all great players either returning from injury or getting towards the end of their careers. I was excited, but not overawed. By now I had become groomed as a professional – you learn to take these things in your stride.

However, I was still aware it was a big game for us because Alex Ferguson had instilled into all the Aberdeen players that beating Rangers and Celtic was the be-all and end-all at every level. "If you beat those guys," he'd say, "you'll end up top of the League." We won 1–0 and my cheek was fine, and I suppose it did me no harm in showing I was prepared to go in where it hurts. Even as a rookie 16-year-old, I guess I'd worked out that it helps to be a little bit mad if you want to make a career between the sticks.

Unfortunately, my spell as Jim Leighton's number two was brief. Understandably, Alex Ferguson felt he needed a more experienced keeper as cover and he brought in Marc de Clerc, a Belgian who had been playing in Holland. He was a real pleasure to work with and brought his own ideas to the training sessions Jim and I had devised, which was great. But his arrival as the club's number two keeper meant I was demoted from the reserves and back to playing in a sort of midweek second string mini-league used to blood young players and rehabilitate first-teamers coming back from injury.

The 1980/81 campaign was another eventful season for Aberdeen and their increasingly impressive manager. As Scottish champions, the Dons had qualified for the European Cup, knocking out Austria Vienna in the first round before losing to Liverpool in round two in October. We lost 1–0 at home and the return leg at Anfield 4–0. It was no disgrace; Liverpool went on to win the trophy for the third time in five years, with the great Ray Clemence in goal, of course.

Watching the games from the stand was about as close as I got to the glamour of the European Cup. As an apprentice I still had my chores to do, including washing the training kit, which, when the weather got cold, included these massive heavy sweaters like fishermens jumpers which took forever to dry. The last job of the week was to make sure the dressing room was spick and span, or shovel snow off the pitch and pathways around Pittodrie if the weather was especially bad.

One of my other tasks was to wash the manager's car. Alex Ferguson had a big silver Mercedes, top of the range, with a leather interior. I used to clean it every Friday. I was lucky, other youth team players would have to wash the minibus, which was a nightmare. I loved being trusted with the boss's car: he'd let me drive it from his parking space over to the other side of the car park to wash it. He didn't, however, know that I used to sneak it out for a quick spin round the industrial streets surrounding Pittodrie. Luckily, he never seemed to check his fuel gauge.

I ended up spending a lot of time in the boss's car. Every now and then after a match Fergie would decide to go out in the evening with his wife Cathy – usually if he wanted to celebrate a good win. Occasionally, the reserves didn't have a game so the apprentices would be on duty at Pittodrie, watching the match and then cleaning out the dressing rooms. Fergie would come in after the game and shout, "Right, who's babysitting for me tonight?"

One Saturday the rest of the lads saw him coming and made a quick getaway, leaving me in the dressing room on my own, broom in hand. Sure enough he demanded to know who was available for babysitting duties. "It looks like it's me tonight, Boss," I said.

The Ferguson family home was in a smart area on the outskirts of Aberdeen. It was an impressive house with lots of Lladro figurines that Fergie collected on his trips around the world, although I think he's more a connoisseur of fine art, fine wine and racehorses these days.

Alex and Cathy have three sons, Mark (then aged 11) and twins Darren and Jason (then aged eight). Mark wasn't too bad but the twins were a little more boisterous. If they got up to mischief I'd make them do press-ups. We sometimes played snooker on their full-size table, but more often than not, we played football in the garden and then watched *Sportscene*, the Scottish version of *Match of the Day*. I hit it off with the lads straight away and soon became Fergie's regular first-choice babysitter – if not first-choice goalkeeper.

Whenever I got the call to babysit I'd go home after the game while the gaffer was doing press and TV interviews at Pittodrie. He'd then pick me up from my digs and drive me back to his house. We'd be listening to the sports news on the radio and he'd ask, "So, how do you feel we did today?" I was quite interested in coaching, so I'd take the opportunity to quiz him about his tactics and formations and he seemed to enjoy the banter. Back at his, Cathy made me feel right at home and always made sure there were sandwiches or a dinner for me before they went out for the night. There were usually a couple of cans of beer in the fridge, but I was never sure if they were for me or not. I was often tempted to drink them, but only ever had one. I thought it might not go down too well with Fergie if I drank both. At that stage he was very much a Campari and lemonade man, although I think he's developed better taste now with his knowledge of fine wines. Mind you, he'd give us players a rollocking for even being in the same room as alcohol.

He never actually tracked me and my mates down in the way that he would years later with Lee Sharpe and co., but drinking was one of his pet hates. He knew it went on, and he definitely had the spies out around the town, but he'd tolerate it. To a degree. I remember him giving Jim Leighton a right bollocking once, just because he'd been seen crossing the road from the off licence to his house with a crate of beer under his arm. I don't think it was the fact that Jim was having a party days before he was due to play again, more that people had clocked him buying booze.

With us kids Fergie was strict but fair. He wanted to help us be the best we could and felt responsible for us, especially as so many of us had come from all over Scotland to be there, and I think he was very aware of the promise he'd made our parents to look after us. So, in that sense, he was more like a dad than a boss a lot of the time, and I felt quite close to him. We'd never discuss girlfriends or anything like that, but I did feel I could talk to him. And he obviously trusted me because a couple of years later, driving to his house, he asked me to take a look at a player called Brian Irvine who was a centre-half at Falkirk at the time. I assumed that he and Archie had already checked him out, but I dutifully went down to Brechin City to watch him play and reported back to the gaffer that I thought he looked the business. He signed him shortly afterwards, in 1985, and Brian went on to score the penalty that won the 1990 Scottish Cup for Aberdeen and become an all-round Dons legend. Whether I can take any credit for that I'm not sure, but I'd like to think so.

Anyway, when I babysat for Alex and Cathy, I'd stay overnight in the spare room, then on Sunday mornings we would all sit down for a traditional Scottish breakfast. Fergie loved his tatty scones, a Glaswegian speciality. He'd have all the papers and read them cover to cover. The sports pages, yes, but also the financial pages – and if I had to pick anyone to be on my pub quiz team it would be Fergie – he read the lot and would always be the first to know who, say, the Prime Minister of Australia was.

My reputation as a babysitter soon spread and before long it wasn't only the Ferguson children I was looking after. I became very good friends with Jim Leighton and he was kind enough to invite me for dinner at his house where I met his wife Linda. He's no fool, Jim. Before long I was babysitting the Leightons' young children Claire and Greg. It didn't stop there. During my time at Pittodrie I also babysat for Gordon Strachan, Alex McLeish and Mark McGhee. They all paid me £10 a pop (even Fergie), but that wasn't why I did it. They were mates and I was happy to help them out, especially when I would have just been watching *Top of the Pops* anyway. Being offered a tenner was embarrassing but I always accepted it.

Don't get me wrong; I did have a social life of my own. Blacko, Billy, Alan and I popped down to our local, the Bankhead Inn, once or twice a week. We weren't big drinkers, though, and normally had just a couple of shandies and a game of pool or darts with the locals. We also went to the Holiday Inn hotel, usually for happy hour on a Saturday night if I wasn't babysitting for once. We got to know the manager well and soon negotiated a deal to use the hotel's health and fitness facilities. I was already developing quite a good eye for a commercial opportunity. I got friendly with the adidas rep who supplied most of the first team with tracksuits and boots and negotiated myself a deal where I got the latest tracksuits. More importantly, I got them before the first team and I used to turn up at training every morning in a different colour or style. They'd never really notice until lunchtime, when I'd casually stroll into the canteen and there would suddenly be shouts of, "Oi! Big Ben! Where the hell did you get that?" as I swaggered around in the latest model. I particularly remember a velvety effect tracksuit, which I had in five different colours. They all went mental and were straight on the phone to the rep!

*   *   *

Marc de Clerc left Pittodrie at the end of the 1980/81 season, but not before netting a goal for the Dons in one of only two games for the club, both victories. He played in a Scottish Cup tie at Berwick Rangers and scored with a big clearance from his area. Not a bad record for a keeper: played two, won two, scored one, conceded none. I was sad to see him go, but his departure paved the way for me to become Jim Leighton's understudy once again.

At that time, coming up to the summer of 1981, I decided I wanted to go on holiday to Corsica. The only problem was I was a bit strapped for cash. So I asked Mr Aberdeen, Teddy Scott. As well as being reserve team manager, Teddy was kit man and did about 150 jobs around the place. He had been at Pittodrie for years and lived and breathed the club. If you ever needed help or advice, Teddy was the man to go to. He'd either come up with a solution or tell you to go and ask the manager, like he did when I explained my problem. I wasn't exactly hopeful that Fergie would give me the cash to splash on getting drunk with my mates, but dutifully trooped up to the manager's office and said to Alex Ferguson, "Boss, I could do with an advance on my wages because I'm off on holiday in a few days."

Fergie thought about it for a moment, looked up from behind his desk and said, "Bryan, if you sign another year on your contract you can have the money today."

My contract was up for renewal, so I signed then and there.

"Well done, son," he said. "Enjoy yourself, behave yourself and come back fit and well for pre-season."

I was delighted. Not only did I have my holiday cash, but I'd signed a new deal which tripled my wages, putting me on roughly £100 a week. I was happy to sign. I knew from the conversations I'd had with other young players I'd met on my international youth call-ups that I wasn't getting ripped off, although I guess I could have haggled for a little bit more. That wasn't an issue for me though: I was being treated fairly and, more to the point, I could go and have a good time on holiday. I was ecstatic. My new contract and Marc's departure sealed my position as the club's number two keeper. Looking back, I think Alex definitely wanted to help me out in that fatherly way he had, but he was also a canny operator – there can't have been a sweeter contract negotiation than that in all his years as a manager!

CHAPTER FOUR

Flying Saucers

By the start of my second season at Aberdeen I was recognised as the club's number two goalkeeper, at just 17 years old. I also got my first taste of senior action.

By finishing second in the league the Dons had qualified for the UEFA Cup, and the draw for the first round paired us with none other than the cup holders, Ipswich Town. Bobby Robson's team had tremendous European pedigree, with some wonderful players like Dutchmen Arnold Muhren and Franz Thijssen, Scottish internationals John Wark and Alan Brazil, Paul Mariner, Eric Gates and Paul Cooper in goal. Even better, unlike the domestic game back then, teams always had a keeper on the bench in Europe, so I travelled to Portman Road for the first leg as cover for Jim.

We drew the first leg 1–1 before beating Ipswich 3–1 in the return at Pittodrie. Knocking the cup holders out was a tremendous result and another sign of Aberdeen's emergence as a European force under Alex Ferguson. I felt very excited to be part of a club that was clearly going places.

The draw for the second round pitted us against the Romanian side, Arges Pitesti. We won the first leg 3–0 at Pittodrie. All very straightforward. The return trip was less comfortable. The lads were truly awful during the first half, conceding two goals to bring the Romanians right back into the tie at 3–2 on aggregate. I sat on the bench wincing as Fergie became increasingly irritated, shaking his head and bawling instructions, demanding an improvement. The gaffer shot up off the bench as the referee blew the whistle for half-time and made straight for the dressing room. He was not happy.

Once everyone was in the dressing room Fergie well and truly let rip.

"What the bloody hell are you lot playing at?" he stormed. "That was absolutely f***ing rubbish. You're bloody well cheating me, you're cheating yourselves and most of all you're cheating the fans. It's not f***king good enough."

His face turned from bright pink to beetroot red as he completely lost the plot, lunging towards the tray of half-time teas and launching them into the air. Teacups, saucers, the teapot, all made of china, went flying across the room. We were forced to duck as the various items of crockery came hurtling towards us, whizzing past our ears before smashing against the wall.

'What the f*** is going on here?' I asked myself.

This was full-blown Fergie fury. Maybe it was the first of his infamous hairdryer treatments. One by one, each player felt the full force of Fergie's anger. We were absolutely dumbstruck. I sat rooted to the spot, not sure where to look, before finally Willie Miller and Alex McLeish got up and invited the boss to calm down.

"OK gaffer," one of them said. "We'll put it right in the second half."

"You'd better put it right," said Fergie. "Or else."

One Gordon Strachan penalty and a John Hewitt goal later and, suddenly, we were back to 2–2 on the night and through to the next round 5–2 on aggregate. The rollicking certainly worked.

I witnessed a few of Fergie's half-time roastings after that, but I can safely say that afternoon in Romania was the worst (or best, perhaps) I've ever seen. It found its way into Dons' folklore, becoming a big hit on the after-dinner circuit with former Aberdeen players, even those who weren't actually there on the day. It's certainly easy to see how the infamous flying boot episode came about with David Beckham at Manchester United a couple of seasons ago. I can picture the scene:

Fergie livid at half-time kicking the first thing that came to him. Cue one flying boot, inadvertently heading in the direction of the England captain's eyebrow!

Whatever his motivational techniques, I couldn't help but admire Fergie as a boss. He was a master tactician and the strategic side of the game came naturally to him. But there was one area where he struggled badly when it came to European matches. For some reason, Fergie had a problem with foreign names. Some of his pronunciations were priceless and it was often as much as we could do not to laugh out loud when he was going through the opposition teams. One of the best came in the next round of the UEFA Cup.

We were playing SV Hamburg. One of their strikers was Horst Hrubesch, which aficionados of the game will know is pronounced 'H-roo-bish'. Fergie just couldn't get his tongue around it and kept referring to him as Horst 'Rubbish'. Every time he said it the lads almost wet themselves. It was the same whenever he came out with one of his mispronunciations, you really had to bite your lip. I'd usually be all right, until I glanced round and made eye contact with one of the club jokers like Neale Cooper or Alex McLeish, who'd make things worse by pulling stupid faces and nodding in Fergie's direction. It was just like being back in the classroom. I lost count of the number of times I had to control my sniggering as Fergie struggled to get to grips with yet another continental name. It wouldn't have paid to laugh out loud, mind. Fergie wasn't good when it came to people taking the mickey. He would have gone ballistic. Herr 'Rubbish' didn't live up to Fergie's translation, either. He scored two at Pittodrie and another in Germany as Hamburg knocked us out of the competition.

The UEFA Cup had been great news on a personal level: Blacko and I earned our first European bonuses! We used the extra cash to treat Mrs Welsh to a slap-up meal. Her son James was a big Dons fan so we invited him as well. We took them to a nice restaurant and had the works: prawn cocktail and mushroom soup, then fillet steak, all rounded off with strawberry gateau. Margaret thought it was wonderful and proceeded to serve us steak every Thursday night after that. We couldn't believe our luck. That little treat was probably the best decision we'd ever made.

Flying Saucers

I got to know James – or Welshy as I called him – very well. He lived about 20 miles away in Inverurie with his wife Irene and their two young sons, Stephen and Stuart. Mrs Welsh often visited them for Sunday lunch and it wasn't long before I was invited to join them. It was a good arrangement. Margaret had a little Volkswagen Polo but she wasn't keen on driving. I didn't have a car, so once I passed my test I was only too happy to act as her chauffeur. Trips to Inverurie became a regular thing. I played squash with Welshy most Sundays and became close friends with him and his family. And it wasn't long before – you guessed it – I found myself babysitting for them.

The first time I looked after Welshy's toddlers was on the evening of Friday 29th October 1982. I'll never forget it. I was watching the television when the phone rang. It was Alan Lyons back home in our digs. He'd taken a call from Archie Knox who wanted to talk to me. It wasn't as if I was doing anything wrong, like chasing girls in a night-club or downing a few pints in a pub, that was totally out of bounds on a Friday night. Babysitting was hardly breaking the rules – or was it? Alan wasn't sure and he didn't want to see me in trouble, good lad that he was, so he covered for me, telling Archie I was asleep in bed.

"Jim Leighton's gone down with flu and might miss tomorrow's match against Hibs," he told me. "Archie says you're to report at Pittodrie with the rest of the first team squad at 8 o'clock sharp."

So this could be it, my big chance. I was on standby to make my first-team debut. But, hold it, I was in Inverurie, more than 20 miles from home, committed to staying out overnight to look after Welshy's children. I put the phone down and thought to myself, "Wow!" Quickly followed by, "Get to bed!"

I scribbled a note to James and Irene.

Might be playing for the first team in Edinburgh tomorrow! Please wake me up at 6 o'clock. Don't forget! Bryan.

I was so excited I didn't sleep a wink. James gave me a nudge in the morning. "Up you get, Big Man. Don't want you being late now, do we?"

I got up and drove Mrs Welsh's car back to my digs. I grabbed my kit and headed to Pittodrie, not knowing if Jim Leighton would be there or not. As much as I liked the bloke, I was hoping he hadn't made it. When I got to the ground and looked around the car park there was no sign of Jim's car. My heart leapt but I was still nervous as I made my way into the ground. Archie Knox stopped me in the corridor. "Big Ben, it's your big day," he said.

"Fantastic," I thought, and then the butterflies kicked in – not so much a flutter, more of an eruption. But I didn't panic. That's not the way I am. I'd been waiting a long time for this moment; now it was all about being focused, staying calm, concentrating on the challenge ahead. Teddy Scott made a point of coming up to me.

"Good luck, Big Man. Just do your best and you'll be fine, absolutely fine."

I knew Teddy would be pleased for me. I also knew he'd love to be there to see me make my debut, but he wasn't travelling with us. He had to look after the reserves as usual. And that was it. At 18 years old, early in my third season with the club, I was on my way to making my full Aberdeen debut.

The drive to Edinburgh took about two and a half hours. I dozed most of the way after the sleepless night before. We got to a hotel next to Edinburgh Zoo where the team often stopped on trips to Hearts and Hibs matches and I had chicken in breadcrumbs for lunch.

When we got to Easter Road it had been pouring with rain all day. The pitch was waterlogged and for a while it looked as if the game would be called off. I wouldn't be making my debut, after all. The referee took a quick look and declared the match would go ahead, despite all the puddles and quagmire of a playing surface. I didn't care. Having come all this way, the last thing I wanted was to miss out on the chance of making my debut, whatever the conditions.

I can't remember a single thing Fergie said before the match. There were plenty of slaps on the back, and the lads all wished me well. "Good luck, Big Man," that sort of thing. But aside from that, it's a blur. All I was interested in was getting on with the game.

We kicked down the famous Easter Road slope in the first half. I was pretty busy in the early stages, coming out for a few crosses and making some good saves without really having to stretch myself. The game itself was something of a lottery. The conditions were terrible and getting worse as the game progressed. It was bordering on farcical as the ball kept getting stuck in the puddles on the pitch. I swear they wouldn't have played it these days.

Flying Saucers

Peter Weir put us 1–0 up in the second half and we seemed to be cruising until Hibs, cheered on by the majority of a 6,000-strong crowd, staged a late flurry. Gary Murray hit a shot from the edge of the box. It was well struck, towards my right-hand post. I dived full length and got my hands to the ball. On any other day it would have been a regulation save, but as I landed on the sodden turf my momentum carried me through the mud and puddles. I got a face full of dirty, cold water and somehow lost control of the ball. It slipped from my grasp and trickled over the line. There wasn't a lot I could do about it; the conditions had done for me. All the same, it didn't look too clever.

Willie Miller and Alex McLeish looked at me as if to say, "You should have saved that, Big Man." They had a point. It was an eminently saveable shot. They knew it. I knew it. It wasn't the sort of goal you wanted to concede on your debut, that's for sure, especially as it cost us the win. After four straight league victories, a 1–1 draw at Hibs wasn't a particularly good result.

I felt I'd been a tad unlucky with the goal, given the conditions. I also thought I'd done a lot of good things during the game. I think Fergie saw it the same way. He didn't say much to me afterwards. I guess he felt it would have been harsh to hammer me on my debut. What's more, I wasn't going to let it get me down. I knew I was a decent keeper and the lads knew I was a decent keeper. There were no recriminations, just the odd consoling pat on the back.

The following week Jim Leighton was back. I don't know what it was about that bloke. He was never, ever injured and it would be a long wait before I got another crack at first-team action. I never resented him for it though. Far from it. We got on fantastically. I enjoyed working with Jim and he seemed to feel the same way about me. There was a mutual respect. More to the point, I couldn't have asked for anyone better to teach me my craft. I picked up so much from Jim during those early days – things like positioning, when to come for crosses and how to organise your defence – that served me well for the rest of my career.

As the 1981/82 season drew to a close we had a chance to qualify for Europe again, but we needed to beat Rangers in the Scottish Cup final. I was never likely to play in the match but I was part of the squad and ended up playing a part in the outcome of the game. There was a cock-up on the kit front which meant we arrived at Hampden without Alex McLeish's boots. One of the lads responsible for packing the gear had thrown a pair marked 'AM' into the boot hamper, assuming they were Alex's. In fact, they belonged to one of the young-sters, Andy Macleod, whose feet were smaller than Alex's. We had a minor crisis on our hands – or feet.

After a few minutes ranting and raving, Archie Knox came up with a solution: "Big Man, you've got your boots with you, haven't you?"

"Yes," I replied.

"Right, Alex. Give Big Ben's boots a try."

Alex slipped my boots on. They were too big, they were size 10 and Alex was a size 9. There was no other option though. Archie grabbed the physio's kit bag and foraged around for a second or two before producing a handful of cotton wool. "Here, stick this in the toes, Big Eck. It'll do the trick."

Alex played the entire 120 minutes in my boots, complete with cotton wool stuffing. And you know what? He only went and scored. So there you are, my right boot scored a goal in the Scottish Cup final. It was a spectacular equaliser, too, a swerving shot on 33 minutes which took us to extra time. We beat Rangers 4–1, ending a decade of Old Firm domination in the competition. More importantly, it meant we qualified for the European Cup Winners' Cup the next season, so I felt I had, in some small way, atoned for my blunder at Hibs at the start of the season.

That cup final was one of my first tastes of football's high life, as it were. Archie and Fergie made a point of making sure all the squad players felt a part of the occasion, almost ordering us to join in the celebrations on the pitch at the end. I was really pleased to see my mates Neale Cooper, Eric Black and John Hewitt doing so well and went round hugging everyone. The champagne flowed freely in the dressing room. We kept topping up the cup, and knocking it back in time-honoured tradition. I don't know which felt better – touching the cup for the first time or slurping champagne out of it. It was a superb day and in all the excitement I probably had more than my fair share of the bubbly. In fact, those celebrations ultimately led to one of my most embarrassing moments as a professional footballer.

That evening the team stayed at the famous Gleneagles hotel just outside Perth. The married players and their wives spent the evening at the hotel, but a couple of us single lads decided to go into Perth for the night. We found a bar and had a few drinks before getting back to the hotel in the early hours of the morning. Having had plenty of champagne after the game and then again on the bus, all washed down with a few pints of lager, I woke up the next morning feeling none too good.

I went down for breakfast on the Sunday morning and helped myself to a huge steaming plateful of sausages, eggs, bacon and black pudding. But no sooner had I taken my first bite than I came over all queasy and, before I could rush out of the room or even put my hand over my mouth, bleurgh, I was sick all over the plate. In front of most of squad. Archie Knox and his wife Janice were sitting at the next table and he gave me a right dirty look.

Nice one, Bryan! I was sitting with Dougie Bell, Gordon Strachan and Eric Black. But not for long – as soon as the previous night's excesses came back to haunt me, the lads shot away from the table. I quickly covered the plate up with a napkin and walked away embarrassed. I got away with it though. Thankfully Fergie wasn't there at the time and nothing was said. Not my finest hour.

Later that afternoon we travelled back to Aberdeen, stopping on the outskirts of the city where we switched to an open-top bus for a celebratory parade through the streets. To begin with I sat at the back of the bus, feeling absolutely awful but trying to disguise my predicament. But slowly the fresh air kicked in, the hangover began to wear off and I moved forward to join in the celebrations, waving to the thousands of Dons' fans lining the streets. They must have been ten deep as we passed through Union Street on our way to Pittodrie where we received a tumultuous reception. I was so proud just to be part of it. The champagne was doing the rounds again, but I politely declined this time. This was my first open-top tour and I was determined to lap it all up, even with a fuzzy head.

We started our 1982/83 European Cup Winners Cup campaign with a tie against Swiss side FC Sion. It was a beautiful place, but their football wasn't so impressive and we thrashed them 11–1 on aggregate thanks to a 7–0 win at Pittodrie followed by a 4–1 stroll in front of a crowd of less than 2,500 in Switzerland. I must admit I was a little surprised and disappointed I didn't get to play in the second leg, given that we were effectively already through, but Alex Ferguson was always one for playing his strongest squad. At least he was then.

Next up we played Dinamo Tirana of Albania. We stayed in the best, if not the only, hotel in Tirana. It was nothing special; a basic two-star place, I'd say. It was clean enough, but even so the gaffer was taking no chances. We took our own chef on the trip, along with food hampers packed with plenty of snacks like Mars bars and crisps – Golden Wonder cheese and onion for me, of course. We were in and out of Tirana as quickly as possible, playing out a goalless draw to win the tie 1–0 on aggregate before flying straight home.

We then played Lech Poznan from Poland, beating them 3–0 on aggregate to take us through to the quarter-finals and a tie against one of the giants of European football, Bayern Munich. This was the big one, a massive game for Aberdeen Football Club and a huge test of Fergie's managerial credentials. Fergie loved the European games, especially opportunities like this to pit his wits against one of the biggest teams on one of the biggest stages. If he could pull off the biggest result in the Dons' history, people would really start to sit up and take notice.

After Tirana and Poznan, Munich was like a five-star holiday. As usual, I trained on the pitch with Jim the night before the game. This time, unlike the previous trips to the Eastern Bloc, the surface was fantastic and we thoroughly enjoyed the session. We weren't the only ones. Alex Ferguson and Archie Knox weren't going to miss out on a chance to have a run-out in one of the most famous stadiums in the world and Fergie insisted we finish things off with a match, just like back home. And this being the famous Olympic Stadium, they couldn't resist joining in. Fergie kept his elbows to himself this time though.

Bayern had some outstanding players, like West German inter-nationals Karl-Heinz Rummenigge and Klaus Augenthaler, but they hardly got a sniff as the boys fought out a tremendous 0–0 draw, thanks in no small way to a brilliant defensive performance. Willie Miller and Alex McLeish were fantastic in the middle of the back four and Jim Leighton made some superb saves. I always took pride in watching Jim play well. We worked so closely together in training that I felt a clean sheet for Jim was a clean sheet for me, too.

Pittodrie was packed to the rafters for the return leg against Bayern a fortnight later. The atmosphere was electric, like nothing I'd experience at the ground before. The noise was deafening, even as we went out for the pre-match warm-up. Fergie had identified Augenthaler as a particular threat because of his phenomenal shot. I could strike a ball well, so the gaffer told me to fire a few at Jim and give him a thorough workout before the game. I was on fire in our warm-up, smacking balls at Jim left, right and centre. Every time I slammed one past him I shouted: "Augenthaler, top corner!" As it happened, the match commentator went on to say much the same thing because Augenthaler scored on the night, putting the Germans ahead after only 10 minutes. It didn't matter; we won a thrilling cup tie 3–2. It was a real helter-skelter game; one of those wonderful occasions Aberdeen fans will never forget.

If Bayern Munich were one of the most famous clubs in the world, our opponents in the semi-final, Waterschei from Belgium, were positively unknown. Naturally, Fergie made sure we knew everything about them by the time the first leg came along, so much so we thrashed them 5–1 at Pittodrie to make the return match something of a formality. We lost 1–0 in Belgium. Not a disaster you might think, but Fergie was apoplectic. He couldn't stand being beaten, even though we'd won through to the final with relative ease. The moment he burst into the dressing room we knew what was coming.

"You bastards," he screamed. "What the f***ing hell was that all about? It might be good enough for you, but it isn't good enough for me. If that's the best you can do you can all f*** off. Now."

Suddenly a bottle of champagne emerged from nowhere.

"Gaffer, we're in the final!" said Archie Knox.

That did the trick. Fergie's face broke into a huge smile, there was an almighty cheer and we all burst out laughing. It was, after all, our first European final. Defeat or no defeat, even Fergie had to celebrate that.

The final was against the mighty Real Madrid in Gothenburg, by far the biggest game in Aberdeen's history, over and above anything the Dons had won in the League or Scottish cups and arguably the biggest game involving a Scottish club since Celtic won the European

Cup in 1967. The city was buzzing; you couldn't go anywhere without being greeted by a mass of red and white flags. Everyone was talking about the cup final and just about everyone, it seemed, would be hopping on the ferry to Scandinavia so they could be there.

We flew to Sweden a couple of days before the game and stayed a few miles outside Gothenburg. The place was called Farsaat or something like that, which I remember because it sounded just like the way Aberdonians say "Where's that?" I also remember that from the minute we arrived in Sweden to the night of the game it absolutely poured down. The pitch was saturated and we weren't allowed to train on it, apart from one brief session on the day before the game.

We were real underdogs: Real Madrid had plenty of great players such as Hector Camacho, Johnny Metgod and Uli Steilike. Madrid's star names were about to be upstaged, though, by my friend Eric Black. Blacko was brilliant: a fleet-footed striker with a real eye for goal. He was only 5'8" but awesome in the air and scored loads of goals with his head. He was on top of his game at this time and starting to catch the eye of several European scouts, and it took him just seven minutes to give us the lead in Gothenburg. Blacko pounced on a cross and slid in at the far post to make it 1–0. I was so proud of him; here was the young lad I'd known since our primary school days scoring a massive goal against Real Madrid in a European final. I jumped off the bench and punched the air in delight, hugging my fellow substitutes John Hewitt and Stuart Kennedy. Stuart had played right through the European run but injured himself before the final. Fergie insisted he took his place on the bench, even though he was never going to play. That was a mark of the man – always striving to do the right thing by the people who'd worked hard for him.

The rain continued to pour down throughout the game, turning a poor pitch into something of a mud bath. I got absolutely drenched sitting on the bench and felt even more miserable when Real Madrid scored from a penalty. Then in the 90th minute they won a free-kick on the edge of the box. Johnny Metgod, who was famous for scoring from powerful free-kicks, shaped up to take it. I put my hands together and said a prayer, "Please God, make him miss." It worked. Metgod hit his shot past the post. Seconds later the ref blew his whistle and the game went into extra time.

Flying Saucers

Just as it looked like we were heading for a penalty shoot-out John Hewitt, Aberdeen born and bred, and our very own super-sub, came on and hit the winner. We went barmy on the bench but then had to sit and count the seconds down to the final whistle. The tension was unbearable as Real poured forward in search of an equaliser. Somehow we held out and eventually the referee blew the final whistle. We all leapt off the bench and raced out of the dug-out to join in the celebrations on the pitch.

Unfortunately I jumped out just as the boss was running past me with his arms aloft in celebration, accidentally knocking him clean over in the process. Poor old Fergie fell flat on his face, straight into a puddle on the speedway track surrounding the pitch. I didn't realise what I'd done at first and carried on running towards the boys on the pitch. It was only when I looked round to see the gaffer getting up, his face and head covered in water and ash from the speedway track, a gooey red mess soaking his hair and streaming down his face, that I realised what I'd done.

The gaffer was wiping the residue from his eyes as he stumbled across the pitch trying to catch up with the rest of the boys. He shot me a dirty look – in more ways than one – as if to say I was in big trouble. This was his finest hour, but I'd reduced him to an undignified mess. As he ran towards me I feared for my immediate future, – or at least my win bonus – but he carried on past me onto the pitch and promptly went round hugging all the players.

It was Fergie's first major European trophy – he always talked about winning trophies, or 'troughies', rather than cups or silverware – and nothing was going to spoil the moment. Mind you, I still remember him desperately trying to wipe all the red ash out of his hair and face before he faced the TV cameras for the post-match interviews.

He never mentioned it after the game, but the incident made me more and more determined that life on the bench was not for me!

CHAPTER FIVE

Mars Bars and Fish Heads

A couple of weeks after Gothenburg, Eric Black, Neale Cooper and I were selected for the Scotland squad for the World Youth Cup in Mexico, under the control of manager Andy Roxburgh and head coach Craig Brown, both of whom I knew pretty well from their involvement in the Scottish schoolboy set-up.

Andy was an interesting character. He insisted we sing a rousing rendition of *Flower of Scotland* before every game to get us nicely psyched up – and he also liked us to eat a Mars bar just before kick off. I guess he thought it would give us an energy boost and there was always one laid out with our kit.

Our opening games against South Korea and Australia were to be played at 8,844 feet above sea level in a place called Toluca, 45 minutes west of Mexico City, which was obviously going to test the stamina of the outfield players. We goalkeepers also faced a challenge: playing with the new adidas Tango ball which was light and really zipped through the air, so players would happily have a go from just about anywhere, pinging in 30- and 40-yard shots at every opportunity.

Our first game was against the Koreans. The majority of the crowd were local Mexicans, although there were a few Scots. Well, as they say, wherever you go in the world you're bound to meet a Scot. Trouble is, the one who must have been hanging around Toluca had clearly upset just about everyone, because it was clear they didn't like us at all – I got absolutely pelted with coins right from the first whistle. Talk about intimidation; it was a nightmare. It would have been really unsettling for a seasoned keeper, but for an 18-year-old in his first major international tournament, it was bewildering.

I did my best to ignore it and concentrate on the game, even picking up the pesos and stashing them in my bag so I could treat the boys to a drink or two later (mind you, when I got to the bar I discovered they were worth virtually nothing). But the coins were only part of the story. I also got hit with a torrent of rotten fruit. Oranges, lemons and limes – you name it, I got it thrown at me. Then, to round it all off, I felt a big thud on the back of my neck and turned to see a plastic bag lying behind me on the pitch. I picked it up and was suddenly overcome by a foul, rancid smell. It was full of rotten fish heads and tails. Charming.

Fergie and Archie Knox had always taught me to patrol my area, effectively acting as a sweeper behind my defenders, so I could escape to the 18-yard line where I was out of the range of the maniacs while the ball was in the Korean half. But when play came towards me I had to backtrack, which was the cue for another torrent of fruit and coins to come flying at me again.

Despite all the distractions, I had one the best games of my life as we won 2–0. South Korea were a decent team and not afraid to try their luck from all angles and distances. Even if I say so myself, I made a succession of really good saves and after the game Andy Roxburgh told me it was the best performance he'd ever seen from a Scottish goalkeeper, at any level. I got a lot of good press in Mexico and in the papers back home.

Two days later we were back at the same stadium for our second match, against Australia. We were very much the favourites and had high hopes of adding to our opening victory, but we went down to a surprise 2–1 defeat. To rub salt into our wounds, the Aussies' winning goal came from a guy called Jim Patikas, who the Aberdeen boys knew quite well because he'd spent a short time on trial at Pittodrie a couple of seasons earlier. The only plus point was that the throwing of rotten fruit eased off a bit. Perhaps they were just replenishing their supplies.

We had to win our final group match to stand a chance of progressing to the quarter-finals, but we were playing the Mexicans in the famous Azteca Stadium, which was packed with more than 100,000 fans. To say they're fanatical about their football in that part of the world is an understatement; even at under-19 level, the atmosphere was absolutely crazy. As soon as we kicked off there was all sorts raining down in my goalmouth again – coins, bottles, the lot. I remember a bottle of Johnnie Walker whizzing past my ear at one stage. I can't believe it was thrown by a Scotsman. Mind you, it *was* empty!

Despite the incredibly intimidating atmosphere we took the lead early in the game thanks to a goal from Steve Clarke, who's now Jose Mourinho's assistant at Chelsea. The locals didn't like it, to put it mildly, and as the game wore on they began to turn on their own players. They burned their Mexican flags and, as we continued to hold out against the Mexican attacks, their fans started hurling coins and bottles at their own players rather than us. It was especially bad when the Mexicans won corner kicks. Every time one of their players ran over to place the ball, a hail of bottles and coins would come flying at him from the crowd. It was so bad that after putting the ball in the corner the poor bloke would have to run out of range of the crowd and then pick his moment before nipping back to take the kick. Once he'd crossed the ball he'd sprint away from the crowd again as quickly as possible! It was farcical, and truly incredible for an under-19 game.

We held on to win 1–0 and qualify for a quarter-final match against Poland. The game was played in the Azteca Stadium again, only this time there was a big difference; the crowd couldn't have been more than about 10,000. What a contrast. Suffice it to say, it was a comparatively quiet affair, free of flying objects, but unfortunately for us Poland scored an early goal and knocked us out of the tournament.

Tours like this might sound glamorous, but all we got to see of Mexico was a quick tour of Mexico City the day after the game (more a mini-shopping expedition than sight-seeing, really) and a barbecue hosted by the local St Andrews Society. We didn't even get to try the local cuisine: we always had our own chefs who would conjure up some fairly plain beef or chicken to avoid the risk of an upset stomach just before a big game. Not that I would have tried the enchiladas or tacos anyway; I wasn't very adventurous with food back then. I was a small-town boy, fond of my mince and tatties. I did try some of the local tequila the night after we lost the quarter-final but soon switched to beer, and the only souvenirs I brought back were some local newspapers plastered with my picture after the Korean game. I still have no idea what the headlines say!

Back home in Scotland, the 1983/84 season brought a mixture of good news and bad. On the plus side, Aberdeen had a fantastic campaign. We were named European Team of the Year in December after we beat Hamburg 2–0 in the Super Cup, and went on to do the Scottish League and Cup double for the first and only time in the club's history. The bad news was I didn't play any part in it – not a single measly game.

In fact, from a personal point of view, I think the most memorable thing about the season was my array of multi-coloured hairstyles. Neale Cooper and me used to go to a hairdressers in Aberdeen called A Cut Above, run by a couple called Margaret and Ian Christie who used to really pamper us. We'd always come out with different coloured hair, which obviously didn't impress the gaffer. He was always having a go at us about it. On one occasion, before a big European tie, Fergie called the team together for a crisis meeting. We had lost to Hibs the previous day and the boss wasn't happy. We were all in the boardroom at Pittodrie on the Sunday morning. Fergie was generally having a bit of a go and then he suddenly turned to Neale and myself in front of all the lads.

"Right, I'm not happy. Gunn and Cooper, if your hair's not back to its usual colour tomorrow, you're not going on the plane on Tuesday."

We couldn't believe it! How on earth could the colour of our hair have anything to do with getting beaten by Hibs? I wouldn't have minded, but I hadn't even played in the game – I just happened to have bleached blond hair, which apparently meant it was my fault. Needless to say, we had our hair dyed back to its normal colour the very next day.

Aberdeen played more than 50 games that season and the bullet-proof Jim Leighton, with his natural locks, didn't miss a single minute. I didn't even get a sniff after we beat Raith Rovers 9–0 in the first leg of a League Cup tie early in the season; Fergie stuck with Jim for the return leg. I don't know if he was expecting a shock comeback by the struggling First Division side, but in the event the Dons scraped through 3–0 at Stark's Park to win through 12–0 on aggregate. Consequently, as great as it was for the club, I can't say I have any particularly outstanding memories of my fourth season at Pittodrie. In a nutshell, I spent the whole year in the reserves.

Mind you, I did have one memorable game turning out for 'the stiffs'. On 12th May 1984, against St Mirren Reserves, I scored a goal! Alex Ferguson knew I was pretty tidy with my feet – I'd often have a kickabout with the other outfield players in training – and had always said he'd happily put me up front in the event of an injury crisis. Well, true to his word I got the nod against St Mirren a week before the cup final against Celtic when he wanted to rest a few players. And not long into my outfield debut, Neil Simpson floated over a free kick which I headed into the top corner past Billy Thompson, who was a Scottish international goalkeeper!

I was ecstatic and ran round the ground punching the air and giving all the staff on the bench, including Fergie, big high fives. I stood there in front of the directors box with my arms aloft, milking the applause. Alex McLeish, Willie Miller and Mark McGhee were giving me a standing ovation. "Nice one, Big Man," they shouted. It was a really special moment. Normally it was me hero-worshipping them.

Unfortunately, I also picked up a nasty ankle injury later in the game. I went in for a crunching tackle and everything felt a bit squelchy in my right boot. I pulled my sock down and there was blood every-where, so I went off and had a few stitches and then came back on again. I've still got the scars. We won the game 2–1. Gordon Strachan was also watching the match, and he must have been suitably impressed because not so long ago he was on television and described me as the best outfield-playing goalkeeper he ever knew. Gordon, for the record, was rubbish in goal!

Despite my goal-scoring heroics, 1983/84 was obviously a bit frustrating but I never let it get to me. Goalkeepers tend to have a more philosophical outlook on the game than perhaps outfield players do. We're competing for just one spot, whereas outfield players have more opportunities to make their mark in a number of positions, so as a young goalkeeper you are already primed for a long period of waiting and understudying.

You have to be very patient and resilient as a goalkeeper – and really just keep your mouth shut, your head down and get on with it. I think my upbringing helped in that respect, as my friends and family were never the sort of people to go over the top about things and neither am I. On the one hand, this meant I was never really fazed by the big occasion – excited, yes, but never overawed. On the other hand, I never got upset about being in the reserves – it was just the way things were, a situation I couldn't change and part and parcel of the job I was employed to do. We may seem hot-headed sometimes when we're screaming at defenders, but I think goalkeepers are by nature (and because of the demands of the job) fairly even-tempered. You get on with it, simple as that, because that's the nature of the beast. It helped that Jim was brilliant, really encouraging and always making me feel that I was a valued part of the team. We were extremely close friends, which is unusual when there are only two of you in such a competitive situation.

Anyway, I had other things to distract me that season. I graduated to the Scottish under-21 team, coached by Walter Smith. I had huge respect for Walter, and not just because of his reputation as a coach and the 600 or so games he'd played for Dundee United – I'd played against him for Aberdeen reserves and I knew what a hard bastard he was. He was great with us kids though – very easy to talk to and relaxed about us having a game of golf when we all met up, although he did have more of a temper than either Andy Roxburgh or Craig Brown.

I made my under-21 debut in a UEFA Championship group qualifying match in East Germany on a snowy November night, so snowy that we had to use an orange ball. Roy Aitken, one of our over-aged players, gave us the lead at half-time but the Germans, roared on by a home crowd of around 500 – yes, 500 – grabbed an equaliser after the break and we ended up with a 1–1 draw. I made quite a few decent saves in difficult conditions and was pleased with my debut, especially as it helped Scotland to remain undefeated in the competition and we qualified for the quarter-finals as group winners.

The first leg of the quarter-final tie against Yugoslavia was played at Pittodrie, which was fantastic for me, especially as more than 11,000 fans turned up to see us win 2–1, a slight improvement on the attendance in East Germany. Mo Johnston and Brian McClair got the goals to set things up nicely for the return.

Three weeks later we met up at the Excelsior hotel at Glasgow airport for an overnight stay ahead of the flight to Belgrade. It was a really important match for the under-21s, so much so that Jock Stein, the full Scotland team manager at the time, was also on the trip to oversee things.

Most of us headed for our rooms and were soon tucked up in bed, as per the rules. All apart from three members of the squad: Mo Johnston, Frank McAvennie and Charlie Nicholas, who had just made his big-money move to Arsenal. They nipped out for a few shandies, but when they returned in the early hours they found themselves locked out of the hotel. They knocked on a side door and an old boy let them in. Charlie and the lads thought he was the night porter, thanked him for letting them in and tucked a tenner into his pocket.

The next morning at breakfast Jock Stein called Charlie, Mo and Frank over to him. "I'd like you to meet a friend of mine," he said, gesturing to the porter from the night before. "Jock McDonald, president of the Scottish FA." Their faces were a picture, but there were no major recriminations as I recall.

Charlie and Mo both played in Yugoslavia. It was another close match and we were trailing 2–1 when the whistle went for the end of normal time. The Yugoslavs then grabbed a winner in extra time to knock us out of the tournament. It was a massive blow because we had some really good players in the team (Charlie, Mo, Richard Gough, Neale Cooper, Brian McClair and Paul McStay) and felt we could have gone on to win it. Did that late night out affect Charlie or Mo? I doubt it. As for me, little did I know at the time but my performances had certainly impressed Walter Smith.

*   *   *

Mars Bars and Fish Heads

It wasn't long before I met up with Charlie Nicholas and Mo Johnston again. In the early 1980s, Ibiza became something of a magnet for footballers and a few of the lads from the under-21 trip went to San Antonio for a couple of weeks in June. It was a footballers' paradise. At least if you were single. In fact, make that a *poseur's* paradise. Charlie, Mo and their mates were real fashion merchants. Leather was very much the thing back then and they'd be dressed up to the nines in leather trousers or leather shorts (thankfully not the full Frankie Goes to Hollywood look). The Glasgow boys were the trendsetters, the rest of us were constantly trying to catch up.

When we met up for internationals most of us would have a normal suit on or even just a tracksuit. Charlie, however, would turn up wearing something outrageous, like leather trousers and a pink shirt. Then Neale Cooper, John Hewitt and I would hit the shops back in Aberdeen and buy the same sort of clothes. The problem was, Charlie was always one step ahead, so by the time we met up again he'd moved on to the next craze. We'd just be getting into something like the New Romantic Duran Duran look, only for Charlie to have moved on to George Michael-style cropped trousers. I always just wore my tracksuit in for training at Aberdeen, otherwise I'd have got hammered by the other lads. I did, however, once turn up for a match at Ibrox in a black leather jacket and trousers, pink shirt and pink leather tie. I kept my *white* leather trousers for even more special occasions, obviously!

I was still wearing some pretty dodgy gear, but the 1984/85 season was marginally better on the domestic front – I actually got to play a couple of first-team games. As usual I warmed the bench in the European Cup where we were drawn against Dinamo Berlin in the first round. We won the first leg 2–1 at Pittodrie before going down by the same score in Germany to take the tie to extra time and then a penalty shoot-out. It was torturous. Willie Miller had to score to keep us in the competition. I couldn't watch: I lay down on the running track in front of the dug-out with my hands over my eyes, praying he would score. Of course, my main concern was for Aberdeen to progress to the next round, but there was also the small issue of my win bonus to consider. We were on big European bonuses and whatever regulars like Willie Miller and Alex McLeish were getting, I would be getting the same just for being part of the squad.

Unlike Willie and Alex, though, Europe offered my only real chance of a decent bonus because I wasn't a regular in the first team and the bonuses in the reserves didn't amount to much more than £10–£20. The bonus for beating Dinamo Berlin was more like £1,000, which was huge money to me. I was depending on it to buy some new clothes, or possibly even a car.

Willie stepped up. I shut my eyes. He missed. No car then.

My two first-team starts that season were both in the League, where Alex Ferguson was desperately hoping to retain the title. We had made a cracking start to the campaign and were comfortably leading the table with only one draw and one defeat from our opening 17 games. We then hit a stuttering run of four matches without a win over Christmas and the New Year. Fergie called me into his office.

"Get yourself ready," he said. "You're in the team tomorrow."

I didn't get too excited: I think he just wanted to give Jim a kick up the backside, freshen things up.

The game was against Hibernian, coincidentally the team I played against on my League debut. Happily, there was no repeat of the sloppy goal I conceded three years earlier at a waterlogged Easter Road; I kept a clean sheet in a 2–0 win at Pittodrie. Just before the next game Fergie took me aside for a quiet word.

"Well done, Big Ben, you did really well against Hibs, but Jim's back in tomorrow I'm afraid."

I could always tell it was hard for him to break the news, but I respected his decision because that was his job. He had always told me that Jim was his number one – I knew it would be very hard, if not impossible, to replace him.

Jim started every game after that until the final league match of the season, at Morton, a full four months later. We had already won the League and I think Fergie must have taken pity on me because he gave me the nod for the trip to Cappielow Park. I might point out that Morton were rock bottom of the table and already relegated so there wasn't exactly much hanging on the result – I think Fergie wanted me to have a win bonus. All the same, we won 2–1 to take the title, finishing a full seven points ahead of Celtic. Aberdeen haven't won the Scottish championship since, so I guess I can at least claim some kudos for playing in that final match of the title-winning campaign – not that I'd played enough games to qualify for a medal!

A couple of weeks after the game at Morton I rounded off a busy season for the under-21s with a European Championship group match in Iceland on the eve of the full international. We lost 2–0, but my main memories of the trip are off the pitch. After the game, most of us headed for a nightclub in Reykjavik which was hosting the Miss Iceland competition. Football and beautiful women – it was a weekend made for Rod Stewart, who just happened to be there as one of the judges.

We got a round of beers and sauntered over to him. "Good to see you boys," he said, grinning. "Tough luck tonight, let's hope for better tomorrow. Mind you, this isn't a bad job is it?" He gestured at the girls and winked.

The Icelandic girls paraded up and down on the stage in front of us. They were stunning and I was lucky enough to be introduced to the girl who won the competition. Her name was Hofi Karlsdottir. She was absolutely gorgeous, with flowing long blonde hair and a fantastic smile – amongst other things. I congratulated her on her victory with a respectful kiss on the cheek (the Glasgow boys would have steamed right in) and wished her all the best for the main Miss World competition. It did the trick: the lovely Hofi went on to win Miss World 1985. Not everyone can say they've met Miss World, George Best would have been proud of me. Or perhaps not – I was far too polite and shy to ask for her phone number.

At the start of the 1985/86 season Alex Ferguson called me into his office to talk to me about my future. "You've done really well, Big Man," he said, "but Jim Leighton is still very much my number one. I want you to do me a favour and stay for another year. If you help me out, trust me, I'll find you a club at the end of it if you want to move then."

I had only played three first-team games in five years as a pro at Aberdeen and, although I was only 21, I was desperately keen for first-team football. But I trusted Fergie when he said he'd look after me, so I happily signed for another year on around £300 a week, plus half a win bonus even if I didn't play, which I thought was very fair of him. He was always very fair and straightforward in his dealings with me.

As it happened, I found myself playing for the Dons at the start of the season. Jim picked up an injury in the opening league match against Hibernian and I came into the side for the next game, a 1–1 draw at Dundee United. I've got the game on video, but I don't feature very often because I didn't have much to do. Aberdeen and Dundee United were similar teams and it was a bit like a boxing match, with little to choose between us. Both clubs were going well at the time; in fact, we were called the 'New Firm' because we were right up there challenging, and beating, Celtic and Rangers.

After Dundee United it was a little like the old 'waiting for a bus' syndrome as, after such a long wait, suddenly the games came thick and fast and I played four matches in just 12 days. Two wins, two draws, two clean sheets, surely I would keep my place now? By the end of August Jim had recovered and duly came straight back into the team. Ah well.

In March, however, I did finally and somewhat unexpectedly make my debut in the European Cup. The first leg of our quarter-final against IFK Gothenburg was at Pittodrie, and as usual I was to be on the bench. There was no sign of the drama to come as I warmed up with Jim on the pitch before kick-off, but when we returned to the dressing room and he put his contact lenses in he found he couldn't see properly. It turned out he'd picked up an eye infection and we soon realised he had a major problem and wouldn't be able to play. So I was in.

It was a huge game but there was no time for nerves, I just went out for a quick warm-up and got on with it. At half-time we were level at 1–1 with young Joe Miller scoring our goal. Pittodrie's European super-sub John Hewitt then came on for Joe. One of my specialities was to release the ball early, drop-kicking it forward as quickly as possible, and not long after John came on I launched a big kick over the top of their defence to put John away. He ran on to score and make it 2–1 to us, with an assist for Big Ben!

We were on the verge of a fantastic result until the last minute when Swedish international Johnny Ekstrom broke clear from the halfway line. He was a tall, gangly centre-forward, but with lightning pace, and he sprinted clear of our back four before taking the ball round my despairing dive and tucking it away to make it 2–2. We drew the return leg 0–0 at the Ullevi Stadium and went out of the competition on away goals. I sometimes wonder what might have been that season; Gothenburg went out to Barcelona on penalties in the semis and the Spanish giants lost the European Cup final to Steaua Bucharest on penalties, so there wasn't much to choose between us.

As the 1985/86 season drew to a close I suddenly got my chance to become a first-team regular when Jim Leighton was involved in another freak incident. He was cleaning out the bottom of his lawn-mower, but he hadn't unplugged it first. His young daughter Claire accidentally switched the socket on, and the blades suddenly whirred into action. Jim pulled his hand away, but not in time to prevent one of the blades catching the top of his finger. If it had happened to almost any other person there's a good chance they would have suffered serious injuries. It was only Jim's rapid reflexes as a goalkeeper that saved him and probably his career.

Even so, the top of Jim's finger was badly injured and he had to have several stitches, which meant he would be out of action for a few weeks. I came in and played the final seven league games of the campaign, starting with back-to-back wins over Motherwell. Sandwiched between those victories there was a hugely important match in the semi-finals of the Scottish Cup. We were one step away from another cup final, but more than that, it was a chance for us to do the cup 'double', having won the Skol League Cup earlier in the season. Our opponents were Hibernian – it's strange how often we seemed to play them when I got into the team – at a neutral venue, Dens Park, Dundee.

I had one of my best games in an Aberdeen shirt, pulling off a series of good saves. The pick of them was quite early on in the game, with the score still 0–0. A shot from the edge of the area was heading for my top right corner until it deflected off Willie Miller's leg and started heading to my left. I was already diving to my right and it seemed a sure-fire goal but I managed to arch my back and change direction in mid-air, stick out my left hand and flick it onto the crossbar. It was a sensational save, and one of the most important I've ever made. My team-mates raced over to congratulate me and I clenched my fists in determination. "Come on!"

We went on to win the tie 3–0 and book our place in the final against Hearts. In the dressing room afterwards Alex Ferguson was ecstatic. After congratulating everyone else, he singled me out for special praise.

"You've helped us win the cup today, Big Ben," he said, slapping me on the back. I was chuffed – Fergie never normally singled out one particular player in front of everyone else – but I kept quiet. I was just doing my job.

We all went out and painted the town red that night, especially once Neale Cooper and I had got rid of the older married lads. Neale, or Big Tatty as we called him, was one of my best mates and the loudest, daftest lad you could ever meet. He was always larking about, telling jokes and everyone loved him. He was a brilliant mimic and did a superb impression of Fergie. The gaffer had this little nervous cough in the build-up to big games and Neale would copy it perfectly.

"You! [Cough cough]. Make sure you keep tight on their full-back. [Cough cough]. And you. [Cough cough]. Get your bloody hair cut." It was hilarious and really relaxed us before a big match. That night he was in excellent form too. "Cough. Big Ben! Cough. It's your [cough] round [cough]. Highlander! Cough. Put down that bloody pint and go [cough] home."

Neale was actually Fergie's blue-eyed boy (and Andy Roxburgh's too – he even likened him to Franz Beckenbauer). He could do amazing things with the ball, swerving passes around opponents, flicking it with the outside of his right boot. He had the star job of looking after Fergie and Archie's kit. Everyone wanted to look after theirs as you were less likely to get battered by them throwing their boots back at you.

We finished our league campaign with a 6–0 thrashing of Clydebank, just a week before the cup final, which I was really looking forward to. The general consensus seemed to be that I'd played well and I certainly felt I'd done enough to justify my place in the team. Having at last enjoyed a decent run of matches I was really building a relationship with the defence and felt I was on top of my game. As far as I was concerned, the next stop was Hampden Park and the final against Hearts, who were absolutely gutted after missing out on the title.

I went out to Our Man, a really trendy clothes shop in Aberdeen and spent ages choosing my suit for the big day. I finally settled on a navy Hoff number, with a pink and lime green stripe and bought matching pink and green shirts and pink and green ties. I got a nice cream raincoat to finish off the outfit. It all set me back a few hundred quid, but I was determined to be looking the business on my big day.

Jim was recovering from his injury and, in the week leading up to the cup final, played in a reserve game at Ibrox. On the Friday morning we turned up to train as usual, all very keyed up and excited about the game the next day. I wasn't prepared for the bombshell about to hit me. Before the session started Fergie called me into his office, looking very serious.

"What's up, Boss?"

He came straight to the point. "I'm sorry I've got to say this, but Jim is playing in the cup final tomorrow."

It was the biggest kick in the teeth I'd ever had. I was absolutely devastated and started welling up. Fergie put his arm round my shoulder.

"I'm really sorry. I know you'll be disappointed, but I've got to think about preparing Jim for Scotland."

Fergie had taken over the national team following the sudden death of Jock Stein, and was taking charge for the World Cup finals in Mexico in a month's time. Jim Leighton was regarded as Scotland's number one keeper so Fergie explained he had to bring him back for the final to prove his fitness ahead of the World Cup.

I could see his logic and wasn't going to rant and rave about it because I had too much respect for both Alex Ferguson and Jim Leighton, but I was crushed. My confidence had been sky-high; now I felt as if the bottom had fallen out of my world. I felt my performances had pushed me ahead of Jim as Aberdeen's number one. I'd really built myself up for the final and had prepared as if I was going to be playing at Hampden. I hadn't even considered being dropped – why would I after the way I had been playing?

"You've done a great job for us, Big Ben, but I understand if you want to move on. You need first-team football. Walter Smith's been in touch and he's very keen to take you to Ibrox."

Walter Smith was the caretaker manager at Rangers while they waited for Graeme Souness to arrive as their new player-manager.

"Just say the word, Big Man, and I'll give him a call. I'm really sorry." He patted me on the back as I left.

I walked out onto the training pitch and told Jim the news. He was sympathetic and gave me a hug. "Unlucky mate. You've done really well." We had a really close relationship so I couldn't feel aggrieved at him, but I didn't want to chat about it either. Jim knew that so he just gave me a pat on the back and we started our warm-up routine as usual. After training I stumbled onto the team bus in shock. It was a long old journey to Glasgow and my mind was whirring. I didn't know how to feel. I was pleased about the possibility of a move to Rangers, one of the biggest clubs in the land, but still shell-shocked at missing out on the final.

The match was a blur. I remember standing on the pitch at Hampden in my nice new suit and not really taking it all in. I felt detached, as though I was watching myself from a great distance. I just didn't feel a part of the occasion. We beat Hearts 3–0, but the celebrations after the match were nothing like other finals I had been associated with. I was totally deflated.

CHAPTER SIX

Who, what, why, when, where?

After the kick in the teeth of missing out on the cup final, I decided I had to go away and get things out of my system. I went off to Greece for a holiday with Neale Cooper and a few other mates from Aberdeen. Just before I left I heard Graeme Souness had finally taken over at Ibrox. The Rangers move seemed a promising opportunity; Souness was clearly his own man and had money to spend so I figured he would be looking to stamp his mark on proceedings by building his own team at Ibrox as soon as possible.

I wasn't wrong. Two days into my holiday I was relaxing on the beach, letting the European sun work its magic on my Scottish skin, when I idly picked up the Scottish *Daily Record*. I nearly dropped the paper. Souness was indeed looking to bring some big names to Ibrox – Terry Butcher and Peter Shilton. Peter Shilton? What the hell was going on? I thought I was being lined up as the new keeper at Rangers? I couldn't believe it and decided to drown my sorrows by sinking a few beers, even though it was still only 11 in the morning.

I woke up the following day with a massive hangover and went straight out to buy the *Daily Record*. This time the paper said Peter Shilton wouldn't be moving to Ibrox after all. Thank God for that. I read on, expecting to see my name, and discovered the reason he wasn't moving to Ibrox was that Rangers had signed Norwich City's goalkeeper Chris Woods. What? There I was, miles from home, and I simply didn't have a clue what was happening to my career. Again I hit the bottle. I vaguely recall lying on the beach, in a drunken stupor, thinking, "Where am I going from here?"

Until then everything in my life had gone so well, right from the moment I'd started playing. Now, I suddenly realised I wasn't in control of my own destiny. To be fair, Chris Woods was one of the best up-and-coming keepers in the game. He'd made his England debut and was in the squad for the World Cup in Mexico that summer. He'd also been an ever-present for Norwich as they won the old Second Division championship. Rangers had paid Norwich £600,000 for him, which was a Scottish record transfer fee at the time. But I was still totally confused.

I was really struggling to get my head round what I would do next and ended up opting for mad Scotsman mode. I spent the rest of the holiday drinking shed-loads and lying on the beach frying under the fierce sun. And I mean literally frying. We all covered ourselves in Mazola cooking oil, convinced we would tan faster. I got well and truly frazzled, but the Ouzo stunned the pain.

Back at Pittodrie for training before the 1986/87 season, I went straight to see Alex Ferguson in his office.

"So what happens now, Boss? Where do I fit in?"

"Don't worry, Big Man, I've already been on the phone to Ken Brown at Norwich City. They're interested in you and we'll see if we can sort something out."

Ken hadn't seen me play, but apparently he was happy to take me on Alex Ferguson's recommendation. The two clubs agreed a transfer fee of £100,000 with a further £50,000 to follow if and when I won my first Scotland cap.

I flew down to Norwich a few days later, feeling quite excited. I didn't know much about the club, other than remembering Justin Fashanu's famous Goal of the Season against Liverpool, but frankly it didn't matter; Norwich City had won promotion and were back in the top league in England. It was an excellent opportunity for regular first-team football.

Ken Brown and his assistant Mel Machin met me at the airport and took me out for a tour of the training ground at Trowse, just outside the city. It wasn't bad (although not a patch on what they've got now) with a weights room and all the usual facilities – although some of the training pitches were on a bit of a hill, which is quite a rare find in East Anglia! They took me on a quick tour of the stadium, where I admired the building site that was the new City Stand (the old one had recently been destroyed by fire) and the portakabin changing rooms in between the City and River End stands, before heading out for a medical with the club doctor at Cromer, 26 miles away up on the north Norfolk coast. Strangely, he X-rayed my knees and back, but not my hands, even though I was a goalkeeper. The middle finger on my left hand looks as though it's dislocated; the result of a training ground accident as a teenager which bent the finger right back. It's never been a problem to me, but I thought it might have raised one or two questions.

Back at the club, Ken took me into his office for a quick chat. Fergie had already done the groundwork for me and negotiated a rise of £100 a week, to £400 a week, plus a £25,000 signing-on fee – peanuts nowadays but big money back then. I was happy to agree the terms, although we didn't sign contracts at that stage. I'd been impressed when I'd seen Ken interviewed on television, and in real life he was a very friendly, happy sort of bloke who seemed to have a real interest in people.

There was just time for a quick picture in front of one of the goals with the local paper, the *Eastern Daily Press*, which ran the photo on their back page later with the headline 'Bryan Gunn tries the Carrow Road goalmouth for size'. Happy and excited, I headed back to Aberdeen, with everyone expecting my move to go through in the next few days. After all the frustration of the cup final and the on-off transfer to Rangers, at last everything seemed to be working out well.

Who, what, why, when, where?

I was ready to make a fresh start and couldn't get down to Norwich quickly enough. Then it happened.

On 16th August, in the third game of the season, Jim Leighton picked up a nasty head injury which would put him out of action for at least a fortnight, possibly more. Suddenly my dream move to Norwich was put on hold. Incredible. After all those years as his understudy, hardly getting a look-in, Jim picked that moment to get injured!

Fergie was very apologetic but I took it on the chin – although I was a little concerned that it might scupper the deal. I was still under contract to Aberdeen, so I just had to get on with it.

I was brought into the team for the Dons' next game, a Skol Cup tie against Alloa a few days later. Mel Machin, Ken Brown's assistant at Norwich, came up to watch me. I spotted him standing at the side of the pitch when I went out to limber up and decided to impress him by going all-out with my warm-up – with all due respect to Alloa, they weren't likely to be the toughest of opponents and we were expected to beat them comfortably on the night. I told the boys to give me a really good workout and I took every cross and saved every shot as if I was playing in a proper match. I was diving about everywhere, saving shots left, right and centre and coming out for crosses as if my life depended on it. It was the warm-up of all warm-ups. Just as well because, sure enough, I hardly had anything to do in the game as we beat Alloa 4–0, apart from one save in the last 15 minutes and, for all I know, Mel might have left by then.

Three days later I should have been with my new team-mates at Norwich City for their opening match of the season at Chelsea, but instead I was running out at Parkhead to play Celtic in front of more than 46,000 – including my parents who had travelled down especially. To play in front of such a crowd was some consolation, I guess. It was a dream come true and felt like real *Boy's Own* stuff.

The atmosphere was amazing. The noise coming from the Jungle – the huge area of terracing where the hard-core Celtic fans stood – was incredible, although I still think the Azteca Stadium was more intimidating. At least here I wasn't getting fish heads chucked at me. I was excited rather than nervous. The TV cameras were there so it was a great opportunity for me to show what I could do and I grabbed the chance with both hands, putting in a top-notch performance as we came under a lot of pressure. I made a couple of good saves from Scottish international Murdo MacLeod, who was notorious for hitting shots from 30-odd yards into the top corner. There were plenty of other big names in the Celtic team, like Tommy Burns, Roy Aitken, Pat Bonner, Brian McClair and Mo Johnston, but we managed to take the lead in the first half thanks to a goal from Joe Miller. As expected, Celtic really came at us in the second half and Murdo MacLeod eventually managed to beat me with a rocket of a shot from about 30 yards out which I didn't see until late. We ended up drawing 1–1, which was a really good result.

I managed to snatch five minutes with my parents after the game and my dad was spilling over with pride. He wasn't really a fan of any particular team, but he knew he'd get some stick when he got back to Invergordon. As in most Scottish towns in those days, you were either Rangers or Celtic, so he knew half his mates wouldn't be speaking to him for a day or so and the other half would be queuing up to buy him drinks.

I was pretty chuffed myself; I'd proved I could play on a big stage and showed I was a decent keeper. It was a great confidence boost for me, knowing I was going to go down to England and hopefully play in front of big crowds at places like Old Trafford and Anfield.

In total I played four games – three wins and that memorable draw at Celtic – and once again I thought I'd come in and done pretty well. But I knew Jim would come straight back into the side for the next game – the Skol Cup quarter-final, against Celtic. For once, though, I wasn't bothered. Jim was fit again and I was finally off to Norwich.

Oh no I wasn't! Just as the deal was about to go through, Aberdeen's number three keeper David Lawrie got injured and Alex Ferguson immediately called it off for a second time. To be fair, we were in the European Cup Winners' Cup again, with a first round tie against Swiss club Sion coming up at Pittodrie, and Fergie needed a reserve keeper on the bench.

In the run-up to the Sion game, I got the chance to strut my stuff again for the reserves as a centre-forward. Not only that, Fergie made me captain, a dubious honour in football as it usually means you'll be playing in the stiffs forever. To be honest, I'm not sure quite why he did it in the run-up to a big European game and weeks away from my big move south, but I was happy as always to help out. It wasn't a memorable affair – we had a player sent off so I had to drop back to centre-back. We lost 2–0 and I capped a great afternoon by getting booked for dissent.

Eventually I watched us beat Sion 2–1 from the bench, at the same time as Norwich were beating Leicester City by the same score at Carrow Road. It was the first of four straight league wins for Norwich, but as they climbed the table I was sitting at Pittodrie kicking my heels, waiting for the second leg of the Sion match. It was the end of September by now, more than a month into the new season. Norwich were going well but I was going nowhere. I was annoyed about the situation, but at the same time what could I do about it? Alex Ferguson was simply doing what was best for his team and I couldn't blame him for that. On 1st October we lost 3–0 in Switzerland to go out of the Cup Winners' Cup 4–2 on aggregate. Obviously, it wasn't good news for Aberdeen, but at least I would finally be able to make my long-awaited move to Norwich.

I flew down to Norfolk to complete my move on Wednesday 15th October 1986, the best part of two months later than originally planned. I was relieved and excited to be on my way at last. There was just one small problem. Norwich were top of the First Division, thanks in part to their keeper Graham Benstead, who had been promoted from the reserves at the start of the season and was evidently doing a good job. It was great to see my new club doing so well, but I was beginning to worry that I'd have problems getting into the team. That wasn't in the script, I was meant to be the Canaries' new number one, but how could they possibly drop a keeper who was doing so well?

My fears were confirmed soon after the plane touched down. Ken Brown greeted me with a big smile.

"Hey Big Man, how are you doing? It's great to have you here. We're just going to pop down to Carrow Road and sign some forms."

I couldn't quite work out what the hurry was, then he hit me with the news – he wanted me to play for the reserves that very night. They had a match against Crystal Palace at Tooting and Mitcham and Ken was keen for me to play, if the club could get the necessary paperwork sorted in time. What Ken didn't know was that I was nursing a monumental hangover from the night before. Neale and some of the other lads had taken me out for a few shandies in Aberdeen the night before to say goodbye and I was suffering big-time. Well, I had no idea they'd expect me to play on my first day. Ouch!

We went straight to Carrow Road to sign my contract, which was duly faxed through to Football League headquarters, then Ken drove me and his assistant Mel Machin down to London in his Volvo. All through the journey Ken blabbered on enthusiastically, filling me in on the team and other details. I was sitting in the back seat, feeling like death warmed up, trying to nod at the right moment. Occasionally, I caught a snippet of conversation ". . . so you'll be going back on the team bus with the other lads . . .", "we've booked you into the Oaklands hotel, it's very nice . . ." but I barely heard a word of what he said. I managed to throw in the occasional grunt to make it look good, but I was desperate to get my head down and grab a quick doze.

Once we got to the ground, we had to check that the League paperwork had come through and there was barely time for handshakes and a quick "I'm Bryan, good to meet you" before I was out on the pitch. I recognised one of my team-mates, Mark Barham, as he was an England international, but that was about it. Thirteen minutes into the game one of our centre-backs, Shaun Elliott, tried to head the ball back to me, but he didn't get enough on it and Palace's John Salako nipped in and tried to take it round me. I wiped him out just inside my area to give away a penalty and they scored from the kick. Great start, Bryan! Fortunately, we hit back to win 3–1, so there was no major damage done, but it was a bit of an embarrassing way to introduce myself to my new colleagues!

I travelled back to Norwich on the team bus and got chatting to Dave Hodgson, a Geordie lad who'd recently joined Norwich from Sunderland and was very friendly. He offered me a lift back to the hotel on the city outskirts, which was much appreciated as we didn't get back until after midnight and I was knackered when I finally collapsed into bed. It had been a hell of a day.

I got to meet the rest of the lads the next morning at a special training session on the Carrow Road pitch. It was packed with press and TV cameras, although I think that had more to do with Norwich being top of the league than my arrival. Most of the lads were really welcoming. The captain, Steve Bruce, immediately invited me round to his house for a meal and introduced me to the rest of the players, who all seemed good lads.

Graham Benstead came over and shook my hand. "All right?" he said, with a smile that said, "You're welcome, Big Man, but if you think you're going to waltz in here and take my place, you've got another think coming." He was polite enough, but distant. I knew straight away we'd never enjoy the kind of close relationship I had with Jim Leighton at Aberdeen. He was only a couple of months or so older than me, had just got his big break and knew I spelled danger. Fair enough. Ken took me to one side at the end of the training session.

"It's great to finally have you here," he said, "but I'm afraid I can't drop Graham. He's done really well for us and obviously we're flying, so I'm sorry, but I'm sticking by him and you're going to have to fight for your place."

Again, fair enough. I couldn't really argue with the manager when the club were top of the league and Fergie had told me Ken was a fair man, so, although I was disappointed, I knew I'd just have to wait for my chance. Like I say, it's just what goalkeepers have to do. Two days later I made my home debut for the reserves as we ran riot in a 7–1 win over QPR.

The next day Norwich lost 2–0 to Wimbledon at Plough Lane. It was City's first really poor performance of the season and Ken Brown was livid. Graham had made a bit of a hash of things for their first goal, scored by John Fashanu, but he wasn't the only one who'd struggled with the Dons' notorious up-and-at-'em approach and there was no suggestion he would be dropped for the next match at Liverpool. On the Friday morning before the game we were training as usual and at the end of the session I stood at the side of the pitch watching a few of the lads knock balls at Graham, who had stayed on for some extra shooting practice. I noticed him dive down for a shot and appear to hurt his shoulder. The physio came over, gave him some treatment, and that seemed to be that.

Twenty-four hours later Kenny Dalglish's Liverpool hit six past him as Norwich were hammered 6–2. Apparently Graham injured his shoulder in the first 10 or 15 minutes of the game. I think some of the damage was done in that incident in training on the Friday, but he obviously wanted to play at Anfield, especially with me having just signed. I wasn't actually at Liverpool for the game as there were no substitute keepers back then, so I had taken the opportunity to go back to Aberdeen to sort a few things out. In fact I was at Dens Park watching the Dons play Dundee and keeping up with events at Anfield on the radio.

That night I took James Welsh, his wife Irene and their sons Stephen and Stuart out for a meal. They went home to Inverurie and I headed to Aberdeen where I was staying at a mate's flat. I'd hired a car for the weekend. It was a two-litre Audi turbo which went like shit off a shovel and, driving on an unfamiliar country lane, I lost it on a corner, careered off the road and ended up in a ditch. Amazingly, I wasn't hurt at all, not even a scratch. The police arrived quickly, and helpfully gave me a lift back to Aberdeen. I flew back to Norwich the next day, none the worse for wear.

That's when I discovered the full extent of Graham's injury: he'd dislocated his shoulder, a particularly bad problem for a keeper. They wanted to keep the full extent of his injury quiet and I decided to keep mum about my little prang too. Ken and Mel had told me before the Liverpool game that, no matter what, I would be making my full debut in the upcoming midweek Full Members Cup tie against Coventry City.

The Coventry game was obviously a big match for me. Graham's injury meant there was suddenly a good chance I could be getting a run in the team, so there was an extra reason for wanting to do well on my debut. I can't say I felt any nerves. I'd been used to big games with Aberdeen and I was just focused on the job in hand. Anyway, this being a midweek cup game, it wasn't a huge crowd. I was keen to get a rapport going with them though and show them what I was all about.

Ever since I was a youngster I'd developed a little ritual, or habit, which I did before every game. So as I ran out onto the Carrow Road pitch for the very first time I did as I always did, ran towards the goal, jumping up as I reached it and making as if to head the crossbar. I don't know how, or why, it started, but it just became the natural thing for me to do. It didn't really get spotted at Pittodrie, but once the Norwich fans noticed that I did it every game it became traditional for them to cheer my little ritual at the beginning of each half. The supporters behind the Barclay End goal were really up for it. They would wait until I got to about the 18-yard line and then start a small "Wooo . . ." which would build into a full-blown "WOOOO . . . AH!" as I leapt up at the crossbar. I loved it, and came pretty close to smacking my head against the woodwork a couple of times. I always enjoyed a fantastic rapport with the Norwich supporters, and I think my unusual routine helped form that special bond.

I got a good reception from the Norwich crowd straightaway, although I didn't exactly endear myself to them from the off in the Coventry match. In fact, I conceded another early penalty – after 13 minutes. Again! Unlucky or what? This time Steve Bruce under-hit a backpass, which Coventry's Micky Gynn intercepted. He ran clean through and tried to go round me. I put out a big hand and sent him crashing. I was going for the ball, but poor Micky ended up in hospital with a dislocated collarbone.

Two games, two penalties conceded. I was so embarrassed. I dreaded to think what the supporters or my team-mates were thinking. Luckily, Kevin Drinkell scored twice as we came back to win 2–1, so again my intervention didn't prove too costly. And there was no chance to find out what my team-mates really thought of me by heading out for a few beers; that would have to wait, as three days later I was to make my League debut, at home to Spurs.

There was a brilliant atmosphere at Carrow Road for the Tottenham game, with more than 20,000 packed into the ground. Again, I can't say I was particularly nervous, but then I'd played in front of more than 46,000 at Celtic only a few weeks before and more than 100,000 in Mexico. I was getting used to big crowds and big occasions and frankly I wanted more of the same. I'd done the hard apprenticeship and learnt a lot and now I was just looking forward to this opportunity. My dad had flown down for the game and, to make things even better, the man in goal at the other end for Spurs was Ray Clemence, one of my all-time heroes. I'd arrived. This was what I'd been waiting for, to be playing on the same pitch as some of the best keepers in the business, pitting myself against them, and I wasn't about to blow my big chance.

It was an entertaining, close game and I was relieved when the 13th minute came and went without me conceding a penalty. Ian Crook played really well in midfield against his old team and finished off a flowing five-man move to put us ahead in the second half. Spurs' boss David Pleat then sent on Glenn Hoddle and it did the trick as they equalised through Nico Claesen, the Belgian international. But Crookie, Hoddle's understudy at Spurs, had a point to prove and capped a fine performance by setting up the winner, knocking in a perfect free-kick for Shaun Elliott to head us in front again. In the dying minutes Nico Claesen met a cross with one of his trademark glancing headers, which he directed downwards towards my right-hand post. It was heading for the corner of the net, but I dived across quickly to save it in front of the River End crowd and when the whistle blew for full-time a minute or two later I turned to the crowd and punched the air with my fists. God, it felt good. I stood there with my arms wide above my head, saluting the fans, enjoying the moment, a massive grin all over my face. Eventually I dragged myself away and went to celebrate with the others. Ray Clemence came up to me and shook my hand. "Well done," he said. "You made a couple of great saves out there today." It was a dream come true: my hero telling me how well I'd played. Fantastic.

A few of the lads hit the town to celebrate that night, ending up in a club called Rick's Place, where I got to witness just how our winger Dale Gordon earned the nickname 'Disco'. He was a local lad, from Great Yarmouth, and when he scored for us – which was often – he'd rush over to his dad in the City Stand and they'd both do this little dance routine. The Disco Dale shuffle became an important – and regular – part of Carrow Road folklore. Another one of the lads out that night was Crookie who wasn't such a smooth mover on the dancefloor, but he was one of the sweetest passers of a ball I've ever played with. I immediately liked him; he was very down to earth. After training, while the rest of us would have a steak or some pasta, Crookie would sit there and have his usual – a coke, a fag and a Polo mint, all at once.

Anyway, we all had a great night, which was made even better by

Who, what, why, when, where?

the fact that I'd recently moved into Dave Hodgson's flat, slap bang in the city centre, so I didn't have very far to stagger home. The only slight downer was that all night I was inundated with people telling me I had a hard act to follow. I hadn't realised when I signed, but Norwich have something of a tradition when it comes to goalkeepers. As well as Chris Woods, the fans couldn't wait to tell me all about the legendary Kevin Keelan, as well as Sandy Kennon and Ken Nethercott who were both heroes of the famous 1959 cup run. I might not have been entirely sober that night but I quickly realised that I was going to have my work cut out to prove myself to the fans and earn my place in such a wonderful dynasty.

CHAPTER SEVEN
Hi-Ho, Hi-Ho . . .

Having established myself in the Norwich first team, the big games came thick and fast, not least just seven days later when Manchester United came to Carrow Road. Coincidentally, it meant a swift reunion with Alex Ferguson. United had sacked Ron Atkinson a couple weeks earlier and Fergie had jumped at the chance to take over at Old Trafford. Of course, I had no idea that Fergie was on the verge of leaving Aberdeen, although as I left Pittodrie he did say, "Are you sure you want to go?" I sometimes wonder if he was trying to say, "If you don't go now, I'll sign you in a few weeks time." Maybe if I hadn't left Aberdeen when I did, he might have signed me for Manchester United. Fergie and I have remained good friends over the years, but I've never asked him about this, probably because I always wanted to believe it was true.

United were only a couple of places off the bottom of the First Division table when they came to Carrow Road, not a position Alex Ferguson was used to. He had a big job on his hands, and here we were, head to head in only my second league match for the Canaries. It was also his second game in charge of United as it happens, and he'd joked to the press during the week leading up to the game that he knew more about me than Ken Brown did. We shook hands before the game and wished each other luck.

I had a great game and kept a clean sheet, despite us being down to ten men because both Ian Culverhouse and Dave Hodgson had gone off injured and these were days when you only had one sub. The lads really dug in. I made a couple of good saves from Peter Davenport and another decent stop when a shot pinged off a couple of defenders and then ricocheted through some more bodies. Despite seeing the ball really late I managed to hold on to it.

The moment of the game, though, came towards the end of the match. We had a corner but United cleared and broke forward quickly. I spotted a run down our right-hand side by Remi Moses and, before the ball was played, saw it was going to come over the top for him to run onto. Remi was on the halfway line in acres of space, and when the ball was played to him he was clean through. Having read the situation, I was off my line in a flash, racing miles out of my area. Remi ran onto the ball, knocked it forward and looked up – and there I was! I'd legged it almost all the way to the halfway line in front of the old South Stand. He was flabbergasted to see me so far from my goal, just a yard or so away from him. He shaped to shoot, aiming to curl the ball round me, but I stood firm, it hit my chest and bounced out for a throw. There was a big 'Ooh' from the Norwich fans who were just as surprised as Remi had been to see me that far out.

Ken Brown, in the dug-out, couldn't believe what he was seeing either, but I was just doing what Fergie had taught me: to be a sweeper, patrolling the edge of my box and coming out when necessary to clean up the danger. We drew 0–0. Fergie and I shook hands.

"Well done, Big Man," he said, giving me a wry smile and a hug.

The *Eastern Daily Press* gave me a great write-up, referring to 'Gunn's heroics' and adding, 'Gunn made a string of fine, sometimes unorthodox saves . . .'

To round off a great day I was named Man of the Match. My team-mates gave me some gentle stick in the club bar afterwards though.

"I nearly died when I saw you on the halfway line," Steve Bruce said. "You nutter! Nice one, mate."

The next day a group of us went to the The Swan in Poringland, just on the outskirts of the city, for a few beers, before heading back to

Steve and Jan Bruce's house for a massive Sunday roast. The pub was covered in pictures of Norwich players and I was delighted to see my mugshot up on the wall – even more so when the legendary barmaid Olive came over and gave me a hug and a kiss. I'd obviously arrived!

I was loving life in Norwich, especially now that I'd moved into Hodgy's flat in Rouen Road. We were only a few minutes from Carrow Road and a short stroll from the city centre, so I was enjoying finding out if the legend about the city having a pub for every day of the year was true. Hodgy and I lived what you might call a typical footballer's lifestyle. We were always eating out: pizzas and pasta were pretty popular, although Hodgy was always sensible with his diet, which in turn helped me. We didn't stay in and cook very often, although I do remember having a go at a 'boil in the bag' meal once. The only problem was I stuck it in the oven rather than boiling it in a saucepan. All very messy, as Hodgy reminded me when he was best man at my wedding.

We were pretty familiar faces at the local nightspots and I hadn't been at Norwich very long when a guy decided to have a go at me in Ritzy's one night. This bloke came up to me and started giving me real stick.

"You're crap, you are. You think you're this big man come down from Scotland, but you're rubbish. Giving away two penalties? We must have been soft to pay any money for you, let alone £100,000."

He was really winding me up. I tried to ignore it and told him to leave it out, but he was right in my face.

"It's true what they say about Scottish keepers – you're all bloody shit. What a waste of money."

He just wouldn't leave me alone and eventually I cracked and punched him in the face. He reeled back, grabbed me and we had a bit of a scuffle before the bouncers arrived and broke it up. Hodgy dragged me away and took me back to the flat, but that wasn't the end of the matter.

The guy either knew where we lived or found out pretty quickly, because he arrived at our flat soon after we got home. There was a security system in the block, which should have stopped him getting in, but he kept pressing all the buzzers and someone must have let him in. Suddenly he was right outside our flat, banging on the door and shouting, "I want Gunn."

Dave Hodgson got hold of one of our bread knives and headed for the door.

"Don't worry, Big Man, I'll sort this out."

He wasn't going to do anything silly, just frighten the bloke off.

"No, I'll handle it. It's my problem," I said and went out into the hallway.

The bloke had completely lost it and was screaming obscenities as he punched me in the stomach. I hit him back and we fought our way down the stairwell and out onto the street. I finally managed to shrug him off there but, as he limped off, he shouted, "I'll stitch you up in the press."

I'd been told this guy had a reputation as something of a local nutter, but he made it clear he wanted me to pay to stop him telling the newspapers about what had happened. I thought about it and decided it would be better if things didn't get into the papers so I wrote the bloke a cheque for £200, I think, which I figured would pay for his shirt and keep him quiet.

On the Monday morning I went straight in to tell Ken Brown before he got to hear about it.

"I don't know how to tell you this, but I had a bit of a fight at the weekend and I decked this guy," I said. "He was giving me stick in a nightclub. What do you think I should do?"

Ken replied, "Don't worry about it, we used to have someone here called Kevin Keelan who used to deck someone every other weekend!"

Good old Ken. Until this day, the story has never became public, which is quite funny as our flat was right opposite the *Eastern Daily Press* offices. All things considered, I'd say the cheque I gave the bloke was money well spent. I had a cut on my hand to show for my troubles, but thankfully it wasn't too bad and it didn't stop me playing.

I got something of a rude introduction to the physical side of English football in a game against Oxford United at Carrow Road a few weeks later. Graham Benstead had recovered from his injury, but I'd done enough against Spurs and United to keep my place in the team. It was a bit tough on Graham, but that's football.

Anyway, Oxford had a big hard case called Billy Whitehurst up front. He was charging about all game, diving into challenges and generally being a very awkward customer indeed. At one stage I ended up in the back of my net when big Billy hit me with a blatant headbutt to the belly region. He sent me crashing, knocking the stuffing out of me in the process. I was stunned and winded, but the referee spotted the foul and gave me a free-kick; I think the only person who's ever hit me anywhere near that hard is Alex Ferguson, back in my Aberdeen days. We went on to beat Oxford 2–1 and keep our place in the top six, before losing heavily to the then-mighty Everton twice in quick succession. They put four goals past us in the League Cup and then again in the league. To rub our noses in it, they returned to Carrow Road to clinch the championship later in the season.

A couple of months later, I got my chance to play at Old Trafford. By this time Fergie had steadied the ship and taken United up and away from the relegation zone. They had beaten Liverpool 1–0 at Anfield on Boxing Day, thanks to a goal from Norman Whiteside. Amazingly, we played them the very next day. Can you imagine that happening now? The lads turned in another tremendous performance, with Kevin Drinkell hitting the only goal of the game in the second half to give us a 1–0 win. Two clean sheets against Manchester United in the same season – not bad! We went fourth in the table thanks to that win. I wonder if Fergie was regretting not making that call?

On Valentine's Day, 1987, Princess Michael of Kent came to Carrow Road to open the rebuilt City Stand ahead of our game against Manchester City. We were introduced to her before the game, Steve Bruce doing the honours. When she got to me she said, "Oh, you're the big Scottish goalkeeper. I've heard lots about you. Good luck today."

"Blimey," I thought, "I've only been here a few months and I've already made an impression with the Royals!"

We were still going well, and on course for a top-six finish as we went into April, but stuttered after consecutive defeats at Spurs and Newcastle. Tottenham beat us 3–0 at White Hart Lane with Clive Allen scoring a hat-trick on his way to hitting an extraordinary 49 goals that season. The night after the match I led a standing ovation from the Norwich boys' table at the PFA dinner as Clive stepped up to receive the Player of the Year award; well deserved after he'd scored a hat-trick against me the day before, I'd say!

Then we got hammered 4–1 by relegation-threatened Newcastle at St James' Park. A young Paul Gascoigne was beginning to make a name for himself and scored their second from a free-kick. While I was organising my wall in front of the Gallowgate End, Gazza had a word with the referee to see if he could take it quickly. He hit it while I was still at my near post screaming at the wall to move right. The ball skidded off the wet surface, clipped the inside of the far post and hit the back of the net before I had a chance to get down to it. Cheeky sod, but clever.

We recovered from those two defeats to create a bit of football history against Liverpool at Carrow Road. The Reds came to Norwich as joint league leaders, but more to the point their legendary striker Ian Rush had a proud record of never having finished on the losing side for Liverpool when he'd scored in a league game. Sure enough, Rushie put them ahead in the first half so the signs weren't good. But we hit back in the second half with goals from Trevor Putney and Kevin Drinkell to win 2–1 and put an end to the great Welshman's incredible record.

We went into our final game of the season in sixth place, just behind Luton, but with a chance of finishing fifth if we won and the Hatters lost. The problem was, our last match was at Arsenal who had a chance of finishing third and had only lost three home games in the league all season.

We travelled down the night before the game and checked into the Post House in Brentwood, Essex. We settled into the hotel and started preparing ourselves for the serious business at hand – flogging our FA Cup final tickets! It was the week before the final between Spurs and Coventry and in those days the FA allocated each club player two tickets. We all got calls from friends or associates wanting tickets, so we pooled our allocation and held out to see who'd put in the highest offer. So there we were, sat in the bar, when one of the lads announced he'd been offered six times face value by a supposed friend of a friend of Stan Flashman. We despatched Ian Crook and

Trevor Putney to meet up with 'Jimmy the Jock' in the car park. They came back half an hour later with a suitcase full of cash and tales of how they thought he was packing something underneath his big leather trenchcoat.

It was standard practice at the time for players to sell on their tickets, but it was all new to me, coming from Scotland. I was a bit wide-eyed about it all, but we all happily handed over our tickets – it was our holiday money.

And our clothes money! Once we'd received the cash, we went into the lounge where a mate of Wayne Biggins produced even more suitcases for us. He was a clothes trader from Sheffield and had loads of designer label clobber, including tons of Matinique gear which was all the rage at the time. There were a few Boss labels as well, but I'm not entirely sure they were genuine. We all bought some gear for our holidays and finally, after a very busy night, hit the sack.

After such careful preparation, the next afternoon we found ourselves 2–1 up at Highbury and on our way to a famous victory, only for Arsenal to get a penalty in the last couple of minutes. Martin Hayes stepped up in front of the old North Bank. He had scored 12 out of 13 spot-kicks for the Gunners that season. Not bad – we hadn't been awarded a penalty all year. I always fancied myself at facing penalties. I had a pretty good record over the years and saved about one in three over the course of my career. My size definitely helped and I really enjoyed the psychological games that went on beforehand. I always tried to ensure I was in control. I'd try to get hold of the ball and then either give it to the referee or throw it casually at the penalty-taker, looping it just enough so that he had to run after it. Anything to delay and unsettle him. I wanted to let him know we were doing things at my tempo and I was in charge. I'd really psych myself up and make an effort to look as big as possible – spreading my hands wide, puffing out my chest – and then have a little bounce on the line while glaring at him as if to say, "Yeah, you reckon?" I'd be talking to myself, too: "Come on, Big Man."

I always saw penalties as a chance to make a name for myself, be a hero, and as Hayes stepped up I really thought, "No problem, I'll save this." But I didn't have to. Hayes hit his shot high . . . too high. The ball clipped the top of my crossbar and went over. We won 2–1 and finished fifth – then the club's highest ever league finish. We had created club history and I was really proud.

We would have qualified for Europe that season, but for the ban on English clubs after the Heysel tragedy. It was the second time in three seasons Norwich had been denied their debut in Europe – the club had also missed out after winning the Milk Cup in 1985. But we weren't going to let that take the shine off our celebrations.

When I'd first joined the club I'd been amazed to discover that the team bus wasn't allowed to leave until there was a crate of Foster's lager on board – well, they were our shirt sponsors! – along with a crate of Webster's bitter and a bottle of gin. I'd never seen anything like it, certainly not on my trips with Aberdeen; it was more like my days as a young player with the Invergordon amateur side. It did the trick, though, because we loved our away trips in that first season – winning eight away games, drawing seven and losing only six, which is pretty good going.

And pretty much whatever the result, we'd always enjoy the journey home. On our way back from London games we'd stop off at a pub in Epping Forest, order fish and chips from the shop next door and sink a couple of pints while we waited for them. After the Arsenal game we were all obviously in high spirits, cracking open a couple of cans on the bus and changing into our new holiday gear. We stopped at Epping Forest as usual, our physio Tim Sheppard went off to get the fish and chips and we headed for the pub to do the little party piece our mad left-back Tony Spearing had devised, and we'd perfected on previous away trips. Tonight it was my turn to lead us off.

I went into the pub dressed in a rather fetching red floral shirt and matching shorts. I had my club tie around my head with my smart matchday shoes and socks on my feet – so, yes, I looked pretty daft. I approached the barman and, as was the tradition, asked for a pint and seven halves of lager. He looked at me a bit strangely but duly started pouring, no doubt wondering what the hell was going on. As he placed the last half on the bar I turned to the door, puffed out my chest and, at the top of my voice, sang, "Hi-Ho! Hi-Hoooo!" At which point seven of the other lads shuffled into the pub in a line, on their knees, singing *"Hi-Ho, Hi-Ho, it's off to work we go . . ."*

As they came past me on their knees, all dressed as stupidly as me in their new holiday gear, I handed out the little half pints of lager. It brought the house down. All the locals – and quite a few Norwich fans who'd worked out where we always stopped – were wetting themselves with laughter. It was all part of the great togetherness we had. I'd enjoyed plenty of good times with the boys at Aberdeen, but nothing quite like this!

Eventually, we all piled back onto the bus for the long, boozy drive back up to Norwich. The beer and gin were flowing freely now and so the singing inevitably started. After the obligatory rousing, if rather rambling, rendition of 'I Am the Music Man', the song where you act out playing a different instrument every round (I had to come up with the fifteenth instrument after about 15 cans of Foster's – not good!), Wayne Biggins took over. He had a fantastic voice and if ever we were feeling a bit low, he'd lighten the mood by belting out a Frank Sinatra number. He kicked off with 'New York, New York' but soon got drowned out. Then Trevor Putney did that Max Bygraves song about the tiny house by the tiny stream, the one which starts, "There's a Tiny House . . .".

Finally it came to my turn. I only knew one song, the very sad 'Nobody's Child' by Sydney Devine. I'd listen to it constantly as a kid because my dad was a massive fan of Sydney and Johnny Cash. A beautiful, heart-wrenching song about a little boy all alone in an orphanage. With lyrics like, "I got no mummy's kisses, I got no daddy's smile, nobody wants me, I'm nobody's child," normally when I sang it on the coach it would completely kill the atmosphere. Wayne and Trevor would be hugging each other and we'd all have tears in our eyes. Tonight, though, we all looked at each other, grinned and cracked open another beer. We'd finished fifth!

CHAPTER EIGHT

Kops and Grobbers

What a difference a year makes! Just 12 months after walking out of Alex Ferguson's office at Aberdeen, thoroughly disappointed at missing out on the Scottish Cup final and not sure where my career was going, here I was celebrating a brilliant first season at Norwich. Life really couldn't have been much better.

To cap it all, I was called up to the full Scotland squad for the Rous Cup, an end-of-season round-robin tournament involving Scotland, England and Brazil. I was Andy Roxburgh's third-choice keeper behind Jim Leighton and Andy Goram and didn't actually get a game, but I was incredibly proud to be involved. I did manage to swap shirts with David Seaman, though, after we drew 0–0 with England at Hampden Park. Like me, David was number three keeper, in his case behind Peter Shilton and Chris Woods. I also bagged a Brazil shirt (number 22 to be exact), which was the trendy thing to have at the time, after we were beaten 2–0 at Hampden. Unfortunately, I've no idea who had been wearing it: their coach came into our dressing room to swap the shirts.

After the match I flew down to Heathrow to meet up with the Norwich boys ahead of a summer tour to America. I felt like an international jet-setter, flying high with a successful First Division club one minute, on international duty the next, and then heading across the Atlantic to the United States. Great stuff.

I was pretty happy in the rest of my life too, having moved out of Dave Hodgson's flat into my own house in St Anne's Road, Framingham Earl, just outside Norwich. Loads of the other lads lived round there, so many in fact that the locals nicknamed it Canary Close. Trevor Putney lived opposite me and I was never short of an invite to go golfing or to the cinema.

Steve Bruce's wife, Jan, was interested in interior design and she kindly came over to do up my house for me. Her mate got a major discount at Laura Ashley, which was all very well but it meant I ended up with a pink house. Pink walls, pink flowery borders, pink carpets, a cream and a pink floral settee – it was like living in Barbie's house. It was the style at the time though, honest, and I was happy to leave it to Jan's judgement; I wasn't exactly Mr Domestic – I practically lived off Marks and Spencer's ready meals.

I was enjoying the limelight that goes with becoming a familiar face. I'd meet the odd pretty girl at a party or in a club, but I was still only 23 so they were never anything serious.

The tour to the States was brilliant. We played in Miami, Seattle (where I played up-front, but didn't score) and Los Angeles, before returning home for a few weeks' holiday and then jetting off for a pre-season tour of Sweden. We had a cracking time in Sweden, training hard in good conditions and playing a few matches that didn't stretch us too much. Everyone enjoyed a few good nights out, which was brilliant for team spirit. That's what the Norwich set-up was all about, working hard and playing hard. Alcohol wasn't as much of an issue then as it is now. Ken Brown's philosophy was that if you could do your job and play your football, that was all right by him. He felt it was important to have a happy squad that bonded together well.

There was definitely a drinking culture at Norwich but it was very much the norm amongst teams at the time. We'd enjoy a lager and come in the next day and sweat it out. I guess if a team from my day took on one of today's sides, with all their modern thinking and philosophy, most people would say we'd be run off the park. I know where I'd put my money though – and we'd definitely win the race to the bar afterwards!

For all our wonderful team spirit and pre-season preparations, the 1987/88 campaign didn't start too well. We kicked off with the toughest possible fixture, against the champions Everton at Goodison Park. We lost 1–0, but it wasn't exactly a disgrace and we returned to Norwich confident of getting our season up and running against Southampton. Again, though, we lost 1–0 at Carrow Road against a team that had two young hopefuls on the bench by the names of Alan Shearer and Matthew Le Tissier.

We won our next game, at home to Coventry City, 3–1, despite big Brian Kilcline smashing a penalty past me. There was nothing subtle about 'Killer's' approach to the game, including the way he took a penalty: he just thumped it as hard as he could.

If we thought that win would act as a springboard for a return to the form of the previous season, we were wrong. We picked up a handful of points in the next few games but things just wouldn't click for us and the rot really set in when we lost four straight games in the league and dropped into the bottom three, with just seven points from ten games. We didn't realise it at the time, but behind the scenes the pressure was really beginning to build for Ken Brown. I don't think any of the players thought he was in danger of getting the sack. Ken had been in the job seven years and was part of the furniture. He was also popular with the fans and it never even crossed our minds that he might lose his job on the back of a few bad results at the start of the season, especially when we then beat Spurs 2–1 at Carrow Road. Claesen again!

After the Spurs match we went to Old Trafford and it looked like we might have turned the corner when we took a half-time lead through Wayne Biggins. Victory against Manchester United away from home would have taken the pressure right off, but it wasn't to be. United were going well, up in the top six, and we conceded two in the second half.

Fergie was still rebuilding and a few days after that defeat I got a phone call from him, asking me about Steve Bruce. He rang my mobile; it was one of the early designs, the size of a brick, with a separate handset and battery. Fergie said:

"Big Man, how good is this Steve Bruce? What do you reckon?"

Brucie was your original centre-half. He was always prepared to stick his head in where it hurt and his nose had been broken umpteen times. He was just like Alex McLeish in that respect, but he also had some of Willie Miller's attributes. McLeish was more aggressive and used to do the heading and attacking, Miller was more skilful and would do the sweeping up; Brucie could do a bit of both.

"Honest opinion," I told Fergie, "if you want a centre-half who can take a goalkeeper's kick down on his chest and stroll out of defence with it, he's your man."

Not that I wanted to see Steve leave; he was our skipper and one of the most important players in the team, but I could only tell the truth when my old boss came calling. And if Brucie had an opportunity to move to one of the biggest clubs in the world I wasn't going to do anything to harm his chances. I'd also got to know Steve and Jan quite well and, guess what, they often asked me to look after their children, Alex and Amy.

While Alex Ferguson considered making a move for Brucie, we were in dire straits. Ken was fired the day after a 2–0 defeat to Charlton Athletic. I can't remember any build-up to it in the press, or Ken being under any real pressure as far as the players were concerned. Steve Bruce had done a piece in the local paper telling fans not to blame Ken for our poor results. He said it was down to us, the players, which was absolutely right. Unfortunately, it's the managers who always seem to pay the price.

We didn't find out about Ken's sacking until the Monday morning at training. Brownie came up and told us himself. He went round all the players, one by one, shaking hands. It was very awkward for both him and us players and we just exchanged brief words. "Keep up the good work", "Good luck, Gaffer."

We were shocked and I was gutted to see him go – after all, he was the man who had given me my big chance. I had a lot to thank Ken for. He was a bubbly character, full of fun. He'd always join in with the antics on the team bus, rather than sit down the front like most managers do. But he was also a really nice, decent man and ours was a really happy club, which Ken had worked hard to create. He was very much on the side of the players, like the time he was so cool about that guy having a go at me in the nightclub. I had really enjoyed working with him.

On reflection, I don't think it helped that Mel Machin had left the club before the start of the season to join Manchester City. Ken and Mel were a good combination. Together they got the best out of players, very much the old 'good cop, bad cop' routine. Mel was a tough coach who worked you hard, never let you slack off in training. On the other hand, Ken would make sure he told you when you'd done well and celebrate with the lads when we had a good result. I felt Norwich had made a mistake in letting him go.

I saw Ken a few weeks later and finally got a chance to tell him how sorry I was that he'd been sacked. I guess I felt it personally because he'd signed me, and shown such faith in me.

The board decided to replace Ken by promoting from within, giving reserve team manager Dave Stringer the job. Dave was highly respected within the club and had enjoyed a great career, having been part of the history-making team that took Norwich City into the top flight for the first time ever by winning the old Second Division title back in 1972.

Dave was also a really nice bloke, much quieter than Ken, although he often had a twinkle in his eye. The handover was very subtle – the first change we noticed was that the bottle of gin disappeared off the team bus for away trips (Dave preferred to have a Foster's). But having been a tough-tackling defender himself, Dave worked hard on organising the defence, urging the players to stick their heads in where it hurt. Ken had always wanted his defenders to pass the ball out of defence, playing stylish, passing football. Dave wanted to keep up the same tradition, but add an extra bit of steel. Over time, I think he helped me to develop and improve as a goalkeeper. We'd stay out for an extra half an hour or so after the main session had finished. It was the good, old-fashioned 'slog your goalkeeper into the ground' routine, forcing you to make 100 saves or so until you couldn't stand up. Despite that, I liked him.

Dave's first game in charge was against Arsenal, who were top of the table, and he threw in two youngsters, Jerry Goss and Dale Gordon, who had played for him when he managed the youth side to victory in the FA Youth Cup in 1983. Gossy was your original hard-working midfielder who would link up with the attackers but also protect the back four, an ideal midfielder. Dale was a skilful winger who could operate on either flank and also went on to become a big favourite at Carrow Road. The gamble nearly paid off; we took the lead but lost 4–2.

Our next match was a trip to Liverpool who were unbeaten in the league and only a couple of points behind Arsenal. I was really excited about playing at Anfield for the first time. When we got there, it was a bit of a let-down – well, the away facilities were anyway. I had imagined really flash dressing-rooms, but they were very basic: one treatment table, a huge communal bath – and carbolic soap. They'd obviously had a lick of paint at the start of the season but other than that they were nothing to write home about.

The stadium itself was pretty inspiring though. I'll never forget running out for the first time in front of the Kop. I touched the 'This is Anfield' sign and ran onto the pitch – a fantastic surface, great for our passing game as well as theirs. The Kop was full right from the point I went out for my warm-up. They had a reputation for giving visiting goalkeepers a great reception and I got a tremendous ovation. I'd seen their reaction to goalkeepers before on television and made sure I gave them plenty of applause in return. As long as you clapped back to them they'd give you a big cheer, which was fantastic. I went on to keep a clean sheet and make a few good saves in front of the Kop in the second half. We put in a tremendous performance to earn an excellent goalless draw, a great result for the team and the start of something extra special for me because it was the first of three successive clean sheets at Anfield. There aren't many goalkeepers who can say they've done that; in fact I believe the only other person is the legendary Gordon Banks. I was incredibly proud to equal the great man's record and it's one of the highlights of my career, without a doubt.

After the game I met up with Bruce Grobbelaar in the players' lounge. He had a little present for me. We share the same initials, and after the previous season's match at Carrow Road I'd noticed he was wearing a gold ring shaped as a big 'BG'. I told him I liked the look of it and he said, "If you fancy one, I'll get one made for you." So we sat there having a beer and he suddenly pulled a 'BG' ring from his pocket. I was dead chuffed, the goalkeeper's union had come up trumps – again.

"Thanks mate, that's awesome."

"No worries," said Bruce.

I went to put it into my pocket but he leaned over and put his hand on my arm.

"That'll be £60, mate." he said.

"Ah," I thought, "it's that kind of present."

No problem. I was still delighted. A clean sheet at Anfield and my own custom-made 'BG' ring; a pretty good afternoon all round. I still wear my 'BG' ring to this day. Mind you, the next time I saw Bruce, I noticed his was now diamond-encrusted!

A week or two later we played Luton on their plastic pitch. It was the first time I'd played on an artificial surface, which I have to say I didn't really like. You never knew what the ball was going to do, especially when it bounced or skidded through on the surface. It was to be Steve Bruce's last match for Norwich City because, sure enough, after a few weeks of behind-the-scenes negotiations, he got his dream move to Manchester United. I hope he appreciates how I helped make it come true for him. We never talked about it but I'm sure he knows I played a part in things. He still owes me a pint!

Steve was one of several great centre-halves I was lucky enough to play behind. My ideal defender is one who will charge down a shot and not turn his back, so they can still see what was happening. You wouldn't expect your goalkeeper to turn his back on the ball from five yards, and it should be no different for a centre-half. Defenders like Steve Bruce and Ian Butterworth would never turn their backs; they would take it in the face – or goolies, if necessary. Alex McLeish and Willie Miller were the same. They were real centre-halves, the kind of blokes who would run through a brick wall for the team.

The week after Steve Bruce left, Robert Fleck arrived from Rangers. He was a great signing and I felt it signified the board's ambition. We'd crossed paths a few times playing against each other in reserve games back in Scotland. Flecky was always the life and soul of the party, great company and really easy to be around. I had a spare bedroom, so offered to take Flecky in as my lodger. We've been good friends ever since.

We didn't stay in the house much, mind you. I was still rubbish at cooking, and Marks and Spencer was now further away, so we ate out all the time. One of our regular venues was The Last Wine Bar in the city centre, where my favourite dish was king prawns in garlic butter. They were fantastic, so much so that I'd often have them as a starter and then again for my main course! Our meals out never seemed to cost me a penny. Flecky always insisted on tossing a coin to see who would pay and I never lost. Maybe I just got lucky every time, or perhaps it had something to do with the fact I didn't charge Flecky anything for his digs – either way, I never paid for a meal in all the time we went out together.

Not that money was a big problem. We were two single lads earning decent wages, which were often bumped up by good bonuses. Our basic pay wasn't anything like the Manchester United, Arsenal or Liverpool lads', but the bonuses were right up there with the best. We had an accumulator system whereby our bonus would increase with each successive victory. We would get £400 for one win, then £500 for winning the next game, on to £600, £700 and so on up to a certain level, where it would stay as long as we kept winning. If we drew, we would stay on the same level; we only went back to the starting level if we lost, so there was every incentive to avoid defeat. It really got the boys focused, I can tell you. Of course, you don't play the game just for the money, but at the same time it helps with team spirit. You only have to mention in the dressing room: "Hey lads, don't forget we're playing for £600 today," and believe me it gets everyone going.

Flecky and Kevin Drinkell hit it off straightaway. They were two strong, direct players, Drinks was probably more of a natural marksman, while Flecky was once described as the scorer of great goals, rather than a great goalscorer, which summed him up quite well. They might have been the jokers of the pack, but they were both very intelligent players and it wasn't long before their goals were lifting us up and away from the danger zone. We beat Chelsea 3–0 at Carrow Road to move out of the bottom three for the first time since Dave took over.

I missed a couple of games early in the New Year after picking up a knee injury in a Simod Cup tie against Millwall. I dived out to make a save on the edge of the box and suddenly their right-back, Keith 'Rhino' Stevens, slid in on top of me with a two-footed tackle and I'd got a gaping hole in my knee. Our physio Tim Sheppard came on to give me treatment, took one look and said, "You're off." I said, "No, Tim, don't worry, just put a plaster on it or wrap it up and I'll be all right."

Thankfully, Tim was one of the best physios in the game and he knew better than me. He said, "No, you've got synovial fluid coming out of it. If you don't get this looked at straightaway you could well lose your leg."

I went off on a stretcher at the Cold Blow Lane end of the Den. It was amazing, there were little kids chucking coins at me and their fans all screaming abuse, shouting things like they'd slept with my wife the night before – I was still single!

Back in Norwich, I spent the night in hospital where the club doctor Hugh Philips cleaned up my knee. I was back in action a couple of games later, but I take my hat off to Tim: without expert medical attention it could have been the end of my career. I've got a nice scar on my knee, but thanks to Tim and Hugh that's all.

Towards the end of the season Dave Stringer signed Andy Linighan from Oldham to bolster the defence. Big Andy was a great character. He was really dry and as fit as you'll get. His debut couldn't have been much tougher; it was at a packed Carrow Road against Manchester United, who were by now up in second place in the table behind Liverpool. We beat them 1–0, thanks to a goal from Robert Fleck. I also did my bit by making an especially satisfying save from Bryan Robson after one of his typical surging runs into the penalty box from midfield. It was in front of the River End and he got to just shy of the penalty spot before letting fly with his famous left boot. I managed to fling myself to my right to push it out for a corner. It's always sweet to beat Manchester United, and even better when your old boss is in charge.

A week later we had another good result against Terry Venables' Spurs, beating them 3–1 at White Hart Lane, with goals from Jerry Goss, Drinks and Flecky, who was scoring for fun by now. Guess who got the Spurs goal, by the way? Yes, Nico Claesen, yet again! I was beginning to get sick of the sight of him and wished he'd bugger off back to Belgium.

By the time Flecky hit his sixth goal in five games in a 4–2 win over Oxford United at Carrow Road, we were up to mid-table and effectively safe from relegation. We then held Liverpool to another goalless draw at Carrow Road, to make it two shut-outs against the Reds in the same season. I was delighted with that, especially as Liverpool went on to win the title that year.

As for Norwich, well, we managed to finish a full 10 points clear of the drop, not exactly a successful campaign, but worth celebrating all the same. Andy Linighan was a great guy, a real man's man who liked to sink a pint or two, so he fitted in with the Norwich lads really well – surprise, surprise! He was certainly in good form, along with the rest of the boys at John O'Neill's testimonial dinner at a hotel in Norwich.

We'd all had a few drinks and towards the end of the evening Andy decided he'd had enough and wanted to go home – there and then. He'd got fed up waiting for a taxi, so decided he would run all the way home to his place at Taverham, the best part of seven or eight miles. We tried to persuade him to wait for a lift, but Andy was nothing if not determined, and once he'd decided he'd had enough, that was it. So off he went, jogging home. He hadn't got very far when one of Norwich's most loyal and dedicated fans, a chap called Colin Tovell, set off in his car to drive home and soon caught up with Andy. Colin's a lovely chap who does loads of unsung work for the club and would do anything for anyone. He rolled down his window and offered to give Big Andy a lift. Andy kept jogging along, so Colin tried again.

"Come on Andy, you can't run all the way home. Hop in."

Andy just kept on going and then, in his typically dry and no-nonsense manner, he turned and said, "F*** off. I'm running home."

Typical Andy. Anyone who knows him from his days at Hartlepool, Oldham, Norwich, Palace or Arsenal can imagine him saying it in his broad northern accent. If you ever upset him you would get this menacing stare from him and you'd say, "All right, Big Man, settle down."

Andy was a brilliant bloke, though, and definitely a centre-half who you would want in front of you. But you know what was really special about that first full season as a Norwich City player? I was voted the supporters' Player of the Season. That was a massive honour: the fans are no mugs, they're the people you're out to impress, and to be their Player of the Season at the end of my first full season was special. It meant I'd turned things round from being a Scottish goalkeeper, with all the baggage that went with that, to following in the footsteps of some great Norwich keepers by getting my name on the trophy along with the likes of Kevin Keelan and Chris Woods. Despite all our problems that year, it was every bit as pleasing as finishing fifth in the league the season before.

CHAPTER NINE

Strawberries and Cream

As ever, at the end of the season I was keen to get away and lap up some sunshine. Luckily for me, Dave Hodgson had moved to Spain, after his short spell at Carrow Road, and invited me over for a week. He was based in Jerez, playing in the Spanish second division, but he also had contacts in the trendy resort of Puerto Banus, Marbella – the holiday hotspot for the rich and famous, as well as footballers. Dave's connections were linked to his time at Anfield and I stayed in the same apartment block as Liverpool coach Roy Evans and his wife Mary. Roy and Mary were lovely and we'd enjoy a few beers around the pool most days, soaking up the rays and chatting about football. I love the Liverpool accent and the Scouse sense of humour.

Dave had to report for training each day, or rather he had to report for treatment every day – he was always injured, that bloke. But once he'd finished in Jerez, Hodgy would travel down to Puerto Banus to meet up with me each night. We'd then go into town for a meal and a few beers. On our first evening together something happened that would change my life for ever.

We were sitting outside a restaurant when something suddenly caught Dave's eye. "Cor, Gunny," he said, "look at that!"

"Look at what?" I said.

"Those three lovely birds coming our way!"

I looked round to see the girls walking towards us. He was right; they were stunning. "Yeah, good shout!" I said.

There were two blondes and a brunette. I'd always had a preference for blondes, but it was the dark-haired girl who immediately caught my eye. She really stood out for me. She was slim, confident and sexy in a very cool, classy way with a sharp, chin-length, dark brown bob. I couldn't keep my eyes off her and kept watching as the girls made their way down the street before stopping at the next restaurant to us. They sat down at a table just a few yards away from us, but they were obscured by a hedge dividing the two restaurants. Luckily, I managed to subtly move my chair to the left and got a good view of the brunette through a small gap in the branches. We soon made eye contact and exchanged a few coy smiles. I don't know if you'd call it love at first sight but something certainly stirred in my loins! At the end of the meal, though, we went our way and the girls went theirs.

Later, after Dave had returned to Jerez, I phoned my mum and dad from a booth on the street. As I ended the call, I heard a noise and looked up to see three girls running towards me. It was the lovely ladies we'd seen earlier.

"Woah!" I said. "What's the problem?" They told me they'd been drinking with a group of Italian guys who'd been buying them champagne. The girls realised the Italians were expecting more in return for their hospitality than they were going to get, so they decided to make a break for it.

"Okay, don't worry, I'll look after you," I said.

"Oh, you're Scottish," said the brunette. She sounded a little bit disappointed. Later she told me she'd originally thought I was Danish or Swedish, because I looked a bit like a Viking. Little did she know about my exotic ancestry.

"Where are you from?" I asked.

"Manchester," said the brunette.

"Ah, Coronation Street!" I said – and then mentally kicked myself.

"We've got to go," said the brunette.

"I'll see you tomorrow!"

Quite why I thought I would see them the next day, I'm not sure. But I did.

I spent most of the following day by the pool at my villa. I kept thinking about the night before, especially the girl with the dark hair. Who was she? Would I see her again? She'd made a real impression on me and I couldn't get her out of my mind. I spent ages getting ready to go out that night, desperately hoping I would bump into the girls again.

I must have been pretty poor company for Dave: I spent most of the evening looking up from our table, hoping to catch a glimpse of the girls, rather than listening to what he had to say. After we'd eaten, we headed to a trendy bar for a nightcap – and finally I spotted her. Thank you, God!

I plucked up the courage to go over and talk to her. She told me her name was Susan. Before long she asked me what I did for a living. I thought about it for a couple of seconds before replying, "Oh, I'm a joiner." I wasn't sure what she thought about football players, so I decided to play safe.

"Oh, that's nice, my brother is a plumber."

Susan told me she was a wedding-dress designer and explained that she was on a hen trip with her friends; Karen was the bride and Debbie, like Susan, was a bridesmaid. The wedding was the following weekend, in Bolton, which was where they were actually from. She said she'd told me they lived in Manchester the previous night because they didn't think I would have heard of Bolton.

By the end of the night Susan and I were really hitting it off and I decided to come clean about what I really did for a living. She was cool with it, although not too sure about Norwich City.

"What division do they play in?" she asked innocently. Susan also told me she'd recently come out of a long-term relationship. She was very much single, in other words, which was great news.

I ended up spending the night in the girls' apartment – for perfectly legitimate reasons, I hasten to add. They told me they'd been frightened by a few strange noises in the complex the previous evening. Obviously, I had to do the chivalrous thing and keep them company – for added security! For the record, one thing did not lead to another: I slept on the couch.

The next morning the girls suggested I join them around their pool, rather than spend the day on my own. The problem was I only had what I'd been wearing the previous evening. Not to worry; Susan promptly produced a pair of her shorts for me to sunbathe in. She'd made them herself; they had blue and white stripes, with three little gold anchor buttons down the front. Very fetching.

The trouble was, although I was in good shape, Susan was only a very trim size 10. Fortunately, the shorts were a loose-fitting, boxer-style cut, or at least they were on her. Luckily, they had an elasticated waist and I just about managed to pour myself into them, by which time they were more like a pair of figure-hugging Speedos! I must have looked like some sort of Page Seven guy. I didn't move around a lot, just sunbathed around the pool. I was worried who might see me and what they might think if they saw me parading around in a pair of girly shorts.

We spent the rest of the day and evening together and had great fun splashing each other in the pool. I was really impressed by Susan. She seemed incredibly grown up for 23. She had her own business – a wedding-dress shop in Bolton – and managed a few staff. She also designed some of the accessories and bridesmaids' dresses so she was obviously creative as well as capable. She had gone to art college, before setting up her business, and done a fair bit of modelling. We just clicked for some reason and got along together really easily.

At the end of the night, Karen and Debbie headed back to their apartment while Susan and I went for a walk around the swimming pool. We lay down on a sunbed, gazing up at the stars. In that instant I knew she was the one for me and popped the question there and then. I just knew it was right. I couldn't stop myself and blurted it out.

"Susan, will you marry me?"

She giggled a bit and then turned to me and said, "Yes!"

And that was it; we'd agreed to get married a little over 48 hours after we'd first met.

I arranged to meet Susan for lunch the next day, when we planned to break our good news to Karen and Debbie. But things didn't quite go to plan.

I was meant to meet Susan at Victor's beach bar at two o'clock. Unfortunately, I got roped into a drinking session around the pool at my apartment. Make that a major drinking session. I was with Hodgy, Roy Evans and a few other characters and it all got a bit out of hand. Two o'clock came and went and I got to the bar to meet Susan a good two hours late.

I began to panic that she would have changed her mind. It wasn't exactly a good sign – our first proper date together, just hours after she'd agreed to marry me, and I was late. Very late. And drunk. Very drunk. It was a piping hot afternoon as I got out of the taxi and approached the bar, where there was good news and bad.

The good news was that she was there. The bad news was that the girls were surrounded by men – lots of them. There were about 20 blokes from an Essex golf club fawning all over them, rubbing suntan lotion into them and having a good laugh with them – and the girls were lapping up all the attention.

Rather nervously, I went up to Susan. "Hi."

"Oh, hello," she said, dismissively.

"Sorry I'm a bit late; I got caught up back at the apartment."

"I thought you weren't coming." She was clearly not impressed.

One of the golfers pushed in between us. "Sorry mate, what are you after?"

"What are you on about? I'm trying to speak to Susan."

"No, you're not with us, what are you doing here?"

"Well, as it happens, Susan and I are getting married when we get back to the UK."

"Sorry pal, I've just asked her to marry me as well. Unlucky."

I wasn't going to be put off and carried on trying to talk to her.

"Look mate," he said, "I'm going to marry her and if you don't go away, I'm going to kneecap you."

I stood my ground and made it quite clear I wasn't going to take any crap from him. He backed down quite quickly.

"Sorry mate. I'm only joking. I'm just here having a good time with the boys."

"That's all right, pal," I said. "No problem."

I turned to Susan. She seemed quite impressed that I'd stood up for myself and gave me a big hug. We went down to the beach and had a kiss and a cuddle, then enjoyed a spot of sunbathing with Karen and Debbie and toasted our good news.

I had to return home to England a couple of days before Susan, but not before her friend Karen, the bride-to-be, had invited me to her wedding to Ian Thorpe in Bolton the following weekend. I was a touch worried about leaving Susan there, but there was nothing I could do about it. I knew I had found the girl I wanted to spend the rest of my life with, and it seemed Susan felt the same about me. Having recently split from her boyfriend, she had returned to live at home with her dad. Sadly, she'd lost her mother a couple of years earlier. Susan gave me her home number and I promised I would call.

By the time Susan returned home, I'd left three messages. Apparently, Susan's dad said to her, "Who's this Bryan and what does he do for a living?"

She told him. "Bloody footballer! I thought I'd brought you up better than that!" he said.

I booked myself a hotel in Bolton for the wedding and drove up on the Friday night. It went really well. Susan and I got closer and closer so I stayed up in Bolton for a few more days, which wasn't a problem because it was early June and I was still on holiday. We decided to make our relationship official by getting engaged. First, though, I wanted to do the right thing and ask her father John for her hand. We arranged a date and time. It turned out to be on a day that England were playing Holland in the European Championships in Germany. When I got to John's house he was outside waving his hands, saying, "Hurry up, Big Man. Come in. You'll miss the football." He was calling me 'Big Man', and we hadn't even met. Susan couldn't believe it, I had been a 'bloody footballer' until then. It had to be a good sign.

The Dutch won 3–1, with Marco Van Basten hitting a hat-trick. Not that I took in much of the action. I went in and sat down. John offered me a beer, and came out with some Carlsberg Special Brew – rocket fuel. I hadn't touched that since I was a teenager. I sat there and forced it down, trying to make conversation without spoiling John's enjoyment of the match.

Susan kept pretending to pop out into the street to talk to some friends. What she was actually doing was catching my attention through the window and mouthing, "Have you asked him yet?" It wasn't easy. I kept waiting for a lull in the action to pick the right moment.

Eventually I just came out with it. "John, I want to marry your daughter. I wondered if that was all right with you?"

He paused a moment and then said in his strong Bolton accent, "Bit bloody soon, isn't it?"

"I know, but we do love each other and want to get married."

"If that's what you want to do, you'll do it," he said.

And that was it; I'd got the old boy's approval.

The next step was to choose an engagement ring. I took Susan shopping in Manchester. Two or three rings caught her eye, but she couldn't decide which one she preferred. It was pretty clear to me which one she really liked – the most expensive one, obviously. We decided to have lunch before making a final decision. On our way to the restaurant I secretly nipped into a building society to withdraw the money. The run of good results in the second half of the previous season meant I'd picked up a few handy win bonuses, so I was able to withdraw enough money for the most expensive ring.

When Susan went off to the loo I took out the wad of notes and stuffed them into her napkin, so that when she opened it up she would find the money there for the ring she really wanted. When she came back to the table she picked up the napkin and flicked it open to place on her lap as she sat down. The cash flew out all over the table and the floor. We both fell about laughing and went off to buy the ring, although I didn't let her have it there and then . . .

A few days later I went up to Scotland to play in Andy Cameron's celebrity charity golf weekend. I took Susan with me and we stayed overnight in a hotel near Erskine Bridge. I took the engagement ring with me and racked my brains trying to come up with an idea of how to propose to her in a special way. I hadn't made any particular plans, but the night before the golf match we had a bath before going down to dinner. I filled the tub up with bubbles and ordered some champagne.

Strawberries and Cream

Susan got into the bath and I then entered the bathroom with a couple of glasses of bubbly before joining her in the bath, which promptly overflowed. I had a plate of strawberries and cream and began to spoon-feed Susan. She was lapping it up, but suddenly grimaced. For a second. Smiling, she pulled the ring from between her teeth and I slipped it onto her finger. We were officially engaged! When we eventually made it down to dinner (I believe we managed to get there in time for dessert!) she revelled in showing off the ring – a beautiful cluster of diamonds.

When we returned from Scotland we booked a cheap holiday to Corfu before I had to return to Norwich for pre-season training. Quite why Susan stayed with me after that holiday, I have no idea. I behaved like a complete prat, playing every practical joke I could think of, including sticking Parmesan cheese up Susan's nose at one stage, which she's never understood, nor forgotten. The accommodation was awful, what you might call cheap but not especially cheerful, but we came back home feeling we were not only madly in love, but had also got to know each other well, too. By any standards, it had been a summer to remember.

CHAPTER TEN

The Saddest Semi

Once the new season got underway it was always going to be difficult to spend much time with Susan. She had her business in Bolton to run and I was based in Norwich. Fortunately, the gaffer appreciated our dilemma and did his best to help, letting me stay up with Susan whenever a fixture took us anywhere near that part of the country – well, he would if we got a good result, so I had an extra incentive! I would travel to games on the team coach with the rest of the lads as normal, but more often than not one of the coaching staff would drive my car up behind the bus for me so I could get back to Norwich for training on the Monday.

Dave Stringer, or 'String Bean' as we called him when he was out of earshot (he wasn't particularly skinny, I guess we just weren't particularly good at nicknames), was happy with the arrangement and occasionally he'd even let me have Mondays off, especially if we'd had a good result. Luckily, we had a great start to the 1988/89 season with four straight wins, including back-to-back victories in the North East at Middlesbrough and Newcastle. Consequently, I was granted a fair bit of what you might call extended leave. It certainly helped with the long-distance romance, but I never abused that privilege and I'd normally get up at 4am on the Monday and drive the 185 miles or so back to Norwich in time for training at 10 o'clock.

There was one occasion, though, when String Bean flatly refused me permission to stay up in Bolton. We were playing Coventry at Highfield Road when David Speedie fell over my arm in the area and referee David Elleray gave a penalty. I wasn't very impressed. I was convinced Speedie had dived and called him a "f***ing cheat". Unfortunately, I didn't leave it there. I turned to Elleray and blurted out, "He's a f***ing cheat and you're a f***ing cheat." Just like my old dad all those years ago, Mr Elleray didn't take kindly to swearing. Having said that, I think it was the fact I'd called him a cheat that really did the damage. And that was it, I was off.

We didn't have a reserve keeper on the bench in those days, so Mark 'Taffy' Bowen went in goal. He was one of the shortest guys in the team and my shirt looked more like a dress on him. Speedie shouted "Chip him" as Brian Kilcline stepped up to take the kick, but he blasted it wide of the post, which would have been hilarious if it wasn't for the fact we went on to lose the game 2–1. Dave Stringer wasn't happy and ordered me to get on the team bus with the rest of the lads for the trip home. I could hardly complain. Mind you, Susan could have: she had to drive back to Norwich behind the team bus!

Every other weekend, of course, we had home games which meant Susan would have to do the travelling, but not until Saturday evening because she had to work. She'd get down about 8 or 9pm and we'd spend the rest of the weekend together before she did the 4am trip back to Bolton on the Monday morning. It was hard work, but well worth it.

On the football front, the season went from strength to strength. We lost only two league games in the first half of the season and led the table for a few weeks before going into the New Year still flying high, second only to Arsenal on goal difference. In January we went to Millwall, who were also going well, only a couple of places below us in the table. It was one of the big games of the weekend and ITV's cameras were at the Den for the match on a Sunday afternoon. It turned out to be one of the most memorable games of my career.

Millwall had plenty of good players in their team at the time, not least Teddy Sheringham who was up front alongside Tony Cascarino. Jimmy Carter and Kevin O'Callaghan supplied the crosses from the wings, while Terry Hurlock typified their tough-tackling spirit in midfield. They were a tough side, for sure, but also had some real quality. The Den was an intimidating place, not exactly one of the most welcoming venues in the world. I'll never forget the look on some of their fans' faces when Susan turned up with some very good friends of ours, the racing driver Will Hoy and his wife, Judy. Susan was wearing a fur coat and Will and Judy were dressed to the nines, more suited for a night out at a posh restaurant in the West End than the rough and ready Cold Blow Lane.

We made a great start to the match, going two up early on with goals from Mark Bowen and Ian Butterworth. Millwall hit back through Cascarino and Carter to make it 2–2 at half-time. The second half was like the Alamo. My goalmouth was under siege from the word go. My gloves seemed to have magnets in them, though, because I somehow managed to stop everything they threw at me. I used just about every part of my body to keep them out – hands, legs, feet, even my face at one point. I must have made about 25 saves in the match and was really pleased with one in particular, a spectacular stop from Terry Hurlock. He cracked a volley towards my top left-hand corner from just outside the box. It came at me like a bullet and I flung myself across the goal and managed to get a hand to it and claw it out. I ended up in the back of the net and someone hacked the ball away to safety. Some Millwall fans thought the ball had crossed the line, but TV replays proved I'd kept it out. It's one of the best saves I ever made. In fact, I count it as my second best ever.

After surviving the fierce onslaught we went up the other end in the dying minutes of the match and snatched the winner. Robert Fleck pounced on a looping ball on the edge of the box to smash home a stunning volley of his own. The 3–2 victory meant we maintained our fantastic form away from home. It was a truly epic game, all the better for being seen by millions on live television. Most people thought I'd done more than enough to take the Man of the Match award, but Ian

The Saddest Semi

St John, who was co-commentating alongside Brian Moore, opted for Terry Hurlock instead. I seem to remember the Saint saying something about having to give it to one of the Millwall players to make sure he got out of the place alive. Maybe that explains it; either that or he was afraid of Terry, who was a fearsome-looking bloke.

Not to worry, we had showed the watching nation what we were made of. The Millwall victory was one of nine in the league on our travels that season, among them tremendous wins at Manchester United and Liverpool, with another clean sheet at Anfield. We were buzzing and at that point in the season it looked like we could push Arsenal all the way for the First Division title.

The game at Old Trafford on 26th October 1988 was particularly memorable for me. We won 2–1 and I saved a penalty. Brian McClair broke into the box from the right and Taffy Bowen brought him down. I'd watched Brian take penalties on video so from the way he was standing I knew he was going to put it to my left. When he hit it I dived full length and managed to parry it. Ian Culverhouse came out of nowhere to clear the danger as McClair pounced on the rebound.

Steve Bruce had kindly sorted out a ticket for Susan, which meant she was sitting with his wife, Jan, among the United players' wives and families. Susan told me she jumped out of her seat when I saved Brian McClair's kick – and then quickly sat down again when she remembered where she was.

I've always thought it's unfair that penalty saves are never recorded. I think the goalkeepers' union should start a campaign to ensure penalty saves are mentioned in the record books along with goal-scorers and things like substitutions. After all, penalty saves can determine the results of games every bit as much as goals. For the record, I saved ten penalties in my career, a fact I would proudly highlight in my testimonial brochure some years later.

Our success was built on a firm defensive foundation. Dave Stringer had moulded a strong back four, with Ian Culverhouse at right-back and Mark Bowen at left-back, while Andy Linighan and our skipper Ian Butterworth formed a formidable central defensive partnership. We defended well, but we also had great players like Mick Phelan and Andy Townsend in midfield. They were brilliant at staging counter-attacks. Up front, Robert Fleck was in outstanding form, but he made as many as he scored and we shared the goals around.

Our team spirit was fantastic. We were able to have a few shandies and a night out every now and then without incurring the wrath of the manager or coaching staff. In fact, it was positively encouraged as part and parcel of team-building. Take New Year's Eve that season, for instance. It was a Saturday that year. We played Middlesbrough at Carrow Road and then drove straight down to London for our next match against QPR on the Monday. We travelled a day early because the match at Loftus Road was an early kick-off.

I don't know if String Bean felt a bit sorry for us because we were away from our families, but he invited us all down to the bar to celebrate the New Year. He even got the first round in – he *must* have been feeling sorry for us. We ended up joining in with a pensioners' party in one of the function rooms – not so much hip and happening as hip replacement. Still, I was boogying on down when I suddenly saw big Andy Linighan lumbering drunkenly towards me, a massive grin on his face. He'd borrowed a flat cap, tweed jacket and massive NHS thick-rimmed glasses off one of the pensioners and was really enjoying strutting his stuff. We fell about laughing, had a few more beers and finally hit the sack around 2am . . . where we indulged in the delights of room service. It was a great night; we thoroughly enjoyed the chance to let our hair down. We'd just about sobered up by the Monday and drew the match against QPR 1–1.

As well as our good league form, we also had a great run in the FA Cup, going all the way to the semi-finals to equal the club's best ever run in the competition back in the 1958/59 season, when the Canaries famously reached the semis as a giant-killing Third Division team. We started our campaign with a 3–1 win at Port Vale and were then drawn against non-League Sutton United in the fourth round. Sutton came to Carrow Road on a real high, having produced the upset of the season by knocking out Coventry in round three. The Sky Blues had won the trophy only a couple of seasons previously, so it was the stuff of fairytales for Sutton and there was a huge amount of hype and interest surrounding our game. They made a few mischievous noises before the match about what they were going to do to us, how they were going to take another big scalp, and there was a great atmosphere inside Carrow Road. On the day, our strikers were just too hot for them; Malcolm Allen hit four and Flecky weighed in with a hat-trick to help us record the biggest FA Cup third round win for some 30 years. The Sutton boys took it in good spirit and I was only too happy to swap my shirt and gloves with their keeper, Trevor Roffey, who seemed quite chuffed about it.

The 8–0 win also equalled the club's record-winning margin, 10-2 against Coventry back in 1930, but as we kept a clean sheet you might say it was our best ever win. I certainly would, being a goalkeeper. We then beat Sheffield United by the odd goal in five in a cracking fifth-round tie at Carrow Road, before beating West Ham 3–1 in the quarter-final replay after drawing the first game 0-0. By the end of March, with only six weeks or so of the season to play, we were still second in the league and in the semi-finals of the FA Cup. Little old Norwich City, unfashionable as ever, were still in with a shout of doing the league and cup double.

April 1989 has to go down as the worst month of my professional career. All of a sudden the wheels came off as we lost back-to-back league games against Liverpool, Nottingham Forest and Coventry, followed by draws against Southampton and Aston Villa. Our title challenge was rapidly evaporating, but the worst thing about that wretched month, by far, came in the FA Cup.

Things got off to a bad start even before the semi-final weekend itself. We travelled to Birmingham on the Thursday, a couple of days ahead of the match against Everton. I was rooming with Flecky, as usual, and we were just enjoying a quiet night watching telly after dinner when Dave Stringer knocked and came in to our room.

"Flecky, I'm really sorry, I don't know how to say this, but I'm afraid it's your dad. He's passed away. If there's anything at all we can do . . ."

Robert was, of course, devastated and went straight home to Scotland to be with his family. I felt terrible for him and hardly slept a wink wondering how he was doing.

The next morning Dave called a team meeting and told the other players. They were all shocked and upset. News like this affects all teams, but we were especially close and Flecky was such a big character – on and off the pitch. We were all obviously gutted for him and,

Safe hands: Proudly displaying the power of the Gunn goalkeeping gene, my dad, James, has no problem holding me (right) and my cousin Ian at our joint christening.

This is me aged 7, from a school photo. Notice the jumper – clearly my stylish fashion sense is already blossoming.

This is me (left), my mum, Jessie, and brother Alan on holiday in Aviemore.

Ian 'Max' McLeod and I knew if we were going to make it as footballers we'd have to put in plenty of practice… on the golf course!

The Invergordon Academy under 15s team line-up, I think the wind blew at the wrong time because my hair did in fact look really cool at this time. My team-mates include Ian 'Max' McLeod (back row, second from right), my fellow Airdrie trialist John Fraser (back row, last on the right) and my fellow naughty choirboy, Alistair Jappy (front row, second from the left).

My trial at Airdrie with Bobby Watson. Notice that I'm not wearing gloves. I'd only use green cotton ones if it was wet.

PRESS AND JOURNAL

(Left) With a pro-contract in the bag, I could finally afford a pair of gloves. If only they could have got me some shorts that fitted!

(Above) Fergie always said I had one of the best shots at Aberdeen, and in 1983 I became the 'Hot Shot Champion of Scotland' at Hampden Park, beating the likes of Brian McClair, Paul Sturrock and Sandy Clark in a shooting competition. Not quite sure why Joe 90 was handing out the trophy though.

"Oops, sorry boss!" Mayhem on the bench in Gothenburg '83 as I send Fergie flying celebrating our European Cup Winners' Cup victory over Real Madrid. I gave him a framed copy of this photo as a thank you for bringing Manchester United to Norwich for my testimonial.

Welcome to Norwich, finally. Ken Brown
picks me up at the airport to drive me
straight to London to play for the reserves…
little did he know I had a stonking hangover.

I knew things were a bit
different in England, but
I had no idea they were
expecting me to save
four balls at a time!

"I do!" I was kilted up in Gunn tartan, of course, when I married Susan in Bolton.

Me and my best man David Hodgson. We were on holiday when I met Susan so it's all his fault!

This was taken for the Norwich programme just after Susan had moved in with me in Norwich. The pink curtains lasted about another week.

After a mad dash to get to Susan's side, I was the
proudest man alive when Francesca was born.

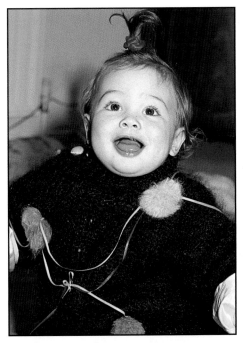

Proud parents at Francesca's christening.

Francesca was a beautiful, happy child.

The arrival of Melissa meant I was
outnumbered 3-1!

This is one of our favourite
pictures, happy times!

EASTERN DAILY PRESS

This photo of me and my old mate Robert Fleck and our daughters Francesca
and Olivia was taken at Stamford Bridge after we had appeared on opposite
sides. Francesca was very ill at the time and we lost her a month later.

I don't know how I got through that first match after
Francesca had died, but everyone was fantastic
including the QPR players and fans. I remember
Darren Peacock having a word as we shook hands
afterwards and I'll never forget that gesture.

With the appeal moving into overdrive my friend, the racing driver Will Hoy, helped us organise an auction where people could bid for a lap around Snetterton in his race car. I had a go, it was terrifying!

Sadly Will is no longer with us. Tragically he died from a brain tumour in 2002.

An auction of donated football memorabilia raised more than £10,000... I wonder where this Scotland shirt of mine is now!

I always liked to look my best for the camera!

Yessss! Celebrating the club's highest ever league finish, 3rd, at Ayresome Park on the last day of the 1992/93 season.

After all that had happened, I was immensely proud to be voted the supporters' Player of the Season for the 1992/93 campaign. The trophy was so big I had to get Susan to help me lift it!

Beating Bayern Munich in the Olympic Stadium is one of my greatest ever memories.

Can you spot me in this picture with the lads
before our 'bad taste' Christmas party?

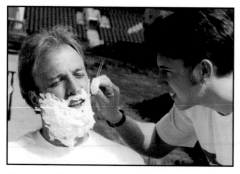

No, not auditions to see who's going to be
Santa Claus in the Canary Store, this was a
charity event at Carrow Road.

Not sure if I'm glancing one
gracefully down the leg side
or getting out plum lbw here!

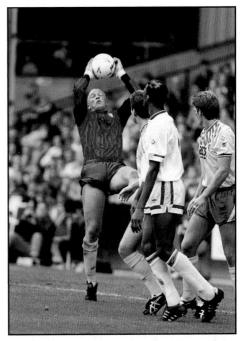

The spirit in the camp at Norwich in those days was second to none.

Another graceful take from yours truly!

'Just strap it up and I'll carry on!" Physio Tim Sheppard wisely ignored my assessment of the situation when I was injured at Nottingham Forest during the 1994/95 season. I missed the rest of the campaign and we were relegated from the FA Premier League.

Fantastic shot of me making a save against Ipswich Town. It
hangs proudly in the Gunn Club, and on the cover of this book!

"Gunny, you are a handsome chap, aren't you!"
Martin O'Neill was an inspirational gaffer.

If you're not going to go in where it hurts in the
East Anglian derby then you never are.

The most embarrassing moment of my career, when a backpass bobbled over my foot and into the net against Ipswich at Portman Road. Still, at least the stats read 'Ullathorne OG'!

A proud moment for me and Melissa as we come
out on the pitch for my testimonial, commemorating
ten incredible years at Norwich City.

Proud dad, beautiful daughter.

Fergie seemed genuinely touched when I gave him the picture of me knocking him flat on his face in Gothenburg. He has been an immense influence on my life and it was a tremendous gesture to bring such a strong United team to Norwich for the match.

"Merci beaucoup, Eric!"

Susan, Melissa and I at the opening of the Francesca
Gunn Laboratory at the University of East Anglia. One
day we hope they'll find a cure for leukaemia here.

Son of a Gunn! Angus is born.

(Top) The happy family. (Above) Three generations of Gunns: Dad, Angus and me.

The whole clan at Angus's christening. (From left to right) James Gunn, Susan, Melissa, Angus, Me, Jessie Gunn and Susan's Dad, John Winward.

Any excuse to dress up! I've come a long way since my days as a Bay City Rollers fan... or have I? These shots were for the PFA magazine, and also to promote my friend Roger Kingsley's designer clothes shop Jonathan Trumbull.

Bryan Gunn and friends… at a meeting of the goalkeepers' union with legends (from right to left), Dave Beasant, Pat Jennings, Phil Parkes, Ray Clemence and Bruce Grobbelaar.

With my old Scotland boss Craig Brown…

… my all-time hero Ray Clemence.

... the men who made it all possible, Sir Alex Ferguson and Ken Brown at Carrow Road during the 2004/05 season when I was working, hence the walkie talkie.

Remember Highbury 1989? Be afraid, Thierry, be very afraid.

... with Alan Hansen.

... with, er, Santa!

Watch out Andy Gray, another Scotsman after your job!

More bling than Charlie Nicholas and Mo Johnston
put together! It was a huge honour to be made
Sheriff of Norwich in 2002.

I exercise my competitive streak out on the golf
course these days... most days, in fact!

The many faces, shirts and hats of Bryan Gunn...
1983/84

1989/90

1995/96

1997/98

1992/93

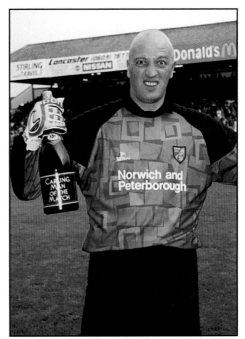

1993/94

2001 (don't ask!)

2002

The Gunn family at home in Framingham Pigot.

Melissa has grown up into a beautiful, intelligent young woman.

Angus gives his defence in the Norwich Academy a rollicking... wonder where he got that from?

although no one said it, we also knew that our chances in the semi had just faded dramatically.

Training was very subdued; naturally our minds weren't really on what we were doing. Everyone was really down and there was none of the usual spark and energy. We were still rather gloomy as we arrived at Villa Park for the game, but tried to put it to the backs of our minds. We wanted to win the match for Flecky, for our fans and ourselves. This was the closest most of us had ever been to an FA Cup final, so we tried to concentrate on the job in hand. The professional approach kicked in as soon as we ran out onto the Villa Park pitch. Our fans had taken over half the ground – the Holte End and most of the adjoining stand was a sea of yellow and green, with flags and inflatable Canaries everywhere and ticker tape raining down on the pitch. Our fans were outstanding; they really out-sang the Everton supporters and I felt a tingle run down my spine as we walked in front of them. I'd played in big games before with Aberdeen and Norwich but, wow, nothing to compare with the atmosphere that day at Villa Park.

I thought about Robert and his family back in Scotland, and knew he would be urging us to go out and book our place at Wembley. Unfortunately, we never really got going and ended up losing to a freak goal. The ball came into the box. I called for it and came out a couple of yards to collect it but Ian Crook, just in front of me, tried to clear it. Poor old Crooky sliced it up in the air and, as it came down, Taffy Bowen and Everton winger Pat Nevin went for it together. I was stranded near the penalty spot and could only watch hopelessly over my shoulder as Nevin got the slightest of touches and the ball trickled over the line and into the net. It seemed to take an eternity; my momentum was still carrying me forward and it was a horrible goal to see going in, as if in slow-motion. It was a poxy goal to concede. I can't remember having a lot to do apart from a point-blank save from Tony Cottee in the second-half, but we didn't play well, and Everton didn't have to do much to beat us. It was really frustrating bearing in mind how well we'd played for so much of the season. Of course, we missed Flecky. He was the sort of player who could change a game for you and he'd been scoring regularly in the previous rounds.

We trooped off the pitch absolutely gutted to have got so close to Wembley only to fail to perform on the day. Whatever level you play, a semi-final is the worst game to lose as you know you were so tantalisingly close. It's a horrible experience; you feel really empty inside. Nobody remembers losing semi-finalists. At least if you reach the final you get to experience the big day and savour the occasion, even if you lose. I felt numb as I came off the pitch. The dressing room was really quiet. Everyone sat slumped, staring dejectedly at the floor. There was no point in ranting and raving.

We sat there in silence for about ten or 15 minutes, our bodies and minds spent. Then one of the coaching staff came into the dressing room. "There's been some crowd trouble at Hillsborough and the match has been abandoned," he said. Liverpool and Nottingham Forest had been playing the other semi-final at the same time as us. To be honest at that stage our thoughts weren't straying any further than our own dressing room, we had no idea of the scale of what had happened in Sheffield.

We were still all cut up about Flecky, as well as the result, as we trooped onto the bus for the trip back to Norwich. The driver turned on the radio as usual. There were more reports of trouble at Hillsborough and we started to realise that something really serious had happened. A couple of the lads' mobiles started buzzing. People were now saying that some fans had been injured, possibly even feared dead. It sounded awful.

As usual, we stopped for a beer on the way home, at a pub near Newport Pagnell. The telly was on and, as I glanced across at it, I froze in horror. Suddenly we became aware of the full scale of the tragedy. Trevor Putney put his arms round me and both of us started crying. It was unbelievably horrific. The rest of the lads sat dumbstruck as we took it all in.

It all got to me again when I got home and reflected on what had happened over the past couple of days: Flecky losing his dad, us losing the semi-final and then this terrible, terrible disaster. I realised how it could easily have been Norwich fans caught up in the horror. A million thoughts went racing through my mind. I felt for those who'd lost people or were still not sure of their loved ones' whereabouts. Susan and loads of the other players' families had been at our game, what if we'd been playing at Hillsborough? I don't mind telling you, I broke down and had a good cry that night.

We won only one more game that season, ironically against Everton three weeks after the semi-final. We beat them 1–0 in the league at Carrow Road, a case of what might have been, I guess, but given the nature of the tragedy it was perhaps only right that Liverpool and Everton met in the FA Cup Final to allow the city to grieve together and pay its respects to the 95 fans who died.

It was insignificant in the grand scheme of things, but we petered out towards the end of the season to finish fourth in the table, drawing 2–2 on the last day of the season with Sheffield Wednesday at Hillsborough. It was stomach-churning to be there, to look at the Leppings Lane end all covered by tarpaulin and remember what had happened that afternoon of 15th April.

We were disappointed that we didn't finish third, but fourth place did mean we'd created club history by finishing in our highest ever position in the top flight. It also meant we'd done enough to qualify for the UEFA Cup. Once again, however, we were denied by the ban on British clubs.

CHAPTER ELEVEN

Skinny-dipping and Muddy Carpets

Norwich City might have missed out on a European adventure once again, but I wasn't to be denied the trip of a lifetime. The next big fixture in my life was coming up in the summer of 1989. After the best part of a year travelling hundreds of miles up and down the country every week on our long-distance romance, Susan and I were getting married. The big day had been set for Sunday, 11th June. It had to be a Sunday, not because of my football commitments but because of Susan's bridal shop. Saturdays are the busiest days of the year in that trade and Susan didn't want her staff or friends to miss out on her big day.

It was a busy time for weddings at Norwich City. My team-mates

Dale Gordon and Paul Cook were also tying the knot that weekend, so we had a joint stag night in Norwich with the rest of the lads, about 40 or so of us heading out on a pub crawl through the city centre. We ended up in the nightclub, Rick's Place. It was a pretty sensible, albeit drunken night. I kept expecting every woman that walked past to be a strippergram but it was disappointingly quiet on that front! A few years beforehand, when I was still at Hodgy's flat, he had organised one for my birthday. I'd received about a dozen or so parking tickets in a short space of time and was just coming out of the showers after training one day, towel wrapped round me, when a policewoman came into the dressing room.

"Bryan Gunn?" she asked.

"Yes, that's me. What's the problem, officer?"

"You've received an excessive number of parking tickets recently, and I'm afraid I'm going to have to ask you to come down to the station with me to answer a few questions."

"Oh. Right. I'll just get changed then," I said and headed for my clothes.

"Mr Gunn, I'm afraid you've been a very naughty boy," she began as the rest of the lads burst into hysterical laughter, and I finally twigged that she was here to take down her particulars, not mine . . .

A few days after the stag do I travelled up to Bolton where Susan's brother Allan offered to put me up for the week ahead of the wedding. That was good news because Allan had a snooker table at home and there was the added attraction of his tasty homebrew, which he served up from a proper beer tap. It was just like being in a pub.

We had invited about 200 people to our wedding, and there was a Scottish invasion the day before, with aunts, uncles, friends and former team-mates travelling down by train to Preston, about 20 miles or so from Bolton. My clan had obviously had a few drinks on the way because they practically fell onto the platform when I arrived to pick them up, especially my dad, who panicked as the train began to pull away from the station and started chasing it along the platform shouting, "My kilt, my kilt! I've left my f***ing kilt on the train!" He hadn't, my brother Alan had it.

Panic over, Dad was introduced to the welcoming party, including

Susan's brothers. He took an instant shine to John, just as I had, and they went straight off together, stopping at a couple of local pubs before arriving at the hotel, eventually.

Several of my former team-mates from Aberdeen also came down: Willie Miller, Alex McLeish, Neale Cooper and Eric Black were all there, along with Jim and Linda Leighton, whose daughter Claire was one of Susan's bridesmaids. Trevor and Lorraine Putney's daughters, Aimee and Hollye, were also bridesmaids and quite a few of my Norwich team-mates were present, including Ian and Kath Butterworth, Robert and Jayne Fleck, and Alan and Jeanette Taylor. Alex and Cathy Ferguson also came, which I was really pleased about, and there were a few of my friends from back home like Ian 'Max' Macleod. With so many great friends around, I had been spoilt for choice when it came to my best man. I could have easily asked Max or Blacko, but opted for Dave Hodgson – after all, he was there when Susan and I had first met. If it had been a year later, I guess Robert Fleck would probably have got the nod.

Word got out that there was a football wedding in town and, come the big day, I don't think Westhoughton knew what had hit it. The press had got a tip that Fergie would be there, along with a few international players, and it was hectic at the church when I arrived, with dozens of photographers jostling for position and crowds of locals curious to see what all the fuss was about. Along with most of the Scottish contingent, I was wearing my kilt (Gunn tartan for me, of course), and I proudly took my place alongside Hodgy at the front of the church to wait for Susan to arrive. I hadn't really had time to be nervous up until then, but luckily Susan and her dad didn't keep me waiting long. They arrived in a lovely vintage car, which must have taken all of 30 seconds to get them there as John lived at 51, Church Street, only a few yards away.

Susan looked a million dollars. I felt so proud when I glanced round to take my first look at her as she reached the altar. She'd designed her own dress, and had it made up for her, and it looked stunning. We had a chimney sweep there to bring us luck, a lad called Ryan who was the son of one of the girls in Susan's shop. He came along carrying a brush, with his little face all blacked up just like a character from *Oliver Twist*. For some reason, the regular vicar couldn't do the honours for us that weekend. His stand-in was none other than one Ian Butterworth! No, not our skipper 'Butts', but the Reverend Ian Butterworth, of the neighbouring parish.

The reception was at the Kilhey Court hotel, a Victorian house overlooking Worthington Lakes in Standish, near Wigan. It was stunning and the whole day went off without a hitch. All our friends and family got on famously with each other and good old Max provided some extra entertainment in the evening when he fell asleep at the table. He was always nodding off when we were youngsters, but, to be fair, he'd be working nightshifts at a fish-processing factory. Little did he know, but just about every guest at the wedding had their picture taken with him, complete with a plant pot on his head.

We were given some very generous wedding presents, including some Lladro and Royal Doulton porcelain from Alex Ferguson and Alex McLeish. Up until the wedding, the only Lladro I had was a special edition model of the World Cup, made for Spain 1982. It had been Hodgy's and he didn't like it, so I ended up with it after I moved into my house. It was pink and light blue – which at least matched the colour scheme of my pink house – but Susan very sensibly sprayed it gold as soon as she moved in. Fergie gave us a lovely Royal Doulton model of a woman with a dove of peace in her hands, which now has pride of place in our guest bedroom.

We flew off on our honeymoon the next day. One night in Amsterdam, where we took a romantic cruise along the canal, followed by a few days in Hong Kong for a shopping spree and then a couple of weeks relaxing by the pool in Bali. I was really looking forward to getting away from the spotlight and just chilling out, but the very first time we ventured to the pool we'd only just laid out our towels when I heard a voice: "Hey, you're Bryan Gunn, aren't you?"

"Blimey," I thought, "I can't go anywhere!"

Steve was a Spurs fan who was also on honeymoon with his wife, Madeline, and we all hit it off immediately, enjoying each other's company over dinner a few times.

They also witnessed Mr and Mrs Gunn's first marital tiff. We were playing mixed doubles tennis. I think I must have been missing bossing my defence: I kept telling Susan what to do, where to stand and where to go. We began to get frustrated with each other, then niggling each other and ended up shouting at each other. We decided to give up on tennis – for the rest of that holiday, at least.

Apart from that, we had a magical time, made extra special by the night we decided it would be really romantic and exciting to go skinny-dipping in the hotel pool. We waited until about midnight, when all was quiet, and crept to the pool as silently as we could, stripped off and were soon frolicking about under the stars to the point where we forgot about anyone else. The moonlight was reflecting off the water and it was a very special memory from our honeymoon.

After our cheeky swim, we grabbed our clothes, made our way back to the hotel and hopped into the lift, wearing nothing but two great big smiles. We reached our floor and the doors opened to reveal four fellow guests, standing there ready to get in. Hastily we clutched our clothes strategically about our persons, muttered an embarrassed "Good evening!" and hurried out of the lift, giggling like children all the way to our room. Good times.

The tennis didn't deter us from risking another sporting adventure, and a few days later we headed off for a game of golf on the hotel's nine-hole pitch and putt course. Susan had only played a few rounds of crazy golf when she was younger. We had just reached the first tee when a tropical rainstorm suddenly hit us and everyone started to run for shelter.

Susan, though, was determined to play. "Never mind a spot of rain," she said. "We're going to do this." Spot of rain? This was the mother of all storms – a torrential downpour.

Susan stepped up to the first tee, steadied herself and swung at the ball. It sailed straight past the first green and carried on all the way towards the second hole, another 50 yards or so further on. My mouth dropped open.

"Where did that come from?"

"I don't know," she said, looking as surprised as she was pleased. And that was it; she was hooked.

As soon as we returned home Susan booked some lessons at Barnham Broom golf club where I was a member. That was great news; I loved the game and now I had a wife who was only too happy to join me for a round or two. Susan quickly became an accomplished player. Her handicap came down almost weekly to a point where she was playing off twelve and good enough to earn a county call-up for Norfolk.

When we got back home, Susan's brother Allan and his wife Kath took over the bridal business and Susan moved to Norfolk to join me at my house in Framingham Earl. Susan had rather different decorating tastes to Jan Bruce and quickly decided the pink had to go. She had a point, mind you. For a start, pink isn't exactly the most practical colour for a lounge, as I had found to my cost when I threw a party at the end of the season before I met Susan.

I'd invited all the Norwich players and my neighbours in St Anne's Road to a housewarming bash one Sunday afternoon. My back garden had just been landscaped, complete with a new lawn and lots of nice plants. It wasn't long before it was wrecked. Some of the local kids came round to join in the fun and spent most of the time playing football in the garden. There had been a downpour overnight and the garden soon turned into a quagmire. The nippers were diving around and doing sliding tackles in the mud, then running into the house, bringing all the dirt in with them. The pink carpet quickly turned black and there were handprints all up the wall – and a few footprints. My team-mate Ruel Fox had brought along some of his pals from Ipswich. They were break-dancers and really went for it.

On the football front, the 1989/90 season was going to be a huge one for me. We'd established ourselves as one of the top teams in the country, on the back of finishing fourth in the league, but there was also the small matter of the World Cup finals coming up in the summer. I still hadn't made my full debut for Scotland, and I was desperate to clinch a place in Andy Roxburgh's squad if we qualified for Italia 90.

After knocking one or two goals past me in previous years, Dave Phillips joined us from Coventry and kicked off his Norwich City career with a goal on his league debut, in a 2–0 win at Sheffield Wednesday on the opening day of the season. Once again we got off to a good start, losing just one of our opening 10 league games. And, once again, we got one up over my old boss – we beat Fergie's Manchester United 2–0 at Carrow Road: Dale Gordon got one and Robert Fleck scored a penalty.

But it was on 4th November 1989 that the season really kicked off, literally. Boy, were there fireworks the afternoon we played Arsenal at Highbury. Malcolm Allen and Dave Phillips put us 2–0 up by half-time, Arsenal hit back after the break, but then Tim Sherwood scored to give us a 3–2 lead as we approached the end of the game. There were about five minutes left when David O'Leary, pushed forward from centre-back, made it 3–3. That was bad enough, but there was worse to follow when they got a really dodgy penalty from a corner in the very last minute of the match. Lee Dixon stepped up to take the kick. I flung myself to my right and saved his shot, only for the ball to rebound straight back to him, jammy sod. Dixon scuffed the follow-up in the general direction of the far corner, where Mark Bowen and Ian Culverhouse went for it along with Gunners' striker Alan Smith. The three of them got in an almighty tangle and the ball, along with all of them, was bundled over the line.

There was a little skirmish between Taffy, Cully and Smith as they tried to untangle themselves from the net and each other, then I noticed Nigel Winterburn having a gloat to Dale Gordon, who promptly pushed him. All of a sudden it was kicking off, big time. Everyone started piling in, right in front of me, inside my penalty area. The only people not involved to begin with were John Lukic, Tony Adams, David O'Leary and me. Eventually, I went over to try to break things up and calm the situation down. But, as I made my way over, I saw the cavalry coming over the half-way line, in the shape of O'Leary and Adams. I felt it was my job to head them off at the pass and moved in, instinctively grabbing Adams with one hand and thumping him with the other. It was absolute bedlam and the poor referee, the aptly named George Tyson, didn't stand a chance, so much so that the police ran onto the pitch to help restore order, pulling Dave Phillips away as he kicked someone up the backside. The only man who kept out of the fracas was John Lukic, who just stood at the other end with his hands behind his back. Sensible man.

Eventually Mr Tyson managed to restore order and, amazingly, no one was sent off – although I guess in the circumstances he would have had to dismiss everyone except Lukic.

We were absolutely gutted as we trooped back into the dressing room after the final whistle blew. One moment we had been 3–2 up and heading for a great win at Highbury, the next we'd been beaten 4–3 by a dubious late penalty after a poor decision by the referee. It's one of the most frustrating things in the game when an official gets it wrong, which Mr Tyson did on that occasion. It cost us dearly and we felt really hard done by.

Dave Stringer didn't bawl us out; he was as annoyed and frustrated as we were about the result. "F***ing gutted," were his exact words. Me and a couple of the other boys joined the Arsenal lads in the players' lounge for a swift half to show there were no hard feelings, but we didn't hang about. They had been really gloating and rubbing our noses in it on the pitch and the last thing we wanted was to have to endure some more of that. We had a quick glass, shook hands and left.

The next morning all the Sunday papers were full of what they were now calling the 'Highbury Brawl'. The photos were splashed across the back pages and I was right in the thick of it all, with an outstretched hand clasping Tony Adams around the neck and a full-blooded fist heading straight for his face. I think I made good contact – I certainly hope so! There was no way I was going to get away with it because I stood out from the rest of the mob, not least because I was wearing a different coloured shirt from everyone else. On top of that, my name was clearly visible on the side of the glove that was very obviously heading in the direction of Tony Adams' nose.

After training on the Monday I was at home with my feet up on the couch when I got a call from Ben Bacon of the *Today* newspaper.

"Bryan," he said, "hard luck at the weekend. I've just been speaking to the Arsenal players and they say the brawl was all your fault because you started it."

"My fault?" I was furious and took the bait, hook, line and sinker. "You're joking. It was their fault. *They* started it, not me."

The following day the headlines screamed: 'Gunn Blames Arsenal'. The papers lapped it up, spinning out the story for the rest of the week. It was hardly surprising; Arsenal were the champions and we were right up there with them at the time.

I was summoned to Lancaster Gate to see the FA. I felt like a naughty schoolboy as I entered a big, oak-panelled room where a number of FA executives sat facing me. They charged me with bringing the game into disrepute – more because of my comments in the paper than the actual fight, I think – asked me if I had anything to say in my defence and warned me about my future conduct. The club's solicitor and the chairman Robert Chase were also there to hear the verdict: Norwich City were fined £50,000 and Arsenal £30,000, although luckily we didn't have any points deducted.

Back at the training ground, the club felt they had to be seen to take action and fined me a fortnight's wages, about £800. I could hardly complain; what I did wasn't very clever, or responsible. It had effectively cost my family money, with *family* being the operative word. By now Susan was pregnant.

We had found out she was expecting early in the season, which was wonderful news. Even better, it seemed we'd timed things perfectly because she was due to give birth towards the end of May – after the end of the season, in other words.

In the last week of April, we were due to play Aston Villa in the penultimate league match of the season. I travelled with the team on the Friday afternoon, as normal, and the first thing I did when I got to the hotel in Birmingham was give Susan a call. I needn't have worried: she was absolutely fine and enjoying a well-deserved break with her feet up, so I decided to do the same and settled in for a night on the bed watching telly.

A couple of hours later she rang back. "Bryan, I've gone into labour. I don't know what you want to do about it, but I'm going to the hospital. You might want to get back here. NOW!"

I immediately called the gaffer and told him I had to get back to Norwich there and then. Dave Stringer was happy, in principle, to let me go home straightaway, but – and it was a big but – we didn't have another goalkeeper. These were the days before substitute keepers, of course, but thinking back it was pretty stupid in the circumstances. Why on earth we didn't take a second keeper on the trip, given Susan's condition, I'll never know. But we didn't, so Dave said he would have to contact our reserve keeper, Mark Walton, and get him to Birmingham before he could let me go.

Fine. Except Mark wasn't at his flat in Colchester. The club tried everyone they could think of to track him down – friends, relatives –

but to no avail. I was beginning to panic and started grumbling about how bloody stupid it all was.

Eventually the Colchester police got involved. They managed to track Mark down and as he hopped into a car to head north, I grabbed the keys to our coach Dave Williams' club car and drove east at something approaching 1,000 miles per hour. The journey was something of a blur; it was as much as I could do to concentrate on the road rather than think about what was happening with Susan back in Norwich. I had a minor scare when I bumped into the back of another car as I approached a roundabout. I got out of the car to check the damage. There was a bit of a scrape on both cars. I explained my predicament to the other driver and exchanged details with him, but he was as good as gold about it, telling me not to worry and wishing me the best of luck. I never did hear from him. Good man. If you're reading this book, thank you very much, pal.

I got back to the Norfolk and Norwich Hospital at about two o'clock in the morning, not knowing what the situation was. Susan was trying to sleep. There was no sign of a baby. I'd made it in time! Then, Sod's Law, nothing significant happened for what seemed like ages. Nonetheless, Susan was very happy to see me. I stayed with her throughout the morning and then around lunchtime things began to gather momentum.

We got lucky on the midwife front. Susan started to go into labour as they were about to change over shifts and the first midwife decided to stay to see things through, along with her colleague, who had come to take over. "Look after him," she said to her colleague, "he's not looking too good." I wasn't; I was really caught up in the emotion of the occasion and one of the midwives ended up mopping my brow as the other looked after Susan.

Finally, at precisely 2.59 on the afternoon of Saturday 28th April, one minute before kick-off, little Francesca Ruth Gunn came into the world. I heard a little scream just as she was born, and it was an amazing feeling as the little bundle was given to me for the first time. There's no experience like it. It's incredible, as any new parent will tell you. We called her Francesca simply because we both like the name and we chose Ruth after Susan's mum.

For the record it finished 3–3 at Villa Park. I can't say I paid much attention to the match but there were various doctors and nurses who kept tuning into Radio Norfolk and coming to tell me what was happening.

A week later I was back for the final match of the season, against Arsenal at Carrow Road. Was there any talk of revenge after the events at Highbury earlier in the season? You bet! We were really fired up for it and there was a great atmosphere in the ground, especially when Ruel Fox put us ahead in the first half. Once again, though, we let them back into it and eventually had to settle for a 2–2 draw. There was some satisfaction for us, though. The draw meant we'd denied the Gunners third place in the table. Even better, they were pipped to third by their arch rivals Spurs. Serves them right!

CHAPTER TWELVE

No Sex Please
...I'm Scottish!

I n an ideal world, it would have been great to spend some time getting to know our new arrival, little Francesca, once the season was over. There wasn't much chance to do that though, because a couple of days after the Arsenal match I was on my way to Aberdeen to join up with the Scotland squad.

We had qualified for the World Cup finals back in November. We needed just a point from our final qualifying match against Norway to ensure we qualified ahead of France. To say it was a tense night at Hampden Park would be a massive understatement. Willed on by 70,000 screaming Scots, Ally McCoist brought the place down when he scored on the stroke of half-time, only for the Norwegians to give us a late scare when they equalised in the 89th minute. I was in the stands, fidgeting nervously for what seemed an eternity as we played out the last few minutes. At last, the referee blew the final whistle. The place erupted. We'd done it. Scotland were going to Italia 90 – and I was going too!

As part of the preparations for the World Cup, Andy Roxburgh decided to give me my full Scotland debut in a friendly against Egypt not long after the Arsenal game. The circumstances couldn't have been better: I was making my debut for Scotland in front of a capacity crowd of 23,000 at Pittodrie, where I'd spent so many years. I would have just about every fan in the ground on my side, and all my folks were coming down from Invergordon for the game, along with my friends like James Welsh from Inverurie and Gordon Irving from Essex. It was everything I could have wished for. Susan brought Francesca up to Scotland and we managed to find a babysitter so Mrs Gunn could see the game.

I couldn't have written the script any better. Here I was, about to make my international debut in front of a supportive crowd, at the club where I'd started my career. Norwich City sent me a good luck message before the game (despite the fact that my full debut would cost them another £50,000 in fees to Aberdeen!), and I also got a supportive fax from Alex Ferguson on Manchester United headed paper. That meant a lot to me.

I met up with the rest of the squad at the Tree Tops, an impressive hotel just outside the city centre. As usual, there was a good buzz about the place: Andy Goram cracking jokes everywhere, and it was good to see old pals like Alex McLeish, Jim Leighton and Stewart McKimmie, all of whom I'd played with at Aberdeen. In fact, I'd played with most of my team-mates before, having come through the ranks with some of them at youth or under-21 level.

The goalkeeping coach, Alan Hodgkinson, tipped me the wink after training on the Monday that I would be playing, and then Andy Roxburgh named the side the day before the game. I was obviously chuffed, and Andy and Jim were delighted for me.

Aberdeen had played Celtic in the Scottish Cup final the previous Saturday but Andy Roxburgh still decided to pick players from both clubs. That meant they hadn't had much rest before the Egypt game, something that might help explain the way things unfolded on the night.

For the record, here's how we lined up on my full debut for Scotland: Bryan Gunn, Stewart McKimmie, Maurice Malpas, Gary Gillespie, Alex McLeish, Richard Gough, Gordon Durie, Jim Bett, Ally McCoist, Paul McStay and Davie Cooper. I puffed out my chest and the hairs on the back of my neck stood to attention as I bellowed out 'Flower of Scotland' before the game. We were facing the main stand and I spotted Susan and my mum and dad in the crowd. I was so proud, so excited. I'd dreamed of this moment ever since I was a little boy – and, although that dream usually involved beating England 2–0 with me saving a penalty kick, I was in good form and hoping to impress on my debut.

Everything was going so well – until we kicked-off. I still shudder when I recall what happened. We conceded a corner early in the game. It was played short to Abdelhamid, who floated a cross towards the back post. I found myself stranded at the near post, but knew Maurice Malpas was behind me and assumed he would head it clear. Unfortunately, Maurice thought I was going to go for it and punch it away or touch it over the bar. I left it to him, he left it to me . . . it was one almighty cock-up and the ball ended up floating over my head, past Maurice and into the net off the far post.

As if that wasn't bad enough, ten minutes later things got worse. Egypt got another corner, and this time it was cleared towards Gordon Durie on the half-way line. Rather than turn to go forward, or try to play a simple pass, for some reason Gordon decided to chip it all the way back to me in the penalty box. It was a suicidal ball. The Egyptian centre-forward, Hossam Hassan, read the back-pass and suddenly the race was on between him and me. We both had our eyes fixed on the ball as it sailed through the air. He was running towards me with the ball coming over his shoulder; I was running straight towards him waiting for the ball to drop. As I got to the edge of my area it fell between the two of us. Neither of us was going to hold back. I went for the ball, double-fisted, determined to punch it clear. Hassan kept coming, his eyes also firmly fixed on the ball. He got his head to it, a fraction of a second before I got there, and nodded the ball over me, just as I clattered him with both fists on the side of his head. The ball went in to make it 2–0 and poor old Hassan ended up in Aberdeen Royal Infirmary, dazed and confused. A bit like me at the time, I think it's fair to say.

It was a disastrous start to my full debut. All my friends and family were in the stands watching, along with more than 20,000 Scottish fans. I knew they were all rooting for me and they in turn knew just how much this game meant to me; how desperate I was to seize the opportunity to show what I could do ahead of the World Cup. I did my best to keep my composure, but it wasn't easy.

We got back into the game in the second half when I launched one of my trademark long kicks upfield. It was flicked on for Ally McCoist, who ran through to make it 2–1. At least I got something right. But just to complete a miserable night, Egypt grabbed another goal towards the end. Youssef broke through from midfield and curled the ball past me from just inside the penalty box. It was another soft goal, and I remember Alex McLeish looking at me and shaking his head. I don't think he was blaming me; it was more a case of frustration, bordering on embarrassment. We really shouldn't have lost to a team like Egypt, but that was it, beaten 3–1 on my debut at Pittodrie.

There were no recriminations after the game, no finger-pointing. Andy Roxburgh just said to me, "Don't worry about it", and told us all that we'd need to play a lot better than that in Italy. But I was absolutely gutted, devastated. It should have been such a wonderful occasion, but everything had gone wrong. I'd arranged to meet all my mates and family after the game at the Holiday Inn hotel in Dyce, close to my old digs in Bucksburn. Nobody said anything about the game. They knew better.

It has to go down as the most disappointing game of my life. As far as I was concerned, I'd blown my big chance. My hopes of playing well on my full debut at what was my football home for so long had turned into a nightmare.

A week or so later the squad headed off to training camp in Malta for the final phase of our World Cup preparations. We played the national team in Valetta, but I didn't get a look-in. Andy Goram started, with Jim coming on as substitute midway through the game. I had to settle for a place on the bench. I was desperate to get another chance, if only to prove what I was capable of and put pressure on Andy as second choice to Jim. By then, though, Andy Roxburgh was looking to play what he considered to be his strongest team and squad, which was understandable. I should also stress I had – and have – nothing but admiration for both Jim Leighton and Andy Goram. Goalkeepers always tend to stick together (okay, apart from me and Graham Benstead!), and Jim and Andy were great with me after the Egypt game. They were really supportive, telling me not to worry about it, but to work hard and look forward rather than back. We were a real goalkeepers' union.

My mate Robert Fleck hadn't made the original squad, but got a late call-up after Davie Cooper was unfortunately forced out of the finals because of injury. It meant we were a striker short so the SOS went out for Flecky to join up with us in Malta. He had been put on stand-by and should have been at home, just in case the call came. But Flecky, being Flecky, had gone on holiday instead, so when the Scotland party tried to contact him they couldn't get through. Knowing I was Flecky's mate, Andy Roxburgh asked me to help track Robert down. I tried every number I had but couldn't get a reply. No one seemed to know where he was. My hotel phone bill went through the roof as I tried everyone I could think of. It was the close season, so I knew there would only be a skeleton staff at the club, but as a last resort I called Carrow Road. Dave Stringer got involved. He did a bit of detective work and eventually discovered Flecky had gone to Dubrovnik in Yugoslavia with his wife Jayne, baby daughter Olivia and his in-laws. Dave gave me the hotel's telephone number and I made the call. Robert was in the bar at the time – surprise, surprise. I said, "Flecky, it's Gunny. Get yourself on a plane to Malta as soon as you can, mate, you're in the World Cup squad."

Robert thought it was a wind-up. His reply was short and sweet: "F*** off!"

I assured him I was serious and persuaded him to join us, pronto. He made it the next day – enough time to join in with the squad for a couple of days and get the holiday out of his system, before we headed off to Italy and the biggest show on earth.

Flecky and I had a lot in common at Italia 90. We were team-mates at Norwich City, of course, but we were also fringe players in the Scotland squad, and both assumed we had little chance of actually playing in the World Cup as we headed for our base at a stunningly picturesque lakeside hotel in Rappalo, near Genoa, where we would be playing our first two games. On top of that, we were both proud new fathers of baby girls: Flecky's daughter Olivia was only six months old at the time. We roomed together and still reckon we must be the only two players in history to end up paying for the privilege of going to the World Cup: our phone bill was astronomical because of the number of calls we made back home, eager to know how our wives and baby daughters were progressing.

I was incredibly proud to be part of the Scotland set-up. It was always going to be frustrating knowing I wasn't likely to get a slice of the action, but every schoolboy footballer dreams of going to the World Cup, and I was no different. It's a very special experience just to be part of the event.

Scotland were drawn in Group C, along with Sweden, Brazil and Costa Rica, who we played in our opening game. On paper, we were the favourites, but you know what they say about football not being played on paper. According to all the reports, their keeper, Gabelo Conejo, was rubbish. Apparently, he didn't like crosses, so the boys were told to pepper his box with high balls and then get big Alan McInally to put him under pressure. So what happened? Conejo had the game of his life, of course, plucking crosses from the air. From inside his six-yard box to the edge of his area, he caught everything with consummate ease. The lads were well on top for most of the game, but just couldn't find a way past him. We were looking at each other on the bench wondering what was going on. They had one chance early in the second half and scored what proved to be the only goal of the game. Unbelievable.

The defeat was shattering, and just as big a setback for the thousands of Scots who made the journey to Italy to support us. Andy Roxburgh gave us the next day off to recover. Apart from the game it was the first chance we'd had to leave the hotel complex, so me, Flecky, Jim Leighton and Stewart McKimmie wandered round the shops in Rappalo for a few hours, buying souvenirs and presents for our kids, before heading back to the hotel to put our feet up. A few of the other lads decided to have a quiet beer to relax and try to get the game out of their systems. Unfortunately, they were spotted in a local bar. It wasn't as if they were lying around drunk, but considering we'd lost I guess it gave out the wrong message to the fans, and the boys got a lot of stick from the press. The hotel got cordoned off after that, to stop the press harassing the lads, and we weren't allowed out at all on our own.

The Costa Rica defeat meant we had to beat Sweden in our next game to stand any chance of progressing to the next stage of the competition. This time we were the underdogs. Andy Roxburgh sprang a few surprises, not least by calling Flecky into the starting line-up. Robert hadn't featured at all until then, not in the qualifying campaign nor the friendlies, but this was his big chance on the biggest stage. I was absolutely delighted for him, and he didn't let his country down. Flecky had a great game, playing his part in a brilliant 2–1 win. Suddenly, we had a chance again, although we still needed at least a draw from our final match against the mighty Brazil. Not easy. Even then, we had to hope Sweden would do us a favour against Costa Rica in their final match, to be played at the same time.

We moved on to Turin for the match against Brazil in the magnificent Stadio Delle Alpi, home to Juventus. It was a big contrast to the Stadio Luigi Ferraris in Genoa, where we'd played our first two games in front of just over 30,000 fans. The Stadio Delle Alpi held more than 60,000, and it was packed for the big showdown. I made sure I took a good look around the stadium as I ran out to help Jim Leighton warm up as usual. The Scotland fans would always get there early, and there was always a warm round of applause for us, which helped me feel more involved.

Brazil had already booked their place in the next round with two straight wins. We figured they didn't really have too much to play for and there was a real confidence in the camp. The Sweden result, and performance, had been a tonic. Brazil were arguably the best team in the world, but we had to believe we could beat them. I remember thinking, "Cor, if we get a result against Brazil I could be out here for another week or so."

Having said that, I had mixed feelings about the outcome. I wasn't a major part of things, and had a wife and newborn baby back home. Professionally, of course, I wanted us to win, but in the back of my mind I have to admit I was thinking, "I can't wait to get home." Any new father would have been the same. It would have been different if

I'd been in the team, as Susan and Francesca would probably have come out to Italy to support me.

The lads put up a great fight against Brazil, and it was still goalless as we went into the closing stages, when Mo Johnston hit a shot from close range. We all leapt to our feet as it beat their keeper Taffarel, only for the ball to hit the underside of the crossbar and stay out. Bollocks. The Brazilians promptly went up the other end and scored. Jim Leighton got his hands to a shot from the edge of the box, but somehow the ball squirmed out of his grip on the greasy surface and Muller followed up to score from the rebound. 1–0. We were dumbstruck. There was very little time for us to come back, and news quickly followed that Costa Rica had beaten Sweden, so even a draw against Brazil wouldn't have been enough. And that was it: once again Scotland were out of the tournament at the first stage.

There couldn't have been a Scotsman in the world who wasn't hugely disappointed to be knocked out that night in Turin. Except me. I was on my way home to my wife and baby. Don't get me wrong, I would have been jumping up and down with the rest of the lads if we'd got a result against Brazil and gone through, but I was positively relishing the prospect of seeing my gorgeous wife and beautiful bouncing baby daughter again. I packed my bags in ten minutes and we left the next morning.

A few days after returning from the World Cup I got a call from my agent, a chap called John Mac. Steve Bruce had introduced him to me shortly after I arrived at Norwich. I'd never bothered with an agent when I was at Aberdeen but it seemed a good idea, especially as he was looking after Steve and helped set up Chris Woods and Dave Watson for big-money moves to Rangers and Everton. John told me, "If you pay me £90 a month, I'll look after everything for you – your finances, everything." I decided to go for the deal, but it wasn't long before I began to wonder if it was worth it. Maybe it's the Scotsman in me, but I never felt I was getting much for my money.

My scepticism was confirmed when I got back from Italia 90. John called me to say he'd agreed a good deal for me on the contract renewal front. "I've been working really hard on this," he said. "I've been speaking to the chairman and this is what's on the table." He then went on to outline the terms of the proposed new contract: £1,000 a week, a £2,500 bonus if I was picked in the Scotland squad and a £5,000 bonus if I actually played or was on the bench, plus a yearly signing-on fee of £50,000, which got paid as an annual lump sum during each close season.

To be fair it wasn't a bad deal. There was just one small problem: I'd already spoken to Dave Stringer about a new contract before I'd gone to the World Cup. We'd sat down on a bench at the Trowse training ground and had a good chat over a cup of tea about new terms. Dave had offered me a new four-year deal: £1,000 a week, a £2,500 bonus if I was picked in the Scotland squad and a £5,000 bonus if I actually played or was on the bench, plus a yearly signing-on fee of £50,000. I sent John a fax politely informing him that I would no longer be needing his services.

Over the years I arranged good deals for gloves and boots myself. I established a good relationship with Uhlsport through a chap called Bernt Killat in Germany, who I had met during my European trips with Aberdeen. I just kept his phone number and gave him a call once I got back to Scotland. Why would I need someone else to do that for me? I wasn't afraid to speak to the marketing managers at the big companies. In a way, I guess, it was breaking a path for my later career, negotiating deals as sponsorship sales manager for Norwich City. It was simply a case of having the confidence to make the approach.

The lads at Norwich obviously appreciated my bargaining skills, because not long after arriving at Carrow Road I became the players' PFA representative and would negotiate things like bonuses on their behalf. I struck a deal which saw us paid an extra £600 for a win, or £1,000 if we won and kept a clean sheet. That was for everyone, not just the goalkeepers. It was very good money back in the late 1980s. Ian Crook was still close to a few players at Tottenham and was able to confirm that, while we certainly weren't as well paid as players at other top clubs, we had one of the best bonus deals in the land. There was no special bonus for a goalkeeper keeping a clean sheet, or for a striker scoring a goal. The only person I remember in all my time at Norwich getting a goalscoring bonus was Chris Sutton.

*   *   *

No Sex Please ... I'm Scottish!

Susan and I hadn't booked a summer holiday because we didn't know exactly when I would be coming home from the World Cup. Okay, we had a reasonably good idea because Scotland have never got past the opening group stage, but miracles can happen so we didn't make any firm plans. Fortunately, Robert Chase offered to sort out a villa for us, in Puerto Banus, owned by his friends, the Docwra family. Morney and Renee Docwra were really kind to us. We'd never met them before but they were good enough to stay on for an extra day to welcome us. They even cooked us home-made steak and kidney pie, served up with a really good vintage Rioja.

The villa was like a home from home. We had satellite TV, which meant I could keep tabs on the World Cup, but my main aim was to make up for lost time and get to know Francesca, who was only a couple of months old. I could hardly take my hands off her. The three of us had a great time on that first family holiday, going for walks and messing around in the pool. I made a real fuss of Francesca, doting on her all week. I was the original proud new dad, and we had loads of fun as a family.

But no sooner had we returned home than I had to report back to pre-season training. I felt I'd hardly had a rest, because of the World Cup. My body obviously agreed because a few games into the new season I began to suffer from a niggling pelvic pain, a dull but persistent ache, which got much worse whenever I had to kick a dead ball. All the years of wear and tear, training day in, day out, were beginning to take their toll. It turned out to be a hernia. In the short term it meant playing with special supportive shorts, which helped a little. Long term, I was advised I would probably need an operation, although I was pretty much an ever-present for most of the season.

Every player will tell you that there are teams that they always seem to do well against, and others who routinely give you a hard time, for whatever reason. At Norwich we always seemed to struggle against Manchester City, but enjoyed plenty of good results against Manchester United and Liverpool. Our bogey team in the early 1990s was Nottingham Forest, managed by the legendary Brian Clough. They came to Carrow Road in January, for our first game of the New Year, and hit six past us, inspired by a young lad called Roy Keane who pulled the strings in midfield and weighed in with two of their goals. That game taught me a lesson. Throughout my time as a professional footballer I always had a rule: no sex on the night before a game. Different players had different views on the subject, but I was adamant – no sex.

Of course my darling wife knew this only too well, but relished the challenge of putting me to the test every now and then.

The night before the Forest match, she succeeded. Susan really went to town, dressing up in her sexiest undies and teasing and tantalising me, so much so that my defence went AWOL, as it were. The next day I was crap against Forest. Mind you, so were the rest of the defence. I can only assume they were at it the night before, as well. But that was that. I never had sex before a game again after that, however hard Susan tried to entice me.

I managed to go some way towards redeeming myself a few weeks later against Derby County at the Baseball Ground, by saving a Dean Saunders penalty. I'd watched him throughout the season and I was sure he was going to just blast it straight down the middle as he had done on quite a few previous occasions. He did just that and I stood firm, parrying the first shot then saving the rebound from point-blank range, before Dave Phillips finally cleared it out of the box. "Awesome, Gunny," he said and, without wanting to sound big-headed, I had to agree. It was definitely one for the scrapbook. We came away with a 0-0 draw, so the lads were quite happy to buy me a few beers that night when we got back to Norwich.

We played Cloughie's team at Carrow Road again that season, in the quarter-finals of the FA Cup. It was much closer this time (no sex the night before, of course), but once again Roy Keane did the damage, knocking us out with the only goal of the game. Our third meeting came in the return league match at Forest towards the end of the season, by which time I was really struggling with my injury. The doctors decided I needed to have a double hernia operation which meant I missed the trip to the City Ground. Just as well. Forest hammered us again, 5–0 this time. In three games during the 1990/91 season Forest beat us three times and put a dozen goals past us in the process.

But it was another game involving Nottingham Forest that season which will always have especially poignant memories for me, even though neither myself nor Norwich City were involved. On 18th May

No Sex Please ... I'm Scottish!

1991, Forest met Tottenham in the FA Cup final at Wembley. I won't forget that day for as long as I live. That afternoon I was at Addenbrooke's Hospital in Cambridge with Susan and Francesca.

CHAPTER THIRTEEN
Francesca

We had absolutely no idea there was anything wrong as I packed my bags for Norwich City's end-of-season tour. We were heading to Puerto Banus, again. Life seemed nigh-on perfect; I was a proud husband and father and, better still, there was the wonderful news that Susan was expecting again. I was also recovering from my hernia operation and felt fit. I got a rude awakening, though, when I jumped onto a diving board at the hotel pool. The pain went through me like a shot. It was excruciating. It felt like I'd creased myself in half. There was little I could do after that except take it easy, sunbathe and take in a spot of pitch and putt with the lads. Could have been worse, I suppose.

The day before we were due to return, the Thursday, I got my daily telephone call from Susan. She was upset; Francesca wasn't well. Apparently she'd been very sleepy and tired. Susan had taken her to our local GP, Dr Sampson, who had done some tests. He was alarmed and said Francesca would have to go to hospital for a more extensive examination the next day. I tried to reassure Susan that everything would be all right. There was sure to be a simple explanation. I mean babies are often tired and sleepy, aren't they? I felt pretty helpless, being so far away, but the good news was I'd be home within 24 hours or so.

Susan took Francesca to the Norfolk and Norwich Hospital the next day, while I flew back to Stansted, from where the team bus picked us up for the trip back to the training ground. A few of the boys had parked their cars there, so I jumped in with Flecky who lived just round the corner from me. I didn't mention my conversation with Susan, but it was very much on my mind, although I didn't consider for one moment that it could be anything serious. Robert dropped me off outside the house. I put the key in the lock and opened the front door. Susan was standing there, waiting for me. I can still picture the moment now: her hair was wet because she'd just been in the shower. She looked worried and upset. I asked her what was going on.

Susan looked at me and broke the news: the doctors suspected Francesca had leukaemia. I was stunned. Leukaemia – what did that mean? I'd heard of it and knew it wasn't good news, but what exactly did it mean? So many questions raced through my head. Just how ill was my baby? What was going on? What could we do about it? Francesca was asleep in her cot. I went straight up to her bedroom, picked her up and gave her a big cuddle. Susan urged me not to wake her, but I just had to hold her in my arms. I looked at Francesca and noticed her eyes were swollen. She obviously wasn't well. She looked a completely different child from the one I had left just a week before.

Dr Sampson came round later that evening to explain more about the illness. He was a lovely, caring man, and did his best to help us understand what the tests had found. Francesca had a form of leukaemia, but evidently the Norfolk and Norwich Hospital wasn't equipped to determine the exact form or seriousness of her condition. We would have to go to Addenbrooke's Hospital in Cambridge the next day to see the specialists and have more tests. Dr Sampson warned us they might even want to start treatment straightaway. We were devastated. There were lots of tears that night. Suffice it to say we hardly slept.

We got up early the next morning and drove to Cambridge with our little girl. Cambridge is roughly 65 miles from Norwich, about an hour and half's drive away. It was a journey that would change our lives for ever. All the way there we were hoping and praying the doctors' diagnosis would be wrong, or at least that the illness wasn't too serious. Francesca slept throughout the journey. When we arrived at Addenbrooke's we made our way to the children's ward, C2, where we'd been told to report. We walked down a long corridor that led to a nurses' station in the middle of the ward. There were separate rooms on either side where I noticed parents sitting at their children's bedsides.

As we approached the nurses' station there was a large fish tank where two little children were playing with some toys. They were both bald and had tubes in their noses and chests, yet seemed totally oblivious as they sat playing happily together on the floor. Susan turned to me and whispered something about Francesca, saying she couldn't imagine her playing contentedly like that without pulling out the tubes or getting them tangled up.

We were met by the sister, a lady called Ginny. She was the archetypal matron; strict, dressed in blue, tall, with silver hair. And very matter of fact. "Hello, you must be the Gunns," she said. "Come with me. You're in here."

Sister Ginny showed us to a room directly across from the nurses' station. There wasn't much in it, just a bed, one chair, a bedside cabinet and a television up on the wall. I was struck by how old-fashioned it all seemed.

It wasn't long before Valerie Broadbent, the senior consultant, came to see us. She told us they would be carrying out tests on Francesca to establish precisely what was wrong. They started by doing a lumbar puncture, an operation which involves taking a specimen of fluid from the base of the spine. It was quite a while before the results came back. We were becoming increasingly anxious; Francesca was looking worse and worse by the hour. The doctors eventually came to the room with the results. It was bad news. Francesca had acute lymphoblastic leukaemia, a particularly aggressive form of the disease. Worse still, she was particularly young to be suffering from it. The previous night had been a hammer blow, now our worst fears were being confirmed. We were numb. The disease was treatable, but there was no time to lose. They would be starting chemotherapy as soon as possible.

Francesca

Dr Broadbent explained that before they began the treatment they would perform an operation on Francesca to give her something called a Hickman line. We didn't know what they meant. They explained that it involved putting a special tube into an artery in her chest to allow the drugs to be fed directly into her bloodstream. Dr Broadbent said it was the kindest way to treat children; the alternative was to inject them with a needle, which would mean having to find a vein each time. Before they could give her the Hickman line, though, they would have to put Francesca on a saline drip overnight to hydrate her and flush her system.

At one point while this was all going on, I happened to look up and notice the FA Cup final was being shown on the TV in the room. I didn't pay much attention, it just happened to be on in the background, but I remember watching as Paul Gascoigne went flying into Gary Charles early in the match. Gazza ended up in agony on the floor and eventually had to be carried off the pitch on a stretcher. It was clear he'd suffered a serious injury, but I remember thinking, "Don't worry, mate. That's nothing compared to what some people are going through right now."

Susan and I spent the night at Francesca's bedside. It wasn't comfortable and we hardly slept at all, but frankly that was the least of our worries. Francesca was very, very sleepy and slipping in and out of consciousness. She looked very poorly. She'd deteriorated rapidly in the 48 hours or so since Susan had telephoned me in Puerto Banus.

The next morning a doctor came in to examine Francesca. We were expecting him to tell us what time she would be going into theatre, but he told us they wouldn't be doing the Hickman line operation after all. We asked him why not. He said it was because they didn't have a surgeon to perform the surgery. Susan hit the roof.

"I don't care who you call, but you call someone now and get them in here. I don't care if he's having his Sunday lunch with his family, my daughter's life is on the line and she's having that operation. You just make sure it happens." She was shaking.

I was just standing there, not really knowing what to do. I guess it's all part of a mother's maternal instinct, to do everything she can for the sake of her child. It wasn't that I didn't feel strongly about the situation, more a case of me not knowing what to do. Susan led the way, without a doubt. There was a nurse in the room at the time and she was nodding as if to say, "Good on you – they do this all the time."

The doctor then went away and Dr Broadbent came to see us. She explained that there had been some crossed wires somewhere along the line. Apparently, Francesca couldn't have the operation because she wasn't well enough and the doctor felt it would be too dangerous; it was nothing to do with a surgeon not being available. Why he hadn't explained that at the time, I have no idea, but Dr Broadbent assured us that was the case and we accepted it.

By now the seriousness of the situation was beginning to hit me. I don't think it had really sunk in when I first arrived home on the Friday night, or during the journey to Addenbrooke's. It felt as if everything was just happening around me, as though I was in a fog. You look around you, but don't take it all in. It was only now, seeing Francesca looking so poorly in a hospital bed, hearing all this talk of operations and realising how ill she was that I began to appreciate the gravity of the situation. We asked the medical staff what the prospects were of beating the disease. They told us Francesca had only had a 30-40 per cent chance of making a full recovery. Straightaway we thought, "Right, we'll be in that 30-40, then." Our daughter was gravely ill, but at least she had a chance. Our view was, "Let's get this treatment done and get through this."

With or without a Hickman line, they had to start the treatment as soon as possible. I remember the nurses coming into the room that Sunday. They were wearing thick gloves and took what looked like chemicals out of specially sealed bags. Francesca's treatment was about to begin. They had to inject the chemotherapy drug into her arm. It was obviously very toxic, and here it was being injected into a little baby girl, *our* little baby girl, barely a year old. Once they'd finished, they put everything away in sealed containers. The doctors told us Francesca would lose her hair. That didn't matter, just so long as she got better. It was the start of a long, desperate battle for her survival.

Our lives had been turned upside down almost overnight. We were facing every parent's worst nightmare. Our precious baby daughter was only 13 months old, a helpless little thing, and here she was facing a fight for her short life. We'd planned a lovely family holiday to Cyprus. It was meant to be the perfect break. Susan would be able to take it easy during her pregnancy, while I kept Francesca occupied. She was becoming a real little character, taking her first steps and muttering a few words. Suddenly, thoughts of splashing around in the sea and enjoying some quality time with my wife and baby were the furthest thing from my mind. The only place we would be going anytime in the near future was Addenbrookes. The hospital would become home for the next few weeks, certainly for Susan and Francesca.

Everything was happening so quickly. They told us that some forms of leukaemia had a 75–85 per cent recovery rate, even back then, but Francesca was suffering from a highly unusual strain and they didn't really know the best way to tackle it, especially given her age.

Dr Broadbent told us there were four different procedures, or plans, for treating the leukaemia. All involved administering chemotherapy, but there were different cycles with various combinations of drugs and timescales. When a child was diagnosed all the results and details were fed into a computer, which then decided which treatment your child should receive. Francesca was put on plan D. It all seemed totally random. We had no way of knowing which plan would be best for Francesca. There was clearly a lot of experimentation going on. We wondered if we should question the process, to ensure we were getting the very best treatment for our daughter, but we had to rely on their judgement. It was really scary thinking that one of the other treatments might possibly work better for Francesca, but we had no idea.

She would have to stay in hospital for at least six weeks. That in turn meant we would be there as well, by her side, day and night, if necessary. We had to think about the practicalities. There were a small number of small flats at the hospital, which relatives could let, but they couldn't guarantee their availability. We could stay in the room with Francesca, but Susan was pregnant and needed her rest. There was only one thing for it: we'd have to find a local hotel.

We stayed with Francesca until late on the Sunday night and made sure she was asleep and comfortable. The treatment had effectively knocked her out. Her life wasn't in danger at that stage and there was little we could do by staying with her. We booked into a nearby hotel that night.

The next morning we returned to the hospital, and then I went back to Norwich to grab some fresh clothes and a few other bits and pieces. That was to become my routine for the next few weeks. I would pop home every now and then to pick up anything we needed, while Susan stayed at the hospital with Francesca for the entire first six-week course of treatment. I was also there most of the time. We would spend the day at the hospital, then go to the hotel for the night and get up early to return to the hospital every morning. It was a pretty mundane existence; we sat by Francesca's bed during the day, keeping her company and chatting to her. She was too young to chat away and often too sleepy and weepy to respond, but we simply had to be there. The only way to break the monotony was to go to the cafeteria for a cup of coffee or something to eat, or take occasional walks round the block. It was a hugely stressful and emotional time, but we knew we had to be positive, for both Francesca's and our own sakes.

The first blast of chemotherapy treatment is the most intensive. Your body and cells are shot to bits and Francesca had to have a week off the treatment to recover. At first it seemed she was responding well. The swelling around her eyes went down and after about three days she was amazingly normal again, happy and smiling. It was wonderful to see her body responding and adjusting. She improved sufficiently for doctors to put a Hickman line in. It's very intrusive, going right into a main artery in the chest. The staff were fantastic, always doing their best to cheer the children up and put a positive spin on things. They tried to make a bit of fun about the Hickman line. I remember they called it her 'Wiggly'. Not that it meant much to Francesca, she was really too young to understand what it was all about.

There were youngsters of all ages in ward C2, from teenagers to toddlers and little babies even younger than Francesca. We were all families with children who were going through the same thing. Over the course of the weeks we got used to seeing the same familiar faces, all facing an almighty battle to overcome this dreadful disease. It was harrowing at times: one day a child might be playing happily in the ward, the next they would be in the cafeteria unable to eat properly because the chemotherapy made them so poorly. Worst of all were the occasions when we'd noticed one of the little faces was missing, and then find out it was because they had lost their fight for life. It was tragic.

You wonder how you would cope if you were faced with such an ordeal, but you just get on with it. You have to. Although we were going through a really tough time, we were relatively fortunate compared to some of the other families. Not everyone could afford to stay in a nearby hotel, for instance, and some didn't have a car. I could travel to and from Norwich whenever I needed to, but other families weren't so lucky. I remember mothers coming to the hospital by bus with a sick child and two or three other youngsters in tow. It made a tough time even more of a struggle. It was something Susan and I felt strongly about. We decided that when Francesca got better, we wanted to do something to help.

In the meantime, and more immediately, there was something else we wanted to do. There was a small playground outside ward C2, but it wasn't really up to much, not helped by the fact some of the parents used it as somewhere to go for a cigarette. There were butt ends all over the place. It was disgusting and wouldn't be allowed these days, I'm glad to say. We decided we would do our best to raise some money to improve things. We kicked things off by donating any cash I got from things like personal appearances, and within a few months we had enough to fund the work. I was invited down to open the new facility. Sister Ginny (who we now realised was a sweetheart, not the austere woman she had seemed at our first meeting!) was there and really appreciated our efforts. It was much better, with a safe rubberised surface and some good kit for the youngsters to play on. Smoking was banned, too.

After the initial intense six-week course of treatment we were allowed home, only for a week a month though. We thought "Wow!" It was so good just to be back in our own home. We could do normal everyday things again, like going to the supermarket. It was fantastic. Francesca was beginning to lose her hair, but she seemed much better in herself, and we were all delighted to be back at home. There were complications though; the chemotherapy really knocks the immune system and means you're particularly susceptible to catching things like colds and sore throats. It meant we often had to go to the Norfolk and Norwich Hospital to collect some strong antibiotics for Francesca. Even so, that first week back home was great. We were so happy. It didn't last long though.

The week flew by only too quickly and we were soon bracing ourselves for the return to Addenbrooke's and three more weeks of treatment. We were on tenterhooks; not just because Francesca was due to have her next blast of chemotherapy, but because we were about to learn how she had responded to the first six weeks of treatment. It was a crucial time. We really needed Francesca to go into remission at that stage if she was to stand a fighting chance of recovering. We were advised that if the patient doesn't go into remission after that first intensive blast of chemo it would be a major setback, almost like a relapse.

Dr Broadbent came to see us with the results. It was more devastating news. Francesca hadn't responded to the treatment. This was a massive blow. She said they would immediately take us off plan D and formulate another course of treatment, specifically for Francesca. We were left under no illusions that her chances of beating the disease had gone down, but we never gave up hoping and praying she would pull through. She was a great little fighter. Together we were determined to battle on and beat the odds, however slim they might be.

There was more incredibly sad news on that first return to Addenbrooke's. During her first six weeks in the hospital, Francesca had met a playmate called Joshua, a bubbly little boy from Ipswich, who also had leukaemia. They were the same age. When we went back we were told he'd died. It was heartbreaking. It was painful to meet so many other children in the same situation, all fighting for their lives. In a sense it was reassuring to know someone else was going through the same thing, but at the same time we almost made a point of not getting to know the other families too well. It's a sort of self-preservation; you've got enough problems of your own, without wanting to share the burden of someone else's suffering. We tended to stay out of the parents' room at the hospital for that very reason –

we would hear all kinds of horror stories in there and we'd taken the decision to be totally positive and focused. We didn't want anything to deflect us from that.

The routine of three weeks in hospital and one week at home continued for the first year. It was something of a rollercoaster ride. We had our good times, and our bad. There were signs of hope, when we thought Francesca was doing well. Her hair came back and you wouldn't have thought there was anything wrong with her. Her treatment varied as the months passed: sometimes it would be another intensive blast of chemo that would knock her out for a couple of days; other times they would give her just an hour or so, on a day visit, which wasn't so bad. Chemotherapy is potent stuff, and children are invariably sick after they've had treatment. Francesca was no different; it always happened around 50 minutes after she'd had chemo. I remember it well. There's a roundabout between Norwich and Cambridge where we always had to stop on our way back to Norfolk. We got used to it, but really felt for those parents who had to take their children home on the bus. It must have been awful and made us even more determined to try to help those in that situation. It's a bad enough ordeal as it is.

Susan stayed with Francesca whenever she was in Addenbrooke's. During her weeks at home we tried to keep everything as normal as we could. We took Francesca to nursery and did our best to treat her like a normal child. We tried not to be too fussy or wrap her in cotton wool. She coped so admirably with all the treatment and everything they threw at her. She really was a strong little girl, a real fighter. When she had her routine 18–month check-up, the same as any other child at that age, the health visitor came round and said she was amazed at how fit and well, how normal, Francesca seemed. She was really doing well. I remember Susan once saying to me, "If you put 10 children in a row, and three of them were going to survive, Francesca would be one of the three."

The first six weeks in Addenbrooke's almost coincided with the close season break. I returned to training, but by and large I was able to come and go as I pleased. Dave Stringer and the club were really supportive. There was never a problem if I needed to get away to go to Cambridge. I guess it helped being a professional footballer. We trained in the morning, which meant I had the afternoons to go to the hospital or sort out whatever needed doing. There was a lot of commuting and, to be honest, football was a welcome release from all the worry of Francesca's illness. Training offered some respite. It was never far from my mind, of course, but at least I could put my attention to something else when I was at work.

It was different for Susan. She was with Francesca just about all the time while also coping with being heavily pregnant. During Francesca's treatment, her Hickman line would be connected to the chemotherapy on a trolley. It meant she could move around during the treatment, which could take several hours. The chemo invariably made Francesca lethargic and weak, so Susan would often have to pick her up and carry her under one arm, while pushing the trolley around the ward with the other. I was concerned about the effect it would have on Susan, given her condition, but she was fit and strong and she coped really well.

To add to the strain we were planning to move into a new house just a couple of weeks or so before our new baby was due. My mum and dad came down from Scotland to help us with the move from St Anne's Road, Framingham Earl, to our new home in the nearby village of Framingham Pigot. It was just as well they were with us, given the way things turned out. We planned the move over a Thursday and Friday towards the end of November 1991. As you would expect, it was a pretty chaotic time and once we'd got all the furniture in I sent Susan off for a swim. She was due to give birth in just a few weeks, and I thought she could do with a couple of hours' relaxation while I helped Mum and Dad put some sheets on the bed and get the house into some sort of order. Once we'd straightened things out, I popped out to meet Susan at the health club. I left Francesca with her nana and papa. She was really excited and inquisitive about her new home, thoroughly enjoying the extra space and running around in our big new garden.

While we were tucking into our lunch Susan began to have a few minor contractions. At first we thought it was because her swim had been a little too strenuous and assumed they would subside. By the time we got home, though, the contractions were coming at closer intervals and getting stronger, so we gathered some necessities and headed straight for the hospital.

Francesca's birth had been natural and relatively plain sailing, but this time there were some minor complications and Susan was whisked straight into theatre. It soon became clear the situation was urgent and I wasn't allowed in with her. I didn't know what was going on as I waited nervously outside the theatre for news. Then, at about ten past six on the evening of Friday 22nd November 1991, Melissa Jayne Gunn was born by emergency caesarean. Susan was still under the anaesthetic when the nurse suddenly appeared with Melissa wrapped tightly in a cotton shawl and ready for her first feed. The nurse handed her to me and gave me a tiny bottle of milk. I kissed my new baby daughter and fed her there and then, sitting right outside the theatre. I was the extremely proud father of two beautiful baby girls.

Although it was a hugely exciting moment, I was obviously concerned about Susan and wanted to know how she was. The staff assured me everything would be fine and a little later she was transferred to the maternity ward. When she came round, I was waiting by her bedside to tell her our wonderful news. I placed Melissa in Susan's arms and we were both overcome with joy. It was a wonderful, emotional moment. Susan was still slightly drowsy so I gave them both a big goodnight kiss and left them to get some rest before heading home to break the good news and tell Francesca she had a new baby sister. Mum and Dad were absolutely delighted for us and for once in my professional life I broke my normally strict Friday night pre-match routine and popped out with Dad for a swift half to wet the baby's head.

After all the excitement, I wasn't at my sharpest by the time we kicked off at Carrow Road the following afternoon. We were playing Coventry City, and I dropped a bit of a clanger in the first half. I made a bit of a hash with a quick throw-out to Dave Phillips. Kevin Gallagher intercepted it and ran through to put the Sky Blues ahead. Thankfully, we hit back after the break with goals from Taffy Bowen and Flecky. They then scored again and it looked as if the game was heading for a 2–2 draw as the seconds ticked away.

There was a young lad on our subs' bench that afternoon hoping to make his debut. He got his chance in the second half and grabbed it with both hands, popping up with the winner in the last few minutes. It would be the first of many goals the youngster would go on to score for Norwich City. His name flashed up on the scoreboard above my head. Chris Sutton had burst onto the scene.

A new house, a new baby and a victorious five-goal thriller, I reckon it has to go down as one of the most memorable 48 hours of my life.

CHAPTER FOURTEEN
A Pain in the Back

L ife became a whole lot easier after the first few months of treatment at Addenbrooke's. Francesca became an outpatient and was able to spend most of the time at home. We had to take her to Addenbrooke's every six weeks for a routine check-up, just for a day, but that was nothing compared with having to live there for three weeks at a time. Francesca was still on chemotherapy, but it was now being administered and co-ordinated in Norwich. At last the whole family were living together at home again: Susan, Francesca, Melissa and me.

On one of our routine visits, shortly after Melissa was born, the doctors suggested it would be a good idea to take a blood sample from her to see if she was a match for Francesca. We didn't realise at the time, but if Francesca carried on responding well to treatment a bone marrow transplant would give her the best chance of beating the disease. If the girls matched, they would be able to harvest Melissa's bone marrow with a view to carrying out a transplant. Naturally, we were prepared to try anything and we agreed to go ahead with the test. They wanted to do it as soon as possible, once Melissa was eight weeks old.

I stayed with Francesca while Susan took Melissa into the treatment room for the blood test. They needed to draw 20 millilitres of blood from her, which I thought was quite a lot from an eight-week-old baby. I'm not good in those circumstances and couldn't handle being in the room while they did the test. I stood outside with Francesca and left them to it. It was tough on Susan. She had to hold Melissa as they put the needle in and took her blood. Melissa let out a loud scream and cried for what seemed like ages. I could hear it all going on and felt terrible, but it had to be done.

Unfortunately, it was all in vain. The match was negative. Even so, we never stopped believing Francesca would get better. There were never any negative thoughts; we simply couldn't allow ourselves to have even the faintest glimmer of doubt.

Throughout this whole time, naturally our concern for Francesca was uppermost in our minds. My way has always been to keep things to myself and to get on with life, but on one occasion I lost control of my emotions for an instant.

Tim Sherwood had organised the 1991 players' Christmas party. We were all in a bar enjoying a few beers, when Tim came over to me.

"Come on, you'll miss the strippers. They've already started upstairs."

"Cheers, mate, but I just don't fancy it. I think I'll stay down here and finish my drink."

"Don't be such a f***ing party pooper. Come on, it'll be a laugh."

"Tim," I said, "please, just leave me alone. I don't want to go up there."

With Francesca gravely ill, I really didn't feel it was the right thing to do, or even something I was particularly interested in. Frankly, I couldn't give a damn.

I think because he'd organised the whole affair, Tim just wanted to make sure everyone was really enjoying it. I assured him I was and again asked him to just leave me be. He wouldn't let it drop.

"Come on, what's wrong with you?"

Suddenly, I just saw red and head-butted him – at which point he saw red too. We pushed and shoved each other for a few seconds but I felt terrible as soon as I'd done it and immediately apologised.

"Look Tim, I'm sorry. I'm just really worried about Francesca, all right?"

"Yeah, fair play Gunny. I'm sorry too. I was just trying to have a laugh."

I really got on well with Tim and liked him as a person, so we shook hands and that was the end of it.

On the football front, 1991/92 was something of a hot and cold season. We hovered around mid-table up until Christmas, but things came to an abrupt end for me early in the New Year. We were playing Sheffield United at Bramall Lane when Mark Bowen knocked the ball across the penalty area to me. Goalkeepers were allowed to pick up back-passes in those days, but as the ball came towards me one of their players ran in to try to intercept it, so I had to move quickly to get there first. I went to pounce on the ball and my knee stuck in the turf as I dived. I continued to stretch and felt my back catapult out of place. I knew immediately that something was badly wrong. I tried to stand up, but once I'd managed to get to my feet I was in agony. I couldn't lift my left leg up above my knee, and it really hurt when I tried to kick the ball upfield. I hobbled around for what seemed like an eternity before there was a break in play. Fortunately, nothing came my way for a while so I grabbed hold of the crossbar and hung down from it, hoping my back would click back into place. It didn't work and I knew I wouldn't be able to carry on. The next time a shot came in I was rooted to the spot, but luckily it flashed just wide of the post. At last, Tim Sheppard was able to get onto the pitch to check me out. It didn't take him long to realise I couldn't continue. We didn't have a substitute keeper on the bench, so striker Darren Beckford took over in goal. He did a pretty good job, too, making several decent saves, but was eventually beaten, just the once, and the lads were unlucky to lose the game 1–0.

Like most goalkeepers I'd had a few back injuries in my time, but until that match they'd been relatively minor. I've lost count of the number of times I had to see a chiropractor the day before a game to have a vertebra clicked back into place.

One of my most painful back injuries came in the craziest of circumstances, though. We were at our Christmas bash one year at Barnham Broom golf and country club, just outside Norwich. As part of the evening's entertainment, Tim Sheppard organised a comedy awards ceremony where every player was given a prize. Mine was a jock strap. Tim joked that it would help cure a slightly embarrassing habit of mine. Norwich City fans will know exactly what I'm talking about; Alex Ferguson and Archie Knox would often give me stick about it. Fergie even mentioned it on my testimonial video.

"Does he still pick his knickers out of his bum?" he asked. "Archie and I used to count the seconds between each pick. I can tell you there weren't many!" It's nice to know he had such good memories of me. I don't know why, but I've always done it, without ever realising I was doing it. If ever the Norwich fans got bored, they would urge me to do it. "Gunny, pick your bum! Gunny, Gunny, pick your bum."

Tim claimed the jock strap would cure the problem and ordered me to try it on there and then. So I did, over my trousers.

You wouldn't think the simple act of putting a jock strap on would be particularly hazardous, but as I bent down to pull it over my trousers I felt something snap in my back. It wasn't much more than a twinge to begin with, but it became progressively more uncomfortable during the night. I found myself having to adjust the way I was standing and then had to prop myself up against the bar as the pain became worse.

Susan was with me, which was just as well because I was really beginning to struggle by the end of the evening, so much so she had to drive us home. By the time we got back I could tell she was tired, so I told her, "You go on ahead. My back's playing up and I think it'll take me a little while to get out of the car."

It took me an age. I could barely walk. I crashed flat out onto the living room floor, hardly able to move. After a while I attempted to get up to go to bed, but I couldn't stand. I had to crawl across the floor to the foot of the stairs where I hauled myself up, step by step. Susan sat at the top of the stairs but there was nothing she could do. It took me a full hour to drag myself upstairs. The pain was excruciating and I was actually in tears.

I was bed-bound for a couple of days before I managed to get out to visit my chiropractor, a chap called Ron Johnson. He was based in Woking, which meant a long drive down from Norwich with a bad back and then another long drive home. Not ideal. Fortunately, Ron weaved his usual magic and sorted me out in time for the game at the weekend. Just as well. It wouldn't have looked too good on Tim if I'd missed the match. I reckon it must be the first case of a physiotherapist causing an injury, rather than curing one. (It didn't work either: I still pick my bum even now!)

Mark Walton came into the team after my injury at Bramall Lane, while I faced several weeks of rest and plenty of manipulation on my back, along with a series of pain-killing epidurals. While I was being treated they discovered I had arthritis in my back, and I was also diagnosed with ankylosing spondylitis. It's a degenerative rheumatic disease where the bones and joints of the spine fuse together and I still have to take tablets for it. If I want to wake up in a fit state in the morning, I simply have to take a pill. If not, it's painful. Apparently, the condition could be hereditary. My mum suffers from similar back problems and takes the same drugs as me. Being a goalkeeper can't have helped, though.

There was little prospect of me playing again that season, but I did make an attempt at a comeback towards the end of the campaign. For the second time in four seasons, Dave Stringer took Norwich City all the way to the semi-finals of the FA Cup, where we were due to meet Sunderland at Hillsborough. I was desperate to play. In reality, there was no chance of being fit in time, but I convinced myself I could make it and even started training. I persuaded Dave to let me travel to Sheffield with the squad. I just wanted to be involved in the occasion. In the end, I didn't even take a late fitness test. It wasn't a wasted journey though; I ended up co-commentating on the match for Radio Norfolk with Roy Waller, which was great fun and made me feel involved.

It turned out to be another hugely disappointing semi-final. Poor Flecky was out of luck again. This time he'd been suffering from a broken rib which had kept him out of action for more than three weeks. Having missed the Everton semi-final three years earlier, he was understandably determined to play this time. Everyone wanted Robert to play. The club tried everything they could to speed the healing process, even bringing in a special oxygen tent in the week leading up to the match. It was a strange contraption, a bit like a Sinclair C5 or the cockpit of a little aeroplane. Flecky would sit inside his oxygen bubble for ages, reading the paper.

I don't know if the oxygen helped, but Robert was passed fit to play in the semi. He wasn't fully match fit, though, and would be the first to admit he didn't have the best of games. He wasn't the only one. Again we didn't do ourselves justice on the day, and again we lost 1–0. It was a crushing blow for the club – and the fans. Like us, they really thought we would make it all the way to Wembley this time – third time lucky, after 1959 and 1989. I went to see the lads after the game. There's no worse place in football than the losers' dressing room after a semi-final. Everybody just sat in silence, staring glumly into space, alone with their thoughts.

To coin a phrase, being out of the Cup meant it was time to concentrate on the league. And we certainly had some concentrating to do. We were too close to the relegation zone for comfort and didn't actually secure enough points to guarantee safety until a 1–1 draw with Wimbledon in the penultimate game of the season. Flecky got the goal. That was just about it, the season all but over, aside from the final match at Leeds United. But we were in for a big shock before the trip to Elland Road.

The news came totally out of the blue. Dave Stringer came in to training on the Monday after the Wimbledon match and told us he was quitting. We were stunned, but Dave explained that he felt he couldn't take the club any further. He said every manager had a sell-by date and he felt he'd reached his. And that was that; he'd made his mind up. He was going. It was a strange time to resign, with just one game of the season left, but I guess Dave felt he'd done his job. He wasn't going to leave until he made sure we were safe and, once we'd got enough points to avoid relegation, I reckon he felt he could walk away with honour and dignity.

Few people have a stronger claim than Dave to the title 'Mr Norwich City'. He's always been a proud and honourable man, with the very best interests of the club at heart. He's a Norfolk boy, born and bred, and knew all about the football club, having gone right through the ranks before becoming the third highest appearance maker in the club's history. Dave was one of those managers you could speak to. He'd been through it all himself as a player.

He was utterly engaging in pre-match team talks. He was a quiet man, but swore a lot in those talks, to the point where one day we ran a sweepstake on how often he would say 'Fookin'. It got to about 30, and he turned to walk away when Tim Sherwood suddenly let out a big cheer as he realised he'd won the money. String Bean realised what we were up to, gave us all a look, as if to say "You sods!" and then said, "You'd better 'fookin' win today." We didn't. Even worse, Tim lost the sweepstake as we all decided that the last expletive counted as part of the team talk. Ha!

But Dave Stringer respected people, and he got the best out of them as a result. Having played in front of the legendary Kevin Keelan for many years, he knew what he wanted from a goalkeeper. He wanted you to come out for crosses, boss your area and be prepared to argue with your defenders. If you were a bit hot-headed, a bit crazy, all the better. That's what Kevin Keelan was like, and I think Dave regarded me in a similar mould, which I can only take as a massive compliment. Dave also had a strong work ethic, which combined well with his coach Dave Williams' tactical awareness and knowledge. Together they were a great team. Old String Bean might have been a bit of surprise choice when he came in on the back of Ken Brown's dismissal, but he did a brilliant job, taking Norwich to a new best-ever finish in the league, as well as two FA Cup semi-finals, in less than five seasons. And the original Mr Norwich City *still* works at Carrow Road on match days. A top man.

Francesca was just over two years old as the 1991/92 season came to an end. She was getting on nicely. At one point during her treatment I had had my hair closely cropped, hoping this might help her feel a little less self-conscious about losing hers. But now her hair was growing back and she appeared to be responding well to the treatment which she was still having every other week. She was a strong little girl and was speaking more as time went by and loved singing along to 'The Wheels on the Bus' and songs from *The Jungle Book*.

A Pain in the Back

With the summer approaching, the doctors encouraged us to go away on a family holiday. I don't know if they knew something we didn't, but they said we should all go away and enjoy a break together, so we booked a week at Cala D'Or in Majorca. It wasn't anything fancy, just a simple self-catering flat at a hotel. It was a really nice spot – the balcony had a lovely view over the sea. We spent most of the time on the beach, jumping in and out of the waves with the girls, splashing about, eating ice-cream, giggling and generally having a great time.

We put a patch over Francesca's chest to cover her Hickman line, which meant she could do anything she wanted. We got a few strange looks from people and one or two asked us what it was, but it wasn't a problem. We just had a lovely time together, the four of us. It was our first experience of a holiday with on-site family entertainment laid on every night. Francesca had a great time at the children's club and we've got lots of lovely pictures of her playing with the other children. It was a wonderful family holiday and, by the time we returned home, things were looking up. Francesca was doing extremely well and I'd just about recovered from my back injury.

The big question on the football front during the close season was who would take over from Dave Stringer. Reserve team boss Mike Walker and coach Dave Williams had stood in for the last match of the season at Leeds, but there was huge interest in the job. Just about everyone seemed to be linked with the club, from Bryan Robson to former Liverpool defender Phil Neal, who actually came to Carrow Road and was photographed with chairman Robert Chase at one stage.

Eventually, Mike was given the job. He brought former Norwich striker John 'Dixie' Deehan back to the club as his assistant. I thought it was a pretty good move, certainly from my personal point of view. Mike had been a goalkeeper during his playing days and had taken me for training sessions while he was reserve team manager. I also got on well with him, so his appointment suited me nicely. I didn't know too much about Dixie, but I was very impressed with some of his training ground techniques. He introduced a lot of fresh ideas and variety to the training ground, routines which really helped players to improve their agility and footwork: things like jumping in and out of ladders and cones. It also helped build up the strength in your legs, which was good for outfield players and goalkeepers alike. As an ex-striker, he also encouraged a lot of shooting and crossing drills, which I was always involved in and enjoyed doing. Even the running routines were enjoyable, which is saying something.

Dixie also trained with a smile on his face, which was a bonus. He spent most of his time working closely with the players on the training ground, while Mike tended to focus on the front-of-house part of the job, doing all the television interviews, that sort of thing. He loved that side of the job – the press and media. That's not to take anything away from Mike: he did all the team talks and also had a lot of say in what we did defensively. Like the two Daves before them, Mike and John were a great combination, although nobody could have imagined just how successful their partnership would become.

There was certainly no sign of things to come after the opening 45 minutes of the new season in the all-new FA Premier League at Highbury. The stadium had effectively been reduced to three sides that season because Arsenal were re-developing the North Stand. We started off kicking towards the infamous mural they'd painted with thousands of supporters to hide the North Stand development, but didn't really come close to threatening Dave Seaman's goal as Steve Bould and Kevin Campbell scored to put the Gunners 2–0 up. Sitting in the dressing room at half-time, all I could think of was damage limitation. I felt our best hope was to avoid conceding further goals in the second half, and then set about improving things in our next game, at home, in midweek. I'm sure most of the lads would have taken 2–0 at that stage and been happy to get back to Carrow Road. Mike and Dixie had other ideas. They had a real go at us and told us to buck our ideas up. Mike decided to change things.

Mark Robins was one of Mike's new signings, joining us from Manchester United on the eve of the season. He had been brought in as a replacement for Robert Fleck, who'd clinched a £2.1million move to Chelsea. I was sorry to see Robert go. He was a fantastic player for Norwich City and one of the all-time favourites at Carrow Road. More than that, he was a great mate. We'd had some brilliant times together. Mark Robins came on at half-time, and to say that he made an instant impact would be a massive understatement. He scored within minutes and then helped inspire one of the most dramatic comebacks I've ever been involved in. Ruel Fox equalised, Dave Phillips made it 3–2 and Mark then pounced on a mistake by Tony Adams on the edge of the box and lobbed Dave Seaman to make it 4–2. I could hardly believe what was happening down the other end of the pitch. The Gunners fans were stunned. In fact it was difficult to tell the real ones from the ones on the mural!

What a cracking start to the season, especially for Mike Walker, John Deehan and new boy Mark Robins. And it got better from there. We went on a brilliant run, losing only one of our opening 10 league games, including a run of five back-to-back wins which took us to the very top of the table by the end of September.

But, while it could hardly have been better at work, things had taken a terrible turn for the worse at home. When we returned from our holiday in Majorca, Francesca seemed fit and healthy, but towards the end of August, just after the start of the season, we'd received a phone call from Addenbrooke's. I was out at the time, playing golf with a friend called John Garbutt, one of Francesca's godfathers. I'm also godfather to his daughter, Katie. Susan took the call from the hospital while she was at home. They told her they'd looked at Francesca's routine results and discovered she had relapsed. The latest check was showing that the cancer cells in her blood had returned. It was dreadful news. The doctor told Susan Francesca's illness was terminal and she was not going to get better. There was no other treatment she could have. Susan was devastated. She called me and asked me to return home, straightaway.

Francesca was at nursery school when I got back. I went into her bedroom with Susan. We sat and talked. And cried. We were terribly upset. We just couldn't imagine being without her. We'd been positive right from the moment we knew she was ill; we'd convinced ourselves she would beat the disease and make a full recovery. Now, for the first time, we faced the prospect of having to accept Francesca wasn't going to get better.

Susan decided we weren't going to accept defeat on the back of a single phone call. She was determined we should speak to the doctors to see if there was any possibility whatsoever that we could do something for Francesca, here in the UK or anywhere else in the world. We couldn't simply give up. That summed Susan up: she fought for Francesca tooth and nail from the word go. I was always there for them and did the best I could, when I could, but Susan was always the one who questioned things. She was the one who wanted to know more about what was going on, and asked questions about why they were doing certain things, or whether they should be trying something else. I tended to believe what the doctors said and accept it. I don't mean I cared any less – far from it – but Susan was much stronger than me. She was a credit throughout the whole trauma of Francesca's battle. I have so much admiration for what she did during those long and painful months.

I called the hospital and told them we were heading to Cambridge immediately. The four of us got in the car and drove straight to Addenbrooke's. When we got there the consultant explained in more detail the extent of the cancer, which confirmed the gravity of the situation. She told us it wasn't possible to do a bone-marrow transplant, because Francesca hadn't gone into remission after the original batch of treatment. That had been the critical stage, although the doctors had never stopped hoping for a miracle and trying new treatments. It was sad, sad news. They told us Francesca only had six to eight weeks to live. Yet she seemed so well at the time.

We came home, obviously devastated, although in an amazing sense there was a feeling of relief. Francesca had lived so much of her young life in hospital, forced to undergo intense treatment for so many months. Suddenly, she wouldn't have to have chemotherapy any more, we wouldn't have to go to hospital any more. It was a glimmer of release, for a short period at least, because it was as if she was leading a normal life again.

After a couple of weeks, Francesca seemed to get better and better. She looked really well. It was as if there was nothing wrong. We prayed to God a miracle might happen. Francesca was a smiley, happy and very pretty little girl with a lovely, bubbly personality. She really did seem to be in the best of health, she looked and acted like there was nothing wrong with her at all. We thought, "This is all rubbish. She's not dying. She can't be." Then, about a fortnight later, the signs began to show that she was deteriorating.

As parents, we did everything we could to make things as normal as possible. I suggested going to Disneyland Paris, but after much thought we decided that if you're not feeling well, the best place to be is at home, especially for a child of just two and a half years. So we just decided to stay at home and do the best we could. Susan's family came down to be with us, as did my mum and dad.

We went out for family weekends, going to the zoo, feeding the ducks and having Sunday lunches. Francesca was very fond of birds and animals. We often took her to Banham Zoo, just outside Norwich, where she always got excited when she saw the pink flamingos and penguins.

Her bedroom was decorated with characters from the Beatrix Potter tales. Her favourite cuddly toy was Jemima Puddleduck. She took Jemima with her wherever she went. She wouldn't go to bed without her. Whenever Susan tried to give Jemima a wash she had a real problem prising her away. Francesca didn't like it at all and it caused a real commotion. Jemima was her most precious possession. They were inseparable.

Francesca would kick a ball with me in the back garden and get excited when she saw her Daddy on television or the front of the match programme. She came to watch me play a couple of times. People would say how lovely she looked; her hair was coming back and growing long and wild. She looked beautiful, but by the end of September we knew she was losing her brave fight for life.

I should have been really excited about our trip to Ewood Park on Saturday 3rd October 1992. Like us, Blackburn Rovers had lost only one of their opening 10 games. We were top of the new FA Premier League, and Rovers, bankrolled by Jack Walker's millions, were second, a couple of points behind us. It was far and away the biggest game of the weekend, but the only thing on my mind as I travelled up to Lancashire on the Friday was Francesca. By now she was gravely ill and having to be sedated to ensure she wasn't in any pain as the cancer cells ravaged her blood. Susan's niece Nichola travelled to Norwich to be with her and the girls while I was away.

We drove up to Blackburn on the team bus. When we got there it was so bleak: the weather, the hotel – everything seemed so dark and dismal, which didn't help given that I wasn't exactly in the right frame of mind. It was one of the darkest nights of my life. It was unlike me; I'm normally a very positive person, but not that evening. Dave Phillips was my room partner, but I hardly spoke to the poor bloke because I was on the phone to Susan most of the night.

Should I have played against Blackburn that weekend? I'm not sure. I'd sat down with Mike Walker in his office a few days earlier and explained the situation. He basically told me, "It's all in your hands, Big Man. You do what you want to do." I felt there was nothing to be gained by not playing, so I joined the boys on the bus for the trip to Blackburn. Whether I was right in the circumstances, I don't know. The club were extremely sensitive and discreet about things, which we appreciated.

We were hammered at Ewood Park. I didn't actually play too badly, neither did the team, but it was one of those days when Blackburn couldn't do anything wrong. They were on fire. Alan Shearer scored two goals, one of which really summed up their day. Shearer got through and went to shoot, but the ball bobbled as he shaped up to curl it round me. It ended up clipping off his foot, turning into the perfect chip which went straight over my head and into the net. When I look back at the video, it doesn't look like a miss-hit, but I know Alan didn't intend to chip me. I'm convinced he was going to try to curl a shot round me. Even when he got it wrong, he got it right!

We were 4–1 down at half-time and ended up losing 7–1. Extraordinary. It was the biggest defeat I'd suffered since that 9–0 thrashing in my schooldays. Blackburn went above us at the top of the table, and in normal circumstances I would have been devastated. Frankly, it didn't matter. I simply wanted to get back to Susan, Francesca and Melissa as quickly as possible. The club appreciated the situation and I flew straight back to Norwich that night on a private plane with Robert Chase and the club's directors.

By the middle of the week it was clear it was only a matter of time before we would lose Francesca. She was very poorly and for a number of nights she slept between Susan and me, in our bed. We lost our little girl in the early hours of the following Monday morning. I was awake at the time. I realised what was happening and woke Susan up. We picked Francesca up and cuddled her. It was heartbreaking. There were floods of tears. It's not something I would wish on anybody. I'm

A Pain in the Back

just glad we were there with her, all together, when it happened.

Francesca had battled so bravely, and we felt we'd done everything we could to help her. But it wasn't to be.

CHAPTER FIFTEEN

Gunn's Golden Goals

I carried Francesca's coffin from the car to the church on my own. The rest of the funeral service, later that week, is a massive blur. I can picture my family and team-mates, along with Sir Alex Ferguson who came down for the ceremony, but the rest is a total haze. We were so grateful for the support, not just on the day, but over the 18 months Francesca was ill.

Robert and Jayne Fleck were wonderful throughout; they gave our family a lot of practical and emotional support. There were others who did so much to help us at such a difficult time, none more so than Ronnie and Janet Gilbert. Janet had been Steve and Jan Bruce's house-keeper when they lived around the corner from me. I guess you could say I inherited Janet when Steve moved on to Manchester United. Her husband Ronnie was our gardener, and together they became invalu-able, especially when the children came along. With Susan's dad up in Bolton and my parents in Scotland, we never had close family to call on, so Ronnie and Janet effectively became the girls' Norfolk granny and grandad. They were always there for us and we'll never forget everything they did.

I missed only one game for Norwich because of Francesca's illness, a League Cup tie against Carlisle at Carrow Road the Wednesday before she died. Our next match was the weekend after the funeral, at home to Queen's Park Rangers. We had to decide if and when I should return to work. Susan and I sat down and discussed it with our vicar, Reverend Brian Hemms. He was a great source of comfort for the family and had visited us every day during the last six weeks of Francesca's life. He was a kind, unassuming man, whose actions spoke volumes – more than any words. Reverend Hemms asked me what I wanted to do. I told him I wanted to play, but didn't want to seem disrespectful to Francesca's memory in any way. He said that if I wanted to play, it would be the right thing to do. So, it was agreed: I would make myself available for the Rangers match.

Susan was one hundred per cent behind the decision. We agreed it was what Francesca would have wanted me to do. She knew me as a footballer. She would often say, "Where's Daddy going?" and we'd tell her I was going to play for Norwich City. She'd been to a few matches and enjoyed it, sitting on her mum's lap, watching games and playing with the other children in the players' lounge. That was a strong motivation for me; to go back and play straightaway rather than sit around feeling desperately sad. I don't know how long that would have gone on for. I could have pulled myself out of playing football and been away for a week, a month, or six months . . . who can tell? I'll never know.

Francesca's funeral was on the Thursday. I went into work the following day and trained with John Deehan on the Friday afternoon. There was no one else, just John and myself. It wasn't easy for me, but it must have been the most difficult session he's ever taken, especially with him being a father as well. I'd already built up a lot of respect for him as a coach, but I held him in even higher regard for the way he handled things that afternoon. We didn't say a lot; we just got on with the job. John coped with the situation admirably. In some ways I'd say it was above and beyond the call of duty.

I honestly don't know how I got through the following day. The lads were incredibly supportive in the dressing room before the game, coming up to me and patting me on the back, wishing me good luck, that kind of thing. I tried my best to focus on preparing for the game, as if it were any other match day. I was fine as we made our way out of the dressing room towards the tunnel. It was as I ran out with the boys that the emotion of the occasion hit me.

I could hear the roar of the crowd. The cheers seemed much louder than normal, especially when I ran towards the goalmouth to my right and jumped up as if to head the crossbar, in my normal trademark fashion. Then, when my name was announced in the team line-ups over the PA system, I got a wonderful reception. And it wasn't just the Norwich supporters; the visiting QPR fans also gave me a fantastic round of applause. That was something special and I knew at that moment I'd made exactly the right decision to get back out there and play.

Susan had cut off a lock of Francesca's hair as a keepsake. I put it in a silver locket, along with a photo of her smiling. I tucked the locket into my glove bag that afternoon and gave the pendant a kiss before I started my warm-up. I kept it in my glove bag from that day on and it became an important part of my pre-match routine. For the rest of my career I'd run out of the tunnel towards the goal, make out as if to head the crossbar, take out the pendant, kiss it, and then put it back before tucking my glove bag into the back of the net.

Like their fans, the QPR players were a different class on the day. Quite a few of them took the trouble to say some kind things, including their skipper Darren Peacock, who came up and embraced me at the end of the game. That gesture was typical of the respect the Rangers lads showed me on the day. Ian Holloway, Les Ferdinand and Ray Wilkins all went out of their way to say something, which I really appreciated. For the record, we won 2–1, but don't ask me about the game itself because I can hardly remember a thing. As it happens, the win took us back to the top of the table, but that wasn't the important thing for me on the day. I was just pleased I played. It was a big step for me; it meant I could go on with things from there.

By the beginning of December, on the back of a four-match winning run, we found ourselves a staggering nine points clear at the top of the Premier League table. Little old Norwich City – unfashionable, stuck out in the sticks, yet a full nine points clear of the chasing pack in the top domestic league in world football, almost halfway through the season. Manchester United were level on 30 points with Aston Villa, who we'd beaten 3–2 at Villa Park during that run of four straight victories. The press were starting to make a few noises about our prospects of going all the way and winning the title. We didn't get carried away; it was more a case of just getting on with the job. We had a fantastic team spirit, a real special bond, which I think Francesca's situation played a part in. Quite a few of the lads had young families, the Butterworths, Crooks and Bowens, and Francesca's illness brought us closer together. Mike Walker was quick to keep our success in perspective and it was very much a case of feet on the ground with the press. "Let's just get to 40 points and make sure we're safe against relegation," he would say. "That's our only target right now."

We were already on 39 points as we prepared to take on Manchester United at Old Trafford, a massive game. Mike just told us to work hard, play our football and let them worry about us, rather than the other way round. It was a close game, with few chances and was settled by one goal. Unfortunately Daryl Sutch misjudged a clearance and the ball fell to Mark Hughes, just eight yards out. He was never going to miss from there and that was it, we lost 1–0.

Win, lose or draw, Mike had already arranged a pre-Christmas break for us in Gran Canaria. We went straight from Old Trafford to Manchester Airport and headed off for a spot of midwinter sunshine. It was my first trip away since Francesca had died and I wasn't entirely sure it was the right thing to do, but it's all part of being a football player. It was very hard on Susan and she was quite upset, but she knew it was important that I joined the rest of the lads.

It was a good relaxing break. We enjoyed a few pleasant drinking sessions; nothing outrageous, but the beer affected some of the boys more than others, like my very good friend Jerry Goss. One evening, after a few beers, Jerry decided it would be a good idea to practise his golf swing. When we got back to the hotel, Gossy went up to Robert Ullathorne's room and decided to borrow his clubs to hit a few balls – there and then. Unlike Jerry, Robert is left-handed, but undeterred Gossy picked up a club, turned it round, got onto the bed and started smashing balls out of the patio windows, up on the second floor of the hotel. Even though he'd had a couple of sherbets, Jerry cracked every shot clean through the open windows, over the hotel swimming pool and into the distance.

The next day, a few of the boys jumped into a cab to go into town. One of them noticed a big crack in the taxi's windscreen and asked the driver how it happened. "Eet's crazeee, just crazeee!" he said. "I was sitting here at the hotel in my taxi when suddenly eet was hit by a golf ball. I can't understand how eet happened, because the golf course eez five miles away!" The lads all burst out laughing.

The trip was great fun and we all became even closer, but it didn't do us a lot of good professionally. We returned home and promptly lost 2–0 to the old enemy Ipswich the week before Christmas and picked up only three points in six games as we went into the New Year. Even so, we were still top of the table. I got the Man of the Match champagne in a 4–2 win over Crystal Palace at Carrow Road, which got us back on track, and then made one of my best ever saves in a 1–0 win at Everton. Tony Cottee hit a spectacular overhead kick at me from point-blank range, which brought the whole of Goodison Park to its feet ready to celebrate. But I dived smartly down to my right, at full stretch, and managed to parry it onto the post, from where the ball rebounded neatly back into my hands. Tony just put his head in his hands in frustration and disbelief. He came over and said, "Great stop," which was nice of him. A few people reckon it's my best save ever and it's certainly in my personal top ten, but not quite the best as far as I'm concerned.

I must have been in pretty good form around that time, because another of my all-time favourite saves came about a month later when I stopped a penalty from Ian Wright in a 1–1 draw against Arsenal at Carrow Road. It was in front of an admiring Barclay End, and I dived, again rather athletically, to my left to claw the ball wide. The crowd loved it. I got lots of, "Scotland's number one! Scotland's, Scotland's number one!" chants and cheers, applause and whistles every time I came near to touching the ball after that.

Manchester United eventually caught us and took over at the top of the table after we were beaten 3–0 at Southampton. But it was still very much a three-way fight for the title, right down to the final half dozen games of the season, when we faced two massive make-or-break matches: Villa and United, back-to-back, both at home, in the space of 13 days. Aside from our almost routine defeat at Wimbledon, we'd been in decent form going into those two games. We knew we had a brilliant opportunity to stake a claim for the title. I hardly dared to dream; if we won those two games we'd have a fantastic chance of becoming the first ever champions of the new FA Premier League.

The Villa match was on a Wednesday night. They were top and we were third, a couple of points behind them. There's always an extra-special atmosphere at Carrow Road in midweek and the place was absolutely buzzing. It turned out to be a fantastic night, especially for our centre-half, John Polston. A couple of hours before the game little Jordan Polston came into the world, then big John Polston went up for a corner in the second half and banged home the only goal of the game. Now that's what I call a good day's work: becoming a dad for the first time and scoring the winning goal in a massive game.

I didn't have too much to do, but I was very pleased with a save I made from Dean Saunders in the first half. He smashed a shot towards the top left-hand corner. I flung myself towards the ball and managed to turn it round the post. If I say so myself, it was one hell of a save. They should have scored in the second half when Garry Parker went round me and had the whole goal to aim at, but he somehow managed to scuff his shot wide. So, a clean sheet, a great win – which meant we'd also done the double over Villa and were back on top of the table – and a proud new dad in the camp. Bring on Manchester United.

United were stuttering, without a win in four games. We had lost only one home match all season, against Ipswich, and were extremely confident. Everyone was billing the United game as the Premier League title decider, and while we weren't buying all the hype we knew it was a huge match. The national press were now camped up at our training ground and we were getting used to living in the glare of the spotlight. There was a real buzz about the city. Everywhere I went people were asking me, "Can we do it, Bryan?" Not just fans, but shopkeepers, businessmen – even little old ladies stopped me in the street to wish us luck.

The Sky TV cameras finally rolled into town on the Monday evening. Win the game, and we would open up a five-point gap over

United. Lose, and they would go back above us at the top of the table.

We were 3–0 down inside the first 20 minutes. This might suggest that Manchester United totally outplayed us. Not true. For a start, it was a close call for offside for all three goals. I had my hand up for every single one. Mind you, so did my defence, who I could just about see on the halfway line.

It was asking a lot to come back from 3–0 against a team like United, but Mark Robins got us back into the match early in the second half and the lads set about salvaging something from the game. Unfortunately, Peter Schmeichel was in brilliant form, as usual, and pulled off several great saves. Back in the dressing room at full-time we were still relatively upbeat. The 3–1 scoreline flattered them a bit and there was still everything to play for. Anyway, there wasn't time to be down about it because we were back in action against Spurs just four days later on Good Friday.

By the time we arrived at White Hart Lane there was an added incentive for doing well. Not long after losing Francesca, we started actively thinking about how we might launch some form of fundraising in her memory. My accountant Keith Colman, who has since become a good friend of the family, came up with a great idea. He suggested we should get the local community involved by inviting people to donate money for each goal Norwich City scored in the final five games of the season. We decided to call it Gunn's Golden Goals.

People could pledge however much they wanted, from a few pence a goal to a pound, or a fiver – whatever. The local *Evening News* agreed to help by printing sponsorship slips along with the names of everyone who made a donation. We hoped to raise about £10,000, which we would pass on to leukaemia research. Unfortunately, the appeal didn't exactly get off to a flying start as we were hammered 5–1 at Spurs, but at least Efan Ekoku's late consolation goal got the fundraising underway. It would do more than that: Efan's goal effectively started what would become Bryan Gunn's Leukaemia Appeal.

Things quickly snowballed. People told their friends and family about Gunn's Golden Goals, encouraging them to do their bit, and things just exploded into a mass of more and more names in the paper.

Even better, the donations kept going up and up. One week the donations would typically be around a fiver, the next week someone would offer a tenner, or £20 a goal, and other people would follow suit. We beat Leeds United 4–2 at Carrow Road in our next game and the appeal was well and truly up and running.

We went into our final match of the season at Middlesbrough, well on our way to reaching our original £10,000 target. By that time Manchester United had already clinched the Premier League title. Fergie's team never looked back after that win at Carrow Road, and finished the season in real style with seven straight victories. Villa had done enough to take second spot, but there was still a big prize on offer as we headed for Middlesbrough's old ground, Ayresome Park. We needed a point to make sure we finished third in the table ahead of Blackburn. It wasn't quite what we'd been hoping for a month earlier, but all the same third place would set yet another new club record, which would be some consolation. Even better, it could also mean qualification for Europe.

Middlesbrough were already relegated, but they were in no mood to go down without a fight on a lovely sunny afternoon in the north-east. Efan Ekoku put us ahead inside a quarter of an hour, but Boro hit back through my old Aberdeen team-mate Willie Falconer. He got in front of me in a flurry of players to equalise. There's a good action shot of the goal which shows me coming out with a double-fist punch, knees in the centre-forward's back, and Willie getting to the ball just ahead of me to nick it over my head. I know it well because autograph hunters still send copies to the club for me to sign.

So Willie's goal made it 1–1, and it got worse when Paul Wilkinson put them ahead. Now we were trailing, knowing we had to get something out of the game. Our fans screamed the place down, urging us on and it worked. Efan scored again to make it 2–2 and then young Andy Johnson, on his debut, charged onto an Ian Crook through-ball and smashed home a brilliant volley. 3–2. It stayed that way until the closing stages when John Hendrie, another Scot, scored an equaliser. What a ding-dong of a match. Panic suddenly set in and for a moment none of us seemed to know if we needed a win or just a draw. We were all looking at each other, wondering if we'd blown it. One minute we were cruising at 3–2 up, next we were all over the place at 3–3.

I've never been so pleased to hear the final whistle, and if we needed confirmation that a draw was enough, we soon got it. Our fans away to my left were going crazy. I started celebrating with the lads on the pitch, and we then went over to the Norwich supporters to celebrate with them. Some of the boys ripped their shirts off and threw them into the crowd. I came off the pitch with next to nothing on: my shirt, gloves, boots, socks, shorts, just about everything apart from my vest and underwear went into the crowd. I was that happy!

To finish third in the all-new Premier League was no mean achievement for a club like Norwich City. It was also the third time I'd been part of a record-breaking team, having previously finished fifth and fourth in the top flight. The three Ians – Butterworth, Culverhouse and Crook – were the only other players to figure in all three teams.

Mike Walker was ecstatic. He'd led us to third spot in his first season in charge and we'd done it in quite some style. Incredibly, we let in 65 and scored 61 in our 42 games, to give us a negative goal difference! Mike had encouraged us to play free-flowing, attacking football, passing our way up the park, and we did play some lovely stuff that season – even if we shipped a few at my end to keep our fans on the edge of their seats.

Although the Boro match was our final league game, it wasn't the end of the season for us. We faced a frustrating wait to see if we'd done enough to clinch a place in Europe. Everything depended on the FA Cup final. In a curious twist of fate, Arsenal and Sheffield Wednesday played each other in the finals of both the League Cup and FA Cup. The Gunners had already beaten Wednesday 2–1 in the League Cup final, which meant they'd booked a place in the UEFA Cup. But if Arsenal won the FA Cup as well, they would qualify for the Cup Winners' Cup, leaving a space in the UEFA Cup for the team who finished third in the Premier League. Namely us. I didn't quite go as far as buying an Arsenal scarf, but it seems the whole of Norfolk became ardent Arsenal fans overnight.

The FA Cup final the following weekend ended in a 1–1 draw, after extra time. Aargh! We had to wait another agonising five days until the replay the next Thursday night. By this stage the rest of my Norwich team-mates had left the country, not because they were too nervous to watch, you understand, but because the club had arranged an end-of-season break in the Cayman Islands. They planned to watch the replay in a restaurant out there. I couldn't be with them because I was on World Cup duty with Scotland, earning my second full cap in a qualifying match in Estonia. Andy Goram was forced out of the trip to Tallinn with a knee injury and I was called up by Andy Roxburgh. It was the perfect way to round off a great season. I felt on top of my game and was really looking forward to resuming my international career. I'd also been named Norwich City's Player of the Season, only the fifth player in the club's history to win it twice. That meant such a lot to me after everything that had happened in the previous months.

The match in Estonia came three years to the day after I had made my full international debut in that fateful game against Egypt at Pittodrie. This time it was a much more enjoyable experience, as I made a couple of decent saves and kept a clean sheet in a 3–0 win, with goals from Kevin Gallacher, John Collins and Scott Booth. It wasn't the most spectacular stadium in the world, just one main stand and a rough pitch, but it was still a special day for me, made all the better because there were lots of Scottish fans, creating a great atmosphere on a brilliant sunny day. Wherever you go with Scotland the fans follow; there was a crowd of just over 5000 in Tallinn and half of them must have been Scots, which was brilliant. It seems the Tartan Army made quite an impression with the locals; according to reports in the Scottish newspapers quite a few of them took a shine to the beautiful Estonian girls and ended up getting married. That's what I call an away victory.

I flew back from Tallinn in time to watch the FA Cup final replay at home the next night. Actually, I was in a restaurant with Susan when the game was played. We'd arranged to go out for a meal with the so-called 'Fandabidozi Club', a group of very good friends who did a lot to help us through the tough times during Francesca's illness. Their friendship and support have been incredibly important to us over the years. My mate Roger Kingsley, from designer clothes shop Jonathan Trumbull, was one of the leading lights, along with Henry Watt and his wife, Tania, and Matthew and Vicky Bradbury. We've been away on a few good trips together, wives and partners, usually with plenty of drink thrown in! We were in Dublin, with a few pints of the dark stuff on board, when someone came up with the idea of calling ourselves the 'Fandabidozi Club'. I was too drunk to remember exactly why, but it was something to do with the catchphrase of the Scottish comedy act, the Krankies.

Anyway, we went to Pinocchio's restaurant in Norwich that night. I remember it well; I was wearing a white grandad Armani shirt and pair of black leather trousers. Luckily the chefs were big football fans and had the radio on in the kitchen. I kept popping in to ask them how the game was going. It was a long, long night as yet again the match went into extra time and then, in the final minute, who should pop up with the winning header, but my old mate Andy Linighan? Arsenal had done the cup double, and Norwich City were at long, long last in Europe. The club had been denied three times because of the ban after Heysel, but this time there was no stopping us, all thanks to one of my old team-mates. Coincidentally, big Andy scored the all-important Wembley winner against another former Canary, goalkeeper Chris Woods, the man I replaced at Norwich.

I was absolutely delirious. Correction. I was out of my head! I was already on a high after the previous night with Scotland, now the champagne was really flowing. We'd achieved great things by finishing third. We'd also earned a tidy bonus for doing so well. We got around £25,000 a man, depending on appearances, for finishing in the top three. On top of that, we had a clause written into our contract at the start of the season saying that if we qualified for Europe we would receive another £25,000, so big Andy's header meant a lot to us. We never believed for a second at the start of the season that we would qualify for a European bonus, but we had and I was deter-mined to celebrate in style.

I ordered champagne all round. There was a slight breakdown in communication, though, which I didn't realise until one of the other diners, the Lady Mayoress of Norwich, Brenda Ferris, came up to me clutching a bottle of bubbly. She planted a huge kiss on my cheek.

"Thank you very much for my champagne, Bryan. I'll have this later!"

I looked around the restaurant and just about everybody seemed to have a bottle of champers, rather than a glass each, which I thought

I'd ordered. What the heck, we'd just qualified for Europe and there was a good bonus on the way. The credit card got stung that night, but at the end of the day it was another magical moment in the history of Norwich – not just the club, but the whole city as well.

By the end of the night, it all became too much. I was overcome with emotion – and alcohol. I needed some time to myself and went to the toilet. I sat there for an hour, literally, on my own, just thinking. Everything hit me. It was the culmination of a year of hugely contrasting emotions, what with Francesca and then the incredible end to the season. Eventually, Henry came in to get me. I just sobbed, "I want my wife."

CHAPTER SIXTEEN
Smelly Socks

When we totted up the money from Gunn's Golden Goals it came to around £15,000, way over our original target of £10,000. And that was just the beginning; the appeal had obviously caught the imagination and hearts of the people of Norwich and Norfolk. Keith Colman certainly wasn't going to let the initiative slip, and wrote to every league club in England and Scotland asking for donations for a charity auction. Just about every club, north and south of the border, replied. In what I can only describe as a glowing testimony to the football fraternity, we received more than 100 items, along with letters of support. They'd heard about our tragedy and were only too happy to help out.

Items came flooding in: shirts from Alan Hansen, Ian Rush, Kevin Keegan, Les Ferdinand and Gary Lineker, who knew something of what we had gone through because his own son, George, had suffered leukaemia around the same time as Francesca. It was a different strain to Francesca's though; George had myeloid leukaemia and thankfully recovered.

We also got a cricket bat from Ian Botham, whom I'd joined on one of his famous marathon leukaemia walks, along with signed footballs and other bits and pieces, including the socks and shirt I'd thrown into the crowd at Middlesbrough, which were donated back to us.

There were more than 200 people in the audience as the local BBC presenter Stewart White and Radio Broadland's Rob Chandler conducted the bidding while I held up the various lots. My socks from the Middlesbrough match hadn't been washed, and consequently had a slight whiff about them! They still fetched a few quid, despite me holding my nose as I held them up for public inspection. One of the highest bids was for Les Ferdinand's signed England shirt, which sold for £300. I heard the bloke who bought it spent the next few months wearing it whenever he went out jogging – it must be the most expensive jogging top ever.

By the end of the night we'd raised another £10,000, which was just stupendous. But it didn't stop there; before we knew it people were arranging all sorts of events. It seemed just about every village fete or school fundraising project that summer wanted to donate their proceeds. Cheques and cash came in from all angles – to the club, the newspaper and the appeal headquarters at Keith's office. The public response was overwhelming. Susan and I were truly touched by all the things people wanted to do to help raise money. It was phenomenal. The Bryan Gunn Leukaemia Appeal was officially up and running.

I make a point of not mentioning specific fundraising events. It wouldn't be fair to single one out, given the sheer numbers of people who've done so much to make the appeal such a success. But every now and then, if I'm speaking at a dinner, or opening a shop or fete, I tell one particular story about our physio Tim Sheppard's young daughters, Hannah, Laura and Francesca. They decided to do their bit for the appeal and set up a little bric-a-brac stall on the path outside their house. Before long, a little old lady came up to them and said, "What are you raising money for?"

"The Bryan Gunn Leukaemia Appeal," they replied.

The elderly woman considered this for a moment, then turned to them and said: "Well, I'm certainly not going to help you buy a gun!"

Bless her cotton socks. She thought they'd said the Buying a Gun Appeal!

To this day I receive cheques at the club, and people make donations when I make guest appearances. It's truly heart-warming. Being in the public eye, I was used to the attention and found it easy to cope with the incredible interest in the appeal. In fact, I would say it actually helped me cope with my grief. It gave me something positive to focus on. Susan was less comfortable. We were invited to a whole host of events, and did our best to get to as many as possible, but the conversation would inevitably turn to Francesca's illness, which Susan found difficult to handle emotionally. As much as we appreciated all the goodwill, Susan preferred to let me get on with things while she kept a lower profile.

I think people cope with grief in different ways. That was certainly the case with Susan and me. We appreciated and supported each other's individual way of coping with our loss; it's been a very positive aspect of our marriage over the years. Susan also had Melissa to care for, of course. She was first and foremost a wife and mother and had her hands full looking after Melissa and, I have to admit, me. I've never been the best in the world on the domestic front, although I like to think I've got a bit better over the years. There was a time when I wouldn't – make that *couldn't* – cook anything more extravagant than a boiled egg. Now I've graduated to scrambled eggs, although, as Susan points out, only on Mother's Day or her birthday. I'm pleased to report I also know how to turn the washing machine on. And the tumble dryer. But that's about it. Washing machine, tumble dryer and eggs. Useless, I know.

With so much money coming in, Keith, Susan and I got together to discuss various ideas as to how best to use it. Susan said she really wanted to do something to help families like those we'd seen struggling to and from the outpatients' department at Addenbrooke's. We thought it would be great if there was a system whereby the youngsters could receive their routine chemotherapy treatment at home, rather than having to keep returning to the hospital. Susan came up with the idea of funding a community nurse who would have the specific job of visiting children suffering from leukaemia to administer the drugs at their homes. It was decided, then; we would advertise for a community oncology outreach sister. Enter Rosie Larkins.

We'd met Rosie at the Norfolk and Norwich Hospital, where she'd helped with Francesca's treatment. She was designated to look after us, and was always there for us from that day on. It was as if Rosie never took a day off, because whenever we visited the hospital she was there. Like all the nurses, Rosie was kind and caring; nothing was too much for her. She did a great job of making us feel comfortable, especially Francesca, so we were absolutely delighted when she applied for the job. From our point of view she was perfect. Susan was asked to represent the appeal on the recruitment board, along with six medical experts. They interviewed three candidates, and decided Rosie was best qualified for the job. She was soon visiting youngsters with leukaemia in and around the Norwich area. Just like Francesca, the children would have to spend several weeks in Cambridge for their first blast of chemotherapy before returning home. That was where Rosie came in: those families no longer had to make those frequent, arduous trips to Addenbrooke's as we'd had to with Francesca.

The appeal was already having a direct effect, which was very gratifying. It funded Rosie's role for three years, after which the position was formally recognised and adopted by the National Health Service, which in turn assumed responsibility for meeting the costs. That was wonderful news. We broadened our scope a few years later to take in the Great Yarmouth area, funding nurse Elly Bond who was based at the James Paget Hospital in Gorleston. It was only a year before the NHS appreciated the importance of that post and made it an integral part of its own operation. I'm very proud to say our initiative has been instrumental in broadening the concept of outreach nurses throughout the country. There were others before we come along, but not many. Now there are.

Of course, our ultimate ambition – then and now – is to conquer the disease. The University of East Anglia in Norwich was doing a lot of research into leukaemia under the guidance of Dr Ian Gibson, now a local MP and good friend of the family. Ian and his fellow scientists had identified a range of projects linked to combating leukaemia, and we were only too happy to provide the cash to fund more students and buy new equipment. We liked the idea because it was specific to Norwich and Norfolk. It meant we could spend the money in the area where it had been raised, which seemed the right thing to do rather than sending it off to a national organisation. In time, it led to the creation of the Francesca Gunn Laboratory which was officially opened at the UEA in September 1994.

Our good friend, the racing driver Will Hoy, also did his bit for the appeal, agreeing to offer guest drives around Snetterton race track. Anglia Television ran a phone-in competition, the prize being a high-speed lap of the track alongside Will, who was a big star in motor racing, having won the British Touring Car Championship. Will and his wife Judy had been to watch me play a few times and we'd gone to see Will racing at various circuits, but this was my first chance to actually experience him in action from close quarters.

I joined Will for an awesome white-knuckle lap of the track. I'd never been driven at those types of speeds, going into bends without braking and feeling like you're going to topple over. I was literally holding the edge of my seat. Will was a brilliant driver and it was great to be in the car alongside him, watching him at work, doing what he did best. It was an amazing experience. It wasn't until I got out of the car that his engineer told me we'd gone round the circuit within a second of Will's lap record – and that was with an extra fourteen and a half stone in the car!

After all that had happened, what with the incredible end to the season, my trips with Scotland and the launch of the appeal, we decided to get away and booked a family holiday in Cyprus in the summer of 1993, just the three of us – Susan, Melissa and me. We were looking forward to some quality time together, somewhere we wouldn't be recognised, where we could enjoy some welcome privacy. I should have known better. No sooner had we got to the Coral Beach resort than we bumped into the Chelsea striker Kerry Dixon, who was on holiday with his family and friends. I didn't know Kerry, aside from playing against him a few times, but we hit it off straightaway and enjoyed a few beers together over the fortnight. We also met Betty Boothroyd, who was Speaker of the House of Commons at the time. Betty was a lovely jovial lady, a really bubbly character who always made a point of saying "Hello" to us over breakfast.

The Coral Beach was one of the best hotels I've ever stayed in, second only to Gleneagles in Scotland, in my book. We missed

Francesca terribly, of course, but it was still wonderful to spend some time together as a family. It reminded us of the holiday we'd had a couple of years previously when Francesca was a baby. I took Melissa into the pool with her little armbands on and splashed around with her as I'd done with Francesca in Puerto Banus. It was a special time.

The locals really took to Melissa, and made a real fuss of her, especially in our favourite restaurant, the Seriani, where we became regulars. The owners were very friendly and loved their football, which was obvious judging by the number of pictures hanging on the wall. I didn't make a point of telling them what I did for a living, but one night a fellow diner spotted me and pointed me out to the waiter. "That's Bryan Gunn over there," he said. "Why haven't you got a picture of him on the wall?"

The waiter came straight over and shook my hand. "Mr Gunn, eet eez so nice to have you here. Please, you send us photo for wall?"

I duly obliged when we got back to England and, sure enough, when we returned to the resort the following year, there I was, hanging proudly on the restaurant wall alongside a gallery of fellow pros. I hope it's still there.

The holiday was over all too soon, and before I knew it I was reporting back for action with Norwich City. The lads were really buzzing, as we boarded a plane for a pre-season tour to the United States. We were to play a four-team tournament at the Mile High Stadium in Denver, Colorado, against the hosts Colorado Foxes, and three guest teams from Europe: Kaiserslauten from Germany, FC Copenhagen from Denmark and us.

During the trip across the Atlantic a few of the lads enjoyed the in-flight hospitality, including Gossy who, as you know by now, undergoes something of a transformation after a few drinks – not quite the Incredible Hulk, but only because he doesn't actually change colour and burst out of his shirt. As we started our descent into Denver, the seatbelt signs came on and we were told to return to our seats. Gossy was among the last to sit down, by which time the only seat left was next to Mark Robins, a quiet lad at the best of times.

For some reason Gossy thought it would be a laugh to grab Robbo in a headlock. When I say headlock, I mean a really tight, arm-firmly-squeezed-around-Mark's-neck, type of headlock. It was no contest; Jerry was a strong lad, while Mark was slightly built, tiny for a striker, really. Gossy sat there with a silly big smile on his face, holding Mark's head in a vice-like grip, so tight the poor bloke couldn't move, no matter how he tried to free himself. Slowly but surely Mark's face became redder, and redder. Then he began to turn blue. Robbo was clearly struggling and the lads realised he needed rescuing. We ordered Gossy to stop it. By the time he let go, Mike Walker had heard the commotion and realised what was going on. The gaffer wasn't best pleased. When we got off the plane Mike called us together. There were no histrionics, that wasn't Mike's style; he very rarely flew off the handle. Instead, he told us in his typically understated, yet authoritative manner, that he was disappointed some of us had overdone the drinks on the flight, and singled out Gossy on the strength of his antics with Robbo.

After training the next day we all got onto the team coach to head back to the hotel, all except Jerry, that is. Mike ordered him to do some extra sprints as punishment for his antics on the plane. The rest of us just laughed. Although that was the standard payback for practically every misdemeanour back then, forcing Gossy, a fitness fanatic, to do extra sprints was like punishing a child by giving them the keys to the sweet shop. He absolutely loved running. Even in the high altitude and intense heat of Colorado, he just kept on going, and going, and eventually Mike had to almost beg him to stop.

Jerry was in the thick of things again a couple of days later as the lads enjoyed a day off between games. We split into different groups, most of us heading to the golf course, while the non-golfers, including Gossy, John Polston and reserve keeper Mark Walton, did a spot of shopping. But only a spot. It turned into a drinking session, with Jerry and Polly doing their best to match Mark pint for pint – quite some feat. By the time the lads all met up again, in a bar near the hotel, the three of them were well and truly smashed.

Polly then decided to take a peek into Jerry's shopping bag and produced a smart top and pair of trousers which Gossy had bought for his wife, Margaret. "Oooh, aren't they lovely," said Polly, holding the clothes up.

Smelly Socks

"Stop taking the mick, you bastard," Jerry shouted. "They're for my wife. Give me the f***ing things back."

Polly refused. Jerry lost it.

He lurched towards Polly and made a grab for the clothes, knocking over a table of drinks in the process. Glasses and bottles went flying in all directions with an almighty chorus of crash, bangs and wallops. That was it. Jerry and Polly – usually the best of mates – squared up to each other, pushing and shoving, shouting and swearing. The bar staff became concerned, clearly wondering what was going to get smashed next. We tried to convince them the boys were really the best of friends and gently ushered them towards the exit, encouraging them to calm down. As they left, we cleared up the broken glasses, handed over a hundred bucks or so to cover the damage and assumed everything would be okay.

We raced after the so-called best mates, but they were at it again, going at it hammer and tongs in the car park. They both ripped off their T-shirts and started trading punches. Before we had a chance to stop them a black-and-white patrol car tore into the car park, sirens blaring, lights flashing. The bar staff had called the police. Two officers jumped out and broke it up. I took on the role of chief cultural attaché, trying to explain things.

"Sorry officers," I said. "They're the best of friends, really. They've just had a little skirmish. We've paid for the damage in the bar and if it's all right with you we'll just be going on our way to the hotel."

I managed to sweet-talk our way out of it, and they let Jerry and Polly off. They have been the best of friends ever since. Honestly, it was all part of the team bonding process on those pre-season trips.

To be fair, you couldn't fault Gossy's ability or temperament when he was playing, and the 1993/94 campaign was going to be a huge season for everyone, none more so than him. After a decade of sterling service at Carrow Road he was looking forward to his testimonial season. Boy, did he pick a year to do it.

CHAPTER SEVENTEEN

Valencia! Oh, Brilliant Save by Gunn!

Of all the highs and lows in Norwich City Football Club's proud 104-year history, there can't have been many better periods than the spell we enjoyed during the first half of the 1993/94 season. We'd just finished third in the Premier League and proved we were one of the top teams in the country, capable of beating anyone on our day. And we were venturing into new territory – preparing for the Canaries' first ever, and well-overdue, European campaign.

Our 'unfashionable' little club was attracting a lot of interest from the national media, not least as we kicked off the new season with the big match of the opening weekend, the visit of champions Manchester

Valencia! Oh, Brilliant Save by Gunn!

United, live on Sky TV. Mike and Dixie didn't have to do too much to get us psyched up. We were still sore from the costly 3–1 defeat towards the end of the previous season. It was a tough start, but an ideal opportunity to get our own back.

No such luck. Having finally managed to win the championship, United were about to become the dominant force in the country under my old gaffer, Alex Ferguson. They beat us 2–0, with Ryan Giggs and Bryan Robson doing the damage either side of half-time. Three days later we travelled to Ewood Park, scene of the nightmare 7–1 hammering the previous season and one of the darkest weekends of my career. This time it was a very different story as we beat Blackburn 3–2. Chris Sutton scored two goals, including a late winner, which was obviously noted by the Rovers' management.

Sutts was rapidly emerging as a star in the making, but he wasn't the only one hitting the headlines with his goal-scoring exploits. The following weekend, at Elland Road, we crushed Leeds United 4–0. Ruel Fox led the way with two goals and Sutts weighed in with another, but the goal of the game, by a long way, came from the right boot of Jerry Goss. It was a peach of a strike at the end of a great passing move which started way back in our half. Jerry smashed a first-time volley into the roof of the net, giving their keeper John Lukic absolutely no chance.

Gossy's strike won *Match of the Day's* Goal of the Month and set the tone for his testimonial season. He was on fire, scoring spectacular and invariably crucial goals for us almost week in and week out. The fans loved him – even more so when he scored the only goal of the game in the first East Anglian derby of the season at Carrow Road. The supporters took to holding up their hands and bowing in tribute to him as they chanted, "Jerry, Jerry, Jerry!" every time Gossy did something special, which was pretty much routine around that time. Jerry enjoyed almost god-like status on the back of his stunning goals and all-action performances. In fact, that's what I've got him down as in my mobile phone. Whenever Gossy calls me, 'God' flashes up on the screen.

The victory over Ipswich made it three straight wins; we were showing signs of continuing where we'd left off the previous season. All we wanted now was a cracking draw in the UEFA Cup. There was a real air of excitement and anticipation. We'd waited such a long time to take our rightful place in Europe, and been denied three times through no fault of our own. There were some massive names in the hat: Juventus, Bayern Munich, Inter Milan, Sporting Lisbon and PSV Eindhoven, to name but a few. Just think where we could be heading.

We got Vitesse Arnhem. We'd all heard of Arnhem, because of its links with the Second World War, but no one knew much about the Dutch team. I recognised one of their players, Hans Gillhaus, who'd played for Aberdeen a couple of seasons after I'd left Pittodrie, but that was it. They had a couple of relative unknowns who would go on to make a name for themselves in time, like goalkeeper Raimond van der Gouw who later played for Manchester United, Phillip Cocu, who joined Barcelona, and winger Glenn Helder who went on to play for Arsenal. At the time, though, they were unheard of outside of Holland. We'd hoped for a slightly more glamorous tie for our first foray into Europe. Ah well. We just had to be professional and get on with it. The first leg would be at Carrow Road in the middle of September.

By this stage, I was playing twice a week. Scotland's World Cup qualifying campaign resumed with a match against Switzerland at Pittodrie. After the back-to-back wins over Estonia Andy Roxburgh kept faith with me. It was great to be back at Pittodrie. The old place was packed to the rafters. The atmosphere was electric; it was a huge game for both sides.

The Swiss were leading Group one at the time, unbeaten and favourites to qualify with Italy, but we knew we would still have a chance of going to the finals in the United States if we could win. The first half went well; I made a couple of good saves to boost my confidence and felt pretty good as we went off after a goalless first half. Andy Roxburgh was pleased with the way things were going and simply told us to keep up the good work, confident we could break them down. John Collins scored early in the second half to put us ahead. Pittodrie went bananas; I was running around punching the air like a wild man. I felt I had the greatest job in the world, doing what I do best and making so many people happy in the process. If only we could hold on to the lead, our World Cup dreams were still alive.

Mid-way through the half Switzerland's star striker Stephane

Valencia! Oh, Brilliant Save by Gunn!

Chapuisat broke clean through and ran towards me one-on-one. He pushed the ball to my left and went to go round me. I had little option but to race out of my goal and try to get there first. As Chapuisat played the ball past me I made a despairing dive and clattered into him in the process. Old habits die hard. Penalty. Georges Bregy gave me no chance from the spot, and the game finished 1–1. Not a bad result given the quality of the opposition, but we had just two games to play, against Italy and Malta, and we knew it was going to be tough to make the finals.

I soon put Scotland to the back of my mind. Back in Norwich, the city was going crazy at the prospect of our first ever European game. The club shop sold out of scarves, flags and banners and, almost everywhere I went, people rushed up to me to wish me luck. John Motson summed it up succinctly as he introduced the BBC's coverage of our UEFA Cup tie against Vitesse Arnhem: "This is the biggest match in Norwich City's history."

I've said before that midweek games at Carrow Road have a special atmosphere, but this time there was an extra buzz in the air. It was noticeably noisier, even from inside the dressing room. One or two of the lads were decidedly nervous, which was understandable. It was a new experience for most of them, just as it was for the Norwich fans. We weren't all novices though. In fact, we had a couple of veritable European veterans in the camp in the shape of Ian Crook and me. Motty informed the viewers that Crooky had won a UEFA Cup medal when he was with Spurs. For some reason he forgot to mention the Cup Winners' Cup medal I picked up at Aberdeen. Very slack, Motty.

Mike Walker and John Deehan had been to watch Arnhem a couple of times and, while their reports weren't as detailed as Fergie's man-by-man, blow-by-blow accounts, they highlighted the individual players to look out for, and warned us they were a good passing side who would try to take the game to us. No sooner had we kicked off than we realised exactly what they meant. In the very first minute they cut right through us with a fast-flowing move, which ended with a shot flashing just wide of my post. I gave the lads one of my trademark rollickings: "Come on you lot, f***ing wake yourselves up." The last thing we wanted to do was concede an away goal.

Arnhem were clearly no mugs, and I had plenty to do without having to make any spectacular saves. Mike had a real blast at us at half-time: "You're showing them too much respect, for f****'s sake. Stop standing off them. Get in their bloody faces." It worked. We upped the ante after the break and took the game to them, knocking the ball around the pitch in our usual confident fashion. Then it happened – our first European goal.

It came from a brilliant move; a series of neat passes finding Mark Bowen on one of his typical overlaps on the edge of their box. Taffy played it in to Gary Megson, who laid it off to Ian Crook. Chippy was a magnificent passer, capable of splitting defences with one killer ball. He lived up to his nickname with a superb, millimetre-perfect lofted pass to Efan Ekoku. I'm not sure what 'the Chief', as we called Efan, was thinking, but he cracked a stunning volley from the angle of the box past Raimond van der Gouw into the far corner of the net. 1–0!

It was a great way to open our European account. I was ecstatic, and ran all the way to the halfway line, grabbed the first team-mate I came to, Ian Culverhouse, and gave him a great big smacker, before suddenly realising they were about to kick off again and sprinting back to my goal.

A few minutes later Vitesse's Helder sprinted through from the halfway line and cut inside from the left wing before hitting a fierce shot from the edge of the area. Fortunately, I got my angles right and managed to get a strong hand to it and parry it away, much to the delight of the supporters in the Barclay Stand behind me who roared their appreciation: "Scotland's number one, Scotland's, Scotland's number one!" That felt great.

With my clean sheet intact, we took hold of the game and doubled our lead with another well-worked goal, which ended with Crooky pulling back a cross for Jerry Goss to make it 2–0. John Polston added a third, and we ran out 3–0 winners. What a start. Norwich City were on their first European cup run, and I was so incredibly proud to be part of it. There were plenty of hugs and slaps on the back in the dressing room afterwards, but Mike was quick to keep our feet on the ground. "Great stuff lads, but don't get too carried away," he said. "It's only half-time in the tie and we've got a Premiership match on

Valencia! Oh, Brilliant Save by Gunn!

Saturday, so nothing silly, eh?" So we didn't do anything silly. We just went out for a few, quiet, sensible, restrained halves of beer . . . or six! It was such a good time, probably the best of my footballing life. As a team we all got on fantastically. We were a really tight-knit bunch, which is such an important ingredient in any successful team.

With the games coming thick and fast, we took a plane to Merseyside before the match with Everton. And we were literally flying at Goodison Park where we turned in an incredible performance. Like us, Everton were going well. They were in the top six of the Premiership and had just beaten Liverpool in the Merseyside derby. Boy, they had no idea what was about to hit them – but then again, neither did we when Paul Rideout gave them an early lead. Even when the Chief pulled us level before half-time there was little sign of what was to come.

The second half has to go down as one the most extraordinary 45 minutes I've ever been part of. We simply tore Everton apart with some fantastic football, probably the best we played during my time at Norwich. The lads grabbed the game by the scruff of the neck, knocking the ball around superbly and hitting some brilliant defence-splitting passes over their back four. I could only stand and admire. Efan Ekoku's pace was a potent part of our game plan; we were always looking to get him away on the counter-attack and it worked a treat that afternoon. I could hardly believe what I was watching as the Chief broke clear three times and beat Neville Southall, with ease, every time. 2–1, 3–1, 4–1 . . . the goals just kept on coming. Efan finished with four and Chris Sutton weighed in with one as we romped to an extraordinary 5–1 win. That's five goals against Neville Southall, one of the best goalkeepers in the world and one of my all-time heroes. I resisted the temptation to swap shirts afterwards.

We flew back from Merseyside. Eventually. Moments after taking off from Speke Airport the pilot came on the radio to tell us there was a problem; the undercarriage hadn't retracted properly. "Gentlemen, we can continue on to Norfolk with the wheels down," he said, "but if it's okay with you I would rather return to the airport and bounce the aircraft onto the runway. That should force the undercarriage up."

If it was okay with us! What were we about to say? "No"? But the news didn't go down very well with some of the lads, especially Mark

Bowen. He wasn't the best of flyers and broke into a heavy sweat. I told him not to worry. "The pilot knows what he's doing, Taff," I said. "Let's just trust him to do his job. We'll be all right."

I looked out of the window to see flashing lights below as fire engines raced along the runway ready for our return, then looked back at Taffy. The poor bloke was in a terrible state: his palms were sweating and he was turning grey. I tried to offer a few reassuring words, but he just couldn't handle it and buried his face in his hands. As we approached the runway, the fire engines were lined up on either side. We touched down, gently bounced onto the tarmac, and then whizzed up again. Sure enough, the undercarriage duly retracted and we were on our way home. Perfect. There were one or two big sighs of relief and a spontaneous round of applause from some quarters.

"But what if the wheels don't come down again when we try to land?" said Taffy. "Erm . . ."

The colour eventually returned to his cheeks when we touched down safely at Norwich airport.

The venue for the return leg of the UEFA Cup tie in Arnhem was hardly a grand arena for Norwich City's first venture into Europe; the stadium was like a typical English non-league ground, very compact with a couple of small stands and not much else. It only held around 10,000 and it felt as if half of them were Norwich fans as we ran out on the night. They were in great voice and were clearly going to enjoy their first trip into Europe. The support that night was fantastic.

The boys produced a great defensive performance, and I made a few decent saves to keep a clean sheet. We had our chances, too, but unfortunately the Chief was as bad that night as he'd been brilliant at Everton and fluffed everything that came his way, which was a shame for the big man because he was being watched by the Nigerian national team manager. Never mind, the goalless draw was more than good enough after our performance in the first leg. Job done, we headed straight back to Norwich, eagerly anticipating the draw for the second round of the UEFA Cup where there were some big names waiting in the wings.

Our good form continued in the league, successive victories against Coventry and Chelsea taking us up to second in the Premiership table

Valencia! Oh, Brilliant Save by Gunn!

by mid-October. They were halcyon days, for both the club and me personally. I was still Scotland's number one. By now Craig Brown had taken over from Andy Roxburgh, and kept faith in me for the massive World Cup qualifier against Italy in Rome, a game we simply couldn't afford to lose.

The day before the match I was sitting in a restaurant in the hotel with the rest of the squad when a waiter came in. "Meester Gunn, Meester Gunn, we have a phone call for you!" It was Susan. She was calling to tell me there had been a torrential downpour back home, so bad that the fields around our house had flooded and water was coming into the kitchen. "What can you do about it?" she asked me.

Hmm. There I was, sat in sunny Rome, enjoying lunch with my international team-mates ahead of a huge World Cup match, and I was being asked to solve a domestic problem hundreds of miles from home. "Er, there's not a lot I can do about it from here, my darling," I told her. I suggested she call a farmer friend of ours, Bev Spratt, who kindly went round to the house with some sandbags and shored the place up. That would have to do until I returned home.

I could have done with a few sandbags in my goal in Rome the next evening. Forget Egypt, Estonia and Switzerland, this was the real thing. It was the biggest test of my international career. We had an outside chance of qualifying for the 1994 finals in the States, but only if we could spring a surprise win against the Italians.

We walked out of the tunnel in Rome's Olympic Stadium to be greeted by more than 60,000 screaming fans. It was a marvellous spectacle. There were flags waving, flares going off and hooters blaring everywhere – a real sense of anticipation and excitement. I'd never experienced anything quite like it, not against Celtic at Parkhead, nor even in that extraordinary youth international against Mexico in front of 100,000 fanatical supporters in the Azteca Stadium.

I wasn't nervous, though. I never suffered like that, not even ahead of really big matches. I just wanted to get on the pitch and concentrate on the job in hand. Most players are the same. You can hear the crowd, of course, but it's not the same as actually being in among the supporters. You don't take the noise in when you're playing, not unless things are going badly and they start to get on your back. That comes across, believe me! Otherwise, it's all about focusing on trying to win the game; talking to your team-mates, commanding your defence, and doing your best to influence the game. Funnily enough, however much noise a crowd makes, you can always hear your team-mates on the pitch.

The Italians had a star-studded line-up; Pagliuca in goal, Costacurta and Baresi at the back, and the dynamic midfield pairing of Roberto and Dino Baggio. We didn't get off to a good start. Roberto Donadoni scored after just three minutes then Pierluigi Casiraghi beat big Brian Irvine to a through-ball and tucked it past me to make it 2–0. But we hit back within a minute through Kevin Gallacher. 2–1. It stayed that way until the final 10 minutes when we pushed forward, knowing we needed at least a point to keep our World Cup hopes alive. As we took the game to the Italians we were caught out at the back and Stefano Eranio smashed an unstoppable 25-yard rising shot which flew past me and into the net. Game over.

To add injury to insult, I ended up with a bandaged head after I raced out to the edge of my box and dived at Roberto Baggio's feet. His knee caught my head and completely stunned me: I was seeing stars for a few seconds and had blood pouring from a cut eye. By the time they finished wrapping the bandage round my head it looked like I was wearing a turban.

I had a few stitches after the game, but that wasn't the only memento I took home courtesy of Signore Baggio, who was famous for his trademark ponytail. I also had long hair at the time which, like Baggio, I tied back when I played. As I left the dressing room after the game I spotted Roberto on the Italian team bus, parked next to the Scotland coach. I fumbled around in my tracksuit, took my hair band out of my pocket and jumped onto their coach. I approached Baggio and gestured to him, offering my hair band and suggesting we swap. He looked a little confused to begin with, but once he understood where I was coming from he broke into a big smile, dug into his kit bag and produced his hair band. Well, it makes a change from exchanging shirts, although I did swap mine with my opposite number Gianluca Pagliuca. Granted, I don't have much cause to wear hair bands these days but I've still got it, along with most of the shirts I've swapped over the years, tucked away in a drawer somewhere.

Having missed out on star quality in the first round of the UEFA

Valencia! Oh, Brilliant Save by Gunn!

Cup, we were more than compensated in round two as we were pulled out of the hat with the mighty Bayern Munich. We were chuffed. I'd been to the Olympic Stadium 10 years earlier, of course, with Aberdeen, when the Dons had earned a goalless draw on the way to winning the Cup Winners' Cup. Back then, I was on the bench as a youngster still trying to make a name for myself. This time, things were very different; I was an integral part of the team and at the peak of my career.

The night before the game we had a session on the pitch under the floodlights. Normally the lads would look to get away from training at the first opportunity, but when it came to the five-a-side at the end, everyone wanted to join in – even Tim Sheppard and Jock Robertson the kit man. They all wanted to savour the occasion and experience of being on the hallowed turf in the Olympic Stadium, a bit like Fergie all those years before.

Jock thoroughly enjoyed himself. He was a lovely old boy, a silver-haired Scot who absolutely lived for the club and went about his job with immense pride and enthusiasm. The game in Munich was as big a match for Jock as it was for everyone else. It was his chance to lay out the kit in one of the most famous dressing-rooms in the world. Unfortunately, Chris Sutton didn't appreciate just how much it meant to him.

After arriving at the stadium for the game the next night, the lads went out on to the pitch get a feel for the surface and generally take it all in. Sutts then went off to answer the call of nature. Soon afterwards, the rest of us returned to the dressing-room to prepare for kick-off, but we could hardly believe our eyes as were greeted by the sight of our star striker and kit man shouting, screaming and squaring up to each other.

Chris had really upset poor Jock, who'd spent ages arranging the kit, hanging up our shirts in order from 1–16 on the pegs, laying various piles of towels and spare socks and shorts on the treatment table with meticulous care and attention. Everything was immaculate – until Sutts came out of the toilet with wet hands and nonchalantly plucked a towel from the middle of the pile on the treatment table, knocking the whole lot over.

Jock went ballistic. He really let rip at Chris, and was pushing him around and threatening to do all sorts of things to him as we walked in.

"You big lanky git," he said. "What did you have to go and do that for?"

It was crazy. Jock was only half the size of Sutts, yet here he was trying to wrestle with him. Chris was doing his best to keep Jock at arms' length: "Calm down, Jock. It was an accident for f***'s sake."

It was a bit like an embarrassed heavyweight holding a frenzied featherweight at bay. We stepped in and reminded them there was the small matter of a UEFA cup match to prepare for. A couple of the lads prised them apart, and moments later everyone was laughing about it. I guess the occasion was getting to everyone.

We didn't prepare any differently from how we would for a standard league game and Mike Walker was his usual cool, calm and collected self, delivering the team talk that night.

"Right lads, this is it. Just go out and pass the ball like you normally do and we'll get a result. Get stuck in and have a good game."

That was it. He hardly ever swore and rarely got worked up before games. He left that to John Deehan, who zipped round everyone, all frenzied excitement, geeing everyone up. Dixie was a bundle of energy and he was contagious. He talked to everyone individually, telling them who to pick up on set pieces, who to watch out for and, in his dry Brummie way, relaxed everyone by taking the mick out of them.

It worked, as usual. We were all calm and focused as we went out onto the pitch. No one had given us a chance. No British club side had ever beaten the mighty Bayern Munich in the Olympic Stadium and we certainly weren't expected to change that.

Oddly, one of the first things I noticed as we kicked off were the mechanical cameras mounted behind the goals. I'd never seen them before. They were moving around all the time, following the ball, which is all well and good but they also made a distinctive whirring noise as they operated. I was conscious of them throughout the game. The cameras are very effective though, providing brilliant TV replays, which was great news for us because they captured genuine contenders for the club's most memorable goal – and save! – as we produced the game of our lives and very possibly the finest result in Norwich City's history.

The goal was simply sensational. It came from that man Gossy. It was still 0-0 mid-way through the first half, when Rob Newman's floated cross was headed away by Lothar Matthaus, towards the edge of their penalty area. It fell straight into Gossy's path, and he caught it perfectly on the volley. I was on the edge of my box, directly behind the line of play as he struck it. It was like watching in slow motion as the ball dipped and headed towards the goal before smacking into the back of the net. It was a wonderful strike. I punched the air and turned round to see our fans behind me going mad. We were 1–0 up, in Munich!

It wasn't just the quality of the shot, but the occasion and importance of the game. We were being watched live on national television back home and at the time it seemed like Norwich City were just about every fan's second favourite club.

Then Ian Crook knocked a free-kick towards the back post. Big Chris Sutton created havoc in the box, tussling with their huge centre-half, Oliver Kreuzer. But as they tangled, the ball floated over to the back post where Taffy Bowen had timed his run to perfection, and he met it with a stooping header. It went straight over Raimond Aumann, my old adversary from Scotland schoolboy days, and into the far corner. I couldn't believe it. I ran around like a madman saluting the Norwich fans behind my goal. Then I looked up towards the score-board. No, I wasn't dreaming. There it was in big bright lights: FC Bayern Munchen 0, Norwich City 2.

Munich got one back, just before half-time, through Christian Nerlinger. It was a bit of a jolt as we headed for the dressing room but, as Mike reminded us, we still had the upper hand. I also did my bit to gee the lads up: "Listen guys, we've been to places like Old Trafford and Anfield and dug in. If we can keep clean sheets there, we can do it here." I then threw in one of my favourite battle-cries. "Come on lads," I shouted, "It's time to get the tin helmets on and dig the trenches."

Most of the second half was played in our half. I was barking orders from the minute we kicked off to the final whistle as Bayern threw everything but the kitchen sink at us. "Man on! Get out of the box! Tight, tight, tight!" It was real backs-to-the-wall stuff, but the boys defended superbly. When Bayern did find a way through, I managed to block everything that came my way. The hands were good that night. They had to be.

As the game went into the last 20 minutes Lothar Matthaus moved forward, prompting attacks from midfield and taking a few pot shots himself. One effort from just outside the area took a deflection for a corner. The ball was floated into my box, where it was headed out to Matthaus, who knocked it wide to Jorghino, unmarked on the right wing. He curled a low cross into a crowded penalty area, towards Adolfo Valencia. The big Columbian was in acres of space, on the edge of the six-yard box, and launched himself at the ball, sending a bullet-like diving header towards my goal from almost point-blank range.

I reacted instinctively, throwing myself towards Valencia and in the general direction of the ball, which smashed into my goolies and rebounded back to Kreuzer who thumped it over the bar. It doesn't matter how you stop them, just as long as you keep them out – that's got to be the number one rule for any goalkeeper. Not for the first time in my career, my wedding tackle had come to the rescue, just as it had against Trevor Brooking all those years ago in my trial match for Ross County. Coincidentally, Trevor was alongside John Motson for the BBC in Munich. We'd set the video and I watched the game as soon as I got home. Motty might have forgotten to mention my medal ahead of the Arnhem match, but I can forgive him because he's responsible for my all-time favourite line of commentary as he called that save: "Valencia! Oh, brilliant save by Gunn. And they've fired the rebound over!" The way Motty exclaims "Valencia!" you just know he's sure they are going to score and there's real surprise and excitement in his voice as I somehow manage to keep it out.

I rate that save from Valencia as my best ever. It wasn't the most spectacular stop I ever made, but it was definitely the most important. The boys couldn't believe it. They all looked at me as if to say, "How did you stop that?" We exchanged a few high-fives, but there was no time to dwell on the moment; we still had a game to win. More to the point, I was just doing my bit as part of a team which was defending for its life. "Come on boys," I bawled. "Keep it going and we'll win this game." And we did.

Every single Norwich City player was a hero that night. It was an historic and ultimately unique victory for both club and country. We were the first British club to beat Bayern Munich in their own Olympic Stadium – and the last now that Bayern have moved to the spanking

Valencia! Oh, Brilliant Save by Gunn!

new Allianz Stadium. That night will stay with me for ever, but perhaps surprisingly the post-match celebrations were pretty low-key. Some of the wives and girlfriends, including Susan, joined us in the hotel for a few drinks, but we had to be professional – once again there was little time to dwell on such a great performance in the middle of such a hectic season.

"One of the finest displays by an English club away from home in recent years," said Motty. No one was arguing.

CHAPTER EIGHTEEN

Dennis the Menace

A rmed with a bulging bag of new kit courtesy of my German sponsors Uhlsport, who were delighted at my performance in their country, I returned to Premiership action with Norwich. I was getting £10,000 a year just for wearing their gloves and boots and when I was introduced to their president after the game, I think he felt he'd got his money's worth.

We were still second in the table behind Manchester United and the games were coming thick and fast. We drew 0-0 against West Ham at Carrow Road, and then played two games at Highbury in the space of four days, earning a replay in the Coca-Cola Cup and then holding Arsenal to a goalless draw in the league. But that clean sheet came at a cost – I picked up an injury making another of my all-time favourite saves. I was keeping goal in front of the famous old North Bank as Ian Wright ran through and smashed a shot at me. I had the ball covered but it took a wicked deflection off Ian Butterworth. I had to instantly change direction, arching my back and flinging myself low to my right to claw the ball away. It was a brilliant save, but I landed awkwardly on my arm and my shoulder popped out.

A shoulder injury is especially bad news for a goalkeeper – just ask Graham Benstead – and at any other time I might have missed a couple of games, but there was no way I was going to be out of action with so many big matches coming up, not least the return against Bayern Munich. The injury was extremely painful and I could hardly lift my arm, but I wasn't going to miss that game for the world and had round-the-clock treatment to ensure I could play.

When the Munich squad flew into Norwich, their president Franz Beckenbauer gave an interview to the local television boys, saying he was confident they would overturn the first leg result, and hinting that it had been a bit of a fluke. He wasn't exactly being disrespectful, but some of our other teutonic friends were. Lothar Matthaus dismissed us as an "ordinary side", and one of the German newspapers claimed we were nothing but a bunch of country bumpkins who were sure to roll over in the return at Carrow Road. Water off a duck's back. Matthaus had a reputation for being arrogant, and we knew we were the underdogs and were happy with that. And who were we, little Norwich, to argue with the legendary Franz Beckenbauer?

The atmosphere inside a sell-out Carrow Road was awesome, the noise was deafening. Mike's pre-match talk was, as usual, simple and to the point. The longer we kept them out, the more frustrated they would become. "Just keep it tight, especially early doors," he said. "We'll be all right, just so long as we don't give away an early goal."

So what do we go and do? We'd played just four minutes when they got a dubious corner. The ball definitely came off one of their players, but the referee gave them the decision. Rob Newman tried to head the cross away, but the ball hit John Polston and fell straight to Valencia's feet. He gave me no chance this time, smashing it on the half-volley and into the corner of the net, past me and a despairing Mark Bowen.

There was a momentary eerie silence from our supporters, then a tremendous surge of noise. I've never ever experienced anything quite like it at Carrow Road. What a roar. I felt the hairs stand up on the back of my neck and actually looked back, did a double take, and wondered for a second where the other 30,000 fans had come from. It was inspirational.

I lifted up my head and shoulders, puffed out my chest and threw the ball back towards the centre circle. I clapped my hands together and started barking at my defenders again. "Come onnnnnn!" I screamed. Bayern had levelled the tie, but we were still ahead thanks to our two away goals, so they stepped up the pressure. I was screaming at my defenders constantly, encouraging and cajoling in equal measure. I'm quite the bossy-boots on a normal match-day, but that night I surpassed myself. The players know you don't have time for niceties, you just shout in shorthand, commanding your area.

I had to make one or two tidy saves in the first half; nothing spectacular, but important stops all the same, given the delicate way the tie was poised. At half-time Mike and Dixie were calm and just told us to be positive, telling us to play our usual game; to pass the ball around as we knew we could and push forward whenever we had the opportunity. We were technically still ahead in the tie, so Bayern would have to come at us, which would leave gaps for us to exploit. The chances were sure to come, Mike said.

He was spot on. Early in the second half Taffy Bowen knocked a cross in from the left, big Chris Sutton got up in front of their centre-half and flicked the ball on to Jerry Goss, who ghosted in between two defenders with perfect timing and side-footed it in. Carrow Road went bonkers. Gossy ran off towards his mum, who was sitting in the front row of the City Stand. All the lads piled in on top of him and he disappeared under a pile of jubilant bodies. I raced to join in the fun, running past the halfway line to reach him – although the closest I could get to him was to give him a pat on the head. Yet again, Gossy was proving the man for the big occasion. Even better, his goal had earned another £425 for my appeal, courtesy of a local bookmaker who'd pledged the money if Gossy scored.

A huge rendition of our famous old anthem, 'On The Ball City', rang out around the ground as our delirious supporters jumped up and down. But the Munich players were far from finished. Lothar Matthaus pushed forward again to try to inspire a fightback, but we kept our discipline and as the game wore on they became increasingly frustrated, especially Matthaus. As the minutes ticked down, he clearly thought they should have had a corner. I grabbed the ball and was in no hurry to take the goal kick. Matthaus got a bit overexcited, accusing me of time-wasting. He started having a real go at me. It was all in German, so I didn't really understand what he was saying, but I got his drift and gave him a bit of verbal in return. "Shut your mouth," I said. Which, to be fair, I think he probably understood.

The referee got in between us, but I reached out and gave Matthaus a little slap on the side of his face which he wasn't very impressed with. Neither was the ref. He booked both of us. Moments later, the final whistle went. We'd done it, beaten Bayern Munich 3–2 over the two legs. I ran around the pitch, hugging everyone and celebrating with the Norwich fans. Herr Matthaus wasn't best pleased. He swapped shirts with Gossy but chucked it at the referee as he trudged off, suggesting he had helped us win the game. I don't know what the German is for sour grapes – sauerkraut?

I swapped shirts with Aumann but didn't get a chance to put it straight on in all the mayhem of the post-match celebrations. There was a great shot on the telly of me with Gossy out on the pitch, both shirtless, arms round each other. My six-pack's not bad, but Gossy's puts me to shame. It captured the moment perfectly; the ecstasy and passion on our faces say it all. We could hardly speak, just kept clenching our fists and going "Yessssssss!" to each other. Gossy was always a man full of emotions, but I couldn't imagine what it must be like to score a goal like that, in a game like that. He must have been on a different stratosphere to even the one I was on. We did a mini lap of honour round the pitch, waving to the crowd, enjoying the moment, still way too pumped to actually think. To round off a perfect night I was given the Man of the Match champagne.

Back in the dressing-room, Mike Walker was completely overcome with emotion. "Bloody brilliant. You were all fantastic, lads. Great stuff," he said as he went round us giving us all huge hugs. He and Dixie had pitted their wits against the best in Germany and come up trumps, so he was thoroughly lapping up the moment – and why not? Mike, or the 'Silver Fox' as we called him, took a lot of pride in his appearance. We used to take the mick, saying that he was straight off the sunbed and into the TV interview. He couldn't wait to face the cameras that night and, fair play to the man, he deserved every moment in that spotlight. Great memories.

The third round draw was a couple of days later, on the Friday, while we were on the team coach on our way to a match at Sheffield United. Dixie organised a sweepstake, and we all coughed up a couple of quid each, making the princely sum of £32 to the winner. The two biggest names in the last 16 were the Italian giants Juventus and Inter Milan, whom I'd drawn out of the hat. Surely it was too much to ask to get another massive club? A huge cheer went up when the news came through, especially from yours truly; we'd been paired with Inter Milan. "You lucky sod," said Ian Culverhouse. "Money always goes to money."

We were really excited. We'd just beaten Bayern Munich, and felt we could take on all-comers and go all the way. Well, why not? We'd played some blinding football against Bayern and confidence was sky-high. The lads reacted like a bunch of overgrown schoolboys and started running through some of Inter's star players; Italian inter-nationals Nicole Berti, Giuseppe Bergomi, and goalkeeper Walter Zenga, who was my favourite foreign keeper. I'd watched a lot of Italian football and liked his style – he had a certain panache and I was relishing the prospect of coming up against him. Inter also had a couple of Dutch stars in the shape of midfielder Wim Jonk and a young striker by the name of Dennis Bergkamp.

If the city had been excited about the Bayern game, it went into melt-down for the Inter match. My mobile was constantly buzzing with friends from near and far wishing us luck. There were queues stretching right round the ground for tickets, yellow and green bunting in just about every shop. By now we'd became accustomed to turning up at training to find three or four film crews and hordes of pressmen, all eager for some kind of soundbite. Were we overawed? No way, we absolutely loved it – especially the gaffer!

A week or so before the first leg against Inter, some of the players took part in an event at an Italian restaurant in Norwich, to raise funds for the Bryan Gunn Leukaemia Appeal. The restaurant was packed, and there was a spontaneous round of applause as Ruel Fox and I waltzed out in our pinnies to take the first orders. It got louder when the crowd spotted Chris Sutton making the pizzas and Efan Ekoku helping out behind the bar. It was a great, fun night – Sky TV were there and we raised hundreds of pounds for the appeal.

Aside from those shenanigans, we prepared for the Inter game as normal. I'd seen and heard enough about Bergkamp to know he was likely to pose a big threat. He had lightning pace and was capable of scoring extraordinary goals. Sure enough, it wasn't long before he served notice of his intentions at a packed Carrow Road, where once again there was a tremendous atmosphere. The Dutchman beat the offside trap and burst clean through, with just me between him and the goal. I stood up as long as I could. It was one-on-one. Bergkamp shaped to shoot, shimmied one way, then the other, waiting for me to go to ground. I went down and spread myself as wide as I could. He tried to place a shot past me and I flicked out my foot and kept it out. One-nil to Gunny!

Suddenly we were under intense pressure. Moments later I had to keep out a crisp shot from Wim Jonk. Then Bergkamp let fly from some 25 yards. The ball was heading for my top left-hand corner, the 'postage stamp' as we call it in the trade. I threw myself to my left and caught it, plucking it out of the air at full stretch. Rob Newman came up and gave me an appreciative thump on the back. "Another one for the cameras, eh Gunny?" he said, grinning, his usual joke whenever I did something out of the ordinary.

Inter had the better chances in the first half and I was happy to go off at half-time with the game still 0-0, but we went close to getting the breakthrough after the restart. It was that man God, again, who smashed a vicious drive from the edge of the box, beating Walter Zenga all ends up. The ball crashed back off the crossbar and was headed back by Ruel Fox to Ian Crook, who hit a sizzling volley just inches over. With our confidence growing by the minute we went all out for a winner, only to be hit on the counter-attack.

Ten minutes from time Ruben Sosa got clear of our back four and sprinted into my penalty box. Rob Newman raced back in hot pursuit, but – great bloke that he is – Rob and racing aren't really words that go together. He struggled to keep up and launched a desperate late lunge, bringing Sosa down for a penalty. Sosa played for it, but we couldn't really complain. The frustrating thing was, Sosa had run wide and there was no way he was going to score from such a tight angle. Bergkamp stepped up and, cool as you like, sent me the wrong way. It ended 1–0 and to make matters worse our three Ians – Culverhouse, Crook and Butterworth – all picked up yellow cards which meant they would miss the second leg in Italy.

We had lost by the narrowest of margins, but despite the defeat we had cemented our reputation as a team that played tremendous football – some of the best seen in the England that season. The rest of the country had been forced to sit up and take notice of us 'carrot-crunchers', and when we took on runaway league leaders Manchester United a few days before heading for the return leg at the San Siro, a record 23 countries took live coverage of the match from Old Trafford.

We took the opportunity to show the watching world what we were made of by matching Fergie's team man-for-man and pass-for-pass in a thrilling 2–2 draw. Eric Cantona was at his masterly best, making both United goals, but he couldn't find a way past me, not even in the last few minutes when he tried to beat me with a clever lob. Everyone in the ground thought it was a goal, but I managed to get a last-ditch hand to it and push it over the bar. "Tres bien, le gardien," said Eric. It's one of the nicest compliments I've ever had from a fellow professional.

Unfortunately it seemed that our growing reputation hadn't spread as far as Italy. Disappointingly, when we arrived at the San Siro for the return leg against Inter it was far from full. While the stadium itself looked impressive with its four corner spiral staircases, the interior was nothing to write home about. Neither was the pitch, as was evident in the very first minute when Mark Bowen hit a gentle back-pass which bobbled all over the place before dribbling just past my post.

The welcome wasn't great either, no exchanging pennants as you do in international matches. I'm sure the directors must have had some hospitality, but when we trained on the pitch the afternoon before the game, the club officials didn't exactly roll out the red carpet. We started at 3pm, the time the game was due to kick off the next day and towards the end of the session it started to get dark. Mike Walker went off to see if he could get the floodlights turned on, but their officials were having none of it, so we finished our session in the rapidly gathering gloom of the night.

Nonetheless, the atmosphere the next night was great with fire-crackers and flares going off and giant flags waving as we walked out for our pre-match warm-up. The setting took your breath away. It was easy to see why it's one of the most famous and impressive stadiums in the world, although Susan told me afterwards that she and the other Norwich fans had been herded into pens for an hour or so before the game and they'd had to smile nicely just to break out to get a bottle of water. She said that behind the façade, the stadium was pretty basic, and there didn't seem to be any female facilities, so she'd had to ask an Italian chap to block the door for her and her mate when they went to the loo in the gents!

Out on the pitch, I headed for our fans in the far corner of the stadium, about 6,000 of them. They started singing, "Gunny, Gunny, give us a song!" I responded by kicking off a rendition of 'On The Ball City!'

That was typical of the tremendous rapport I had with the Norwich fans. I often got them going if things needed livening up, especially at Carrow Road over the years. I'd look round and tap my head. The fans knew it was a cue for a song and they'd always respond, usually by singing:

> Bryan Gunn, Bryan Gunn,
> Bryan, Bryan Gunn,
> He's got no hair,
> But we don't care,
> Bryan, Bryan Gunn!

I was revelling in the moment. Okay, so we had a weakened team due to the suspensions of the three Ians, but we still fancied our chances. And, boy, did we have a lot of chances. Chris Sutton and Efan Ekoku could have scored but Inter soaked up everything we threw at them, and once again caught us with a sucker punch near the end. Bergkamp ran onto a pass on the halfway line and set off like a gazelle down the left wing. He sprinted towards the box where Colin Woodthorpe was back-peddling and caught in two minds: should he stand his ground and cut out a possible through ball to Sosa, or commit himself to trying to tackle Bergkamp? A split second later Bergkamp curled a shot from the edge of the area towards my far post. I dived at full stretch to my left and got a hand to it, but there was nothing I could do to keep it out. It was pure quality; a perfect finish from a Dutch master and taste of what Arsenal fans would come to enjoy on a regular basis after his move to Highbury.

The final whistle went and my whole body went with it. I just slumped. My head, shoulders, chest – I was just doubled over. We had played really well over the two games and didn't deserve to lose. I couldn't stop the tears and crouched on the ground for a moment, before pulling myself together and going over to salute our tremendous fans. Most of the team were in tears, including Mike Walker who was really struggling to contain himself as he was interviewed by a TV crew on the pitch. It's an overused word in football, but we were well and truly 'gutted'. I walked around applauding our fans, but all that I could think was "If only". If only I'd saved that penalty at Carrow Road. If only Sutts' shot had gone in. It was a horrible moment. Inter went on to win the UEFA Cup. For us, it was the end of a proud European run. We didn't realise it was also the beginning of the end of Mike Walker's time at Carrow Road.

I guess the signs were there almost from the moment we stepped off the plane on our return from Milan. The defeat hit us hard, especially Mike. Having tasted big-time European action he wanted more of the same, for himself and Norwich City. When he faced the press at Norwich airport he wasn't particularly interested in talking about what had happened in the San Siro. He was more keen to talk about the future and seized the moment to tell the world he wanted to build on the club's successful run, coming out with his now famous "It's time to release the purse strings" call to club chairman Robert Chase.

Mike wanted cash to strengthen the squad and he let everybody know it. As one of his senior players, I was right behind him, but it was never going to happen. The chairman made it clear the money wasn't there and their relationship soon became prickly, with the press suggesting there was a distinct difference of opinion as to how the club should progress. Mike also had an issue with what he was getting as manager compared with the players. Most of us were on long-term deals while he was on a year-on-year rolling contract. Mike was playing a key role in the club's success and was frustrated that he wasn't enjoying the same level of reward, or job security. He had a point.

The weekend after the match against Inter Milan I joined Mike for a trip to London for the BBC Sports Personality of the Year awards. He didn't give the slightest hint that he was considering his future as we were chauffeur-driven down to London on the Sunday night. We were due to play Leeds at Carrow Road in a live televised game 24 hours later. After arriving at the BBC, we were directed to the hospitality room where the champagne was flowing freely. A waitress came up to me with a tray of bubbly. I looked sideways at Mike before accepting a glass; he gave me a knowing grin and a nod to say it was okay.

I bumped into the Norwich heavyweight boxer Herbie Hide and saw my golfing hero Colin Montgomery from a distance, but just as I was about to rush up to him, we were ushered in for the filming. Norwich City got a special mention for doing so well in Europe, and Mike and I gave a royal wave and grin as the cameras focused on us, then enjoyed a couple more drinks before making our way home, arriving back in Norwich at about 2 o'clock in the morning. It wasn't exactly routine preparation ahead of an important league match, but the bubbly didn't do me any harm.

In fact, I was still fizzing as we took on Leeds on the Monday night. I made a cracking double save from a free kick. Tony Dorigo's screaming shot came flying through the wall and I touched it onto the post, only for the rebound to fall to Rod Wallace who smashed it back at me. This time I pushed it up onto the bar and the ball bounced back into the box again, where there was an almighty scramble before we eventually cleared it. We won the game 2–1 to complete a Premiership double over Leeds. That capped off a great night. It had started with 15-year-old Hayley Johnson presenting me with a cheque for £650 for the appeal before the game. She'd been diagnosed with leukaemia when she was just five years old. Now, 10 years later, she was living proof that research and improved treatment worked.

We lost a bizarre local derby at Ipswich a few days before

Christmas. It was all-square at 1–1 when they won a late corner. Gary Megson came back to help defend it, but managed to head the ball past me and into the net for their winner.

The following night I celebrated my 30th birthday at a special party organised by Susan. It was meant to be a surprise, but a few days earlier I had been sure something was wrong. I'd decided to confront Susan about it as she had been fretting for a while and had got to the point where she couldn't sleep.

"Come on, what's the problem?" I said. "If you're having an affair, tell me!"

"I'm certainly not having an affair," she snapped straight back. "If you want to know, I'm actually organising a surprise birthday party – for you!"

She'd been so worried about things going wrong, or someone letting the secret out. You can imagine how awful I felt. There was still a big surprise in store for me come the night of the party when a stretch limo turned up in our drive. I thought it had come to pick us up, only for my mum and dad to step out of the car. I was gobsmacked; it was a fantastic surprise.

I hadn't seen them for months. There were big hugs all round and plenty of tears on both sides. It turned out my folks had arrived in Norwich the previous day and were staying in a nearby bed and breakfast. What's more, I'd come desperately close to bumping into my dad that very morning when we'd both set out to visit Francesca's grave at the same time. Dad was walking to Francesca's church as I was driving there. He spotted my car and had to dive behind a hedge to make sure I didn't see him.

Early in the New Year, press reports began to link Mike Walker with a move to Everton. The Toffees were struggling near the foot of the table and had sacked Howard Kendall. Mike was keen to hear what they had to say, but Robert Chase refused them permission to talk to Mike. There were all sorts of rumours and suggestions about what was going on, which didn't go down too well in the dressing room. We didn't want Mike to go. He was a big part of what we'd achieved, and we were all looking forward to the future and building on our success. Some of the lads had signed long-term contracts on the back of what we'd been part of with Mike, assuming he would be there for the long term. By the time we played Newcastle at home in early January speculation over Mike's future was reaching a frenzy.

It seemed as if everything we'd worked for was about to come crashing down around our ears. We were all pretty despondent as we trained in the week leading up to the Newcastle game. We all liked Mike; he was charming, liked to mix with the boys, work hard and play hard. We used to joke that he could smell the TV cameras – he'd always come over the hill just as we were finishing training and join in a five-a-side if the TV crews were there – but we had the utmost respect for him and what he'd achieved, and what we'd achieved under him. The last thing we wanted to do was lose that winning formula.

In the middle of all this speculation, a few days before the Newcastle game, I got a call out of the blue from my mate John Wooton.

"Hello Gunny. Can you sort me out a couple of tickets for the game?"

"Sure, how many do you need?"

"Well, there's me and the missus and Natasha and Robbie. You'll need to be discreet though."

He went on to explain that the Robbie in question was none other than Robbie Williams, then still with Take That. John's wife at the time was a model and had a good friend called Natasha, who was *extremely* good friends with Robbie. The members of Take That weren't allowed to have girlfriends – at least they were actively discouraged from being seen in public with girls, as their management felt it wouldn't go down too well with their adoring fans. Natasha was Robbie's girlfriend at the time, and the couple frequently stayed with John and his wife on their farm, using the place as a retreat where they were unlikely to be spotted. It was a lovely remote spot where they could chill without any hassle from the paparazzi.

Robbie, of course, is a big football fan – a massive Port Vale supporter – but back then he didn't often get the chance to go to a game. So when John mentioned he was a good friend of mine and asked if he fancied a trip to Carrow Road, he jumped at the chance. Hence the call. There was no special security and I got him a ticket in with the players' wives, near the so-called 'Snakepit' area of the ground, where some of the more vociferous fans sit.

Robbie turned up incognito in a puffa jacket and one of those funny balaclava-type hats that cover most of your face. After the game, Susan and I joined him, John and the team in the players' lounge and it wasn't long before people started clocking him and queuing up for his autograph. Robbie was charming, and only too happy to sign anything thrust into his hand and pose for pictures for those lucky enough to be in the players' lounge that night. He was a really nice bloke and very complimentary about the club and its facilities; if anything he was quite quiet and shy. Ian Butterworth made sure he got a photo for his daughter Olivia, as did Mark Bowen for his daughter Danielle. I must admit, I was a bit remiss. Melissa, I apologise.

Susan, on the other hand, was delighted. After the game all the Fandabidozi club, along with Robbie and Natasha, went to a restaurant. As we enjoyed a delicious three-course meal and various bottles of wine, the conversation turned to the fact that it would be Susan's birthday in two days' time and Robbie decided to serenade her. I'll never forget the look on Susan's face as he got to his feet, turned to her with that famous twinkle in his eye and that cheeky smile, and started singing, "Happy birthday to you . . ." She's never forgotten it. What a pity we didn't have a video camera that night.

It was back down to earth with a bump two days later. On the Friday morning, as the lads prepared to board the team bus for an FA Cup third round tie at Wycombe, Mike came to the training ground and broke the news that he was off. Obviously, we'd been living with the rumours, but we were totally shell-shocked, and sat there in silence as he told us. Mike was a man of few words. He just said: "Thanks for everything lads, but I'm going." That was it, just like that. He was off.

It was crazy to lose Mike in the way we did. I have nothing but respect for Robert Chase, for the way that he treated me and the other players, but I think in this instance he was wrong to allow Mike to escape. The lads were surprised that more hadn't been done to keep him, but we would never have said as much in the press. It just wouldn't have been the done thing. I think we needed to take the gamble, to take that extra step, go that extra mile. Who knows what would have happened if the board had loosened the purse strings? Nobody can say for sure, but I would bet good money that now we would be an established Premiership side like Charlton or Bolton – or perhaps even better. I really wish I had said something at the time. Maybe Robert Chase thought that we could continue the club's success without Mike Walker. Players are usually the last to be consulted in these affairs. In the dressing room we knew how big a blow losing Mike would be – maybe we should have stuck our necks out and said so at the time.

Mike just wanted to be rewarded for what he'd achieved. Just like us. I never held that against him. It reminded me of something Alex Ferguson said to me when I joined Norwich. He told me to see the move as a stepping stone to a bigger club. The fact was Norwich had become a big club; we'd finished fifth, fourth and third in the top flight of English football and qualified for Europe. There was no need to move on; Norwich were the third best team in the country. Sadly, it's hard to imagine the club ever challenging for third place in the Premiership again, the way football has changed since those heady days.

John Deehan took over team affairs, which at least meant we had a degree of continuity. We were delighted. Dixie was great to work with and always had a smile on his face. Whatever we got up to in training, whether it was a tough physical workout, running through set plays, tactics or just simple ball work, we always had a special prize for the so-called Donkey of the Day. At the end of the session the lads would have a quick vote and award an old yellow shirt with 'Donkey of the Day' written on it, in recognition of either one almighty cock-up or a generally all-round naff performance.

One morning, I had an outstanding session, saving everything that came my way. We rounded things off with the usual five-a-side. Towards the end of training I back-peddled as I went to make a save and hit my head on the crossbar. The goal collapsed and the bar came crashing down on top of me. Everyone thought it was hilarious and promptly voted me Donkey of the Day.

"That was brilliant, Gunny," said Jon Newsome. "Here, have this," he added, throwing the yellow bib at me.

I didn't think it was funny. In fact I was really angry about it. They'd totally overlooked what I'd done in the rest of the session. "You know what you lot can do with that," I bawled. "F*** off, that's what."

At first the lads thought I was joking. I stomped into the dressing room, grabbed Crookie's lighter from his trouser pocket and emerged holding the shirt in one hand and the lighter in the other. "Here's what you can do with your f***ing shirt," I said as I set fire to it.

The lads looked at me as if I'd lost my marbles. "Bollocks to the lot of you," I shouted, as I threw the charred remains to the floor and stormed back to the changing rooms.

"All right, Gunny," said John Deehan. "No need to throw your toys out of the pram. It's only a bit of fun."

He was right, of course. I don't know why I let it get to me. I must have got out of the wrong side of the bed that day.

"By the way, Gunny," said Dixie, "make sure you find a replacement shirt by Monday. You donkey."

In Dixie's first game in charge, we won 2–0 in the cup tie at Wycombe Wanderers, who were managed by an aspiring young manager by the name of Martin O'Neill. Chris Sutton got both goals. He was in a rich vein of form and turning a few heads with his goalscoring exploits. The vultures were beginning to hover, so the club gave Sutts a new contract which rewarded him with a £500 bonus every time he scored in an attempt to discourage him from going anywhere. Chris ended up with 28 goals that season, so he pocketed a few extra quid.

But the second half of the season petered out, not helped by a run of seven straight draws during which I saw red, in more ways than one, against Liverpool. I was sent off at Carrow Road for handling the ball outside the box. Steve McManaman beat the offside trap and flicked the ball over me. I put my hand up and it caught me on the arm, although I tried to make out the ball hit me in the face. Dermot Gallagher wasn't fooled and promptly produced the red card.

Ronnie Whelan raced towards the ref shouting out, "Send the Scottish twat off!" I bumped into him at a dinner recently where he was a guest speaker. His opening line was, "Good to see Bryan Gunn again. The last time I was in Norwich he wanted to rip my f***ing head off!" Which was true. If there hadn't have been three or four players in my way! The dismissal spoilt my one hundred per cent appearance record that season. I was suspended for the 3–3 draw against Swindon a couple of weeks later – the only match I missed in 54 games.

A few weeks later, Mike Walker returned to Carrow Road with Everton for a live televised midweek match. Everton desperately needed the points and Sky gave it a huge build-up. We hadn't won in 10 league games, but heaped yet more pressure on our former boss by winning 3–0. Ian Culverhouse even scored, just to rub poor Mike's nose in it – one of only two goals Cully scored in almost 10 years with the club!

Our last away game of the season was at Anfield, in the final match before they bulldozed the famous old Kop terrace. We won 1–0, courtesy of another stunning goal from Jerry Goss who smashed an unstoppable shot past David James, right in front of the Kop. I was delighted to keep yet another clean sheet at Anfield, but no one seems to remember that. It's always Jerry's goal people talk about. Fair enough. It was a fitting way for him to round off a stunning testimonial season where spectacular goals had become his speciality.

Our final game of that eventful 1993/94 season was against Oldham at Carrow Road. I'm lucky I can remember anything about it; I nearly knocked myself out before we'd kicked off. As per my usual routine, I ran out of the tunnel onto the pitch towards my goal, leaping up as if to head the crossbar at the Barclay End. As it was the last game of the season, I thought I'd have a bit of fun by making out I'd actually connected with the bar. All jolly good fun, except I overdid it, cracking my head against the woodwork so hard I could actually see stars. The fans thought it was hysterically funny. I tried to be cool by pretending I'd done it deliberately, wobbling about on my legs. The fact is it bloody well hurt. A lot.

I was still dazed as we kicked off. It then dawned on me that Oldham were one of several teams involved in the relegation scrap on that final day. I thought, "Hold it, I'd better get my head clear. It's not fair on the other sides if I let one in because I'm not concentrating." We drew a dull game 1–1. In the end Ipswich, Everton and Southampton all did enough to stay up, even if Oldham had beaten us.

And that was it, the end of an incredible season which had just about the lot: international appearances, the marvellous UEFA Cup run, a change of managers, God's extraordinary goals, thousands of pounds raised for the appeal – and a peach of a bruise on my forehead for good measure!

CHAPTER NINETEEN

Broken Leg, Shattered Club

It was a gloriously sunny summer's afternoon as we made our way from Norwich along the A47 towards West Norfolk. The Gunn clan had been invited to a barbeque with the rest of the Fandabidozi brigade. The weather was perfect as Susan, Melissa and I headed towards our friend John Wooton's secluded farm, tucked away in a village between Downham Market and King's Lynn. Suddenly, my mobile phone rang. It was my old boss, Alex Ferguson.

"Hey Big Ben," he said, in his growling Scottish brogue. "How are you doing?"

We exchanged pleasantries, but I knew he was after something and sure enough he came straight to the point.

"What about this Chris Sutton? We need to try and get him up here – what do you reckon?"

Sutts was a man in demand on the back of the hatful of goals he'd bagged for us in the previous couple of seasons. Robert Chase had been adamant his star striker wasn't for sale, going as far as to say that if Chris left the club before the start of the season, then so would he. But the big clubs weren't taking 'no' for an answer. There was an almighty clamour for Sutts' signature, with Arsenal, Liverpool, Everton, Spurs, Blackburn and now possibly Manchester United all in the race to sign him.

I knew from talking to Chris that a hugely lucrative offer was already on the table from Blackburn. He was on about £1,200 a week at Carrow Road, but Blackburn were offering him ten times that and Kenny Dalglish, with the benefit of Sir Jack Walker's millions, had made a £5 million bid. Chris Sutton, the local boy made good, was about to become Britain's most expensive footballer ever.

I knew it was futile, but I let Fergie down gently, and promised him I'd have a word.

"Sorry, Boss," I said – even years later, I still refer to him as 'Boss' or 'Gaffer'. "I think it's too late; I'll do my best, but I think the deal's already been done with Kenny Dalglish."

Fergie, typically, wasn't going to accept he was beaten there and then.

"Well, have a chat with the boy. Tell him not to sign anything, not until he's had a word with me."

I knew there was no point me calling Sutts though. The deal with Blackburn was too far down the line. For once I wasn't able to help Fergie out.

We had a brilliant afternoon at John Wooton's farm. Robbie Williams was there with Natasha and was full of fun, just like he is whenever you see him on the TV these days. There was a plank wrapped in bubble-wrap across the middle of the pool where we staged duels against each other with wet pillows. The rules were simple: knock your opponent into the water and you've won. Robbie challenged me to a pillow fight, so up we got and promptly started trying to thump the living daylights out of each other. Being much bigger than him, it was easy for me to get a few blows in. I started to hit him with a few playful blows and had him in stitches when I followed each hit with a shout of "Take That!", and then again, "Take That!" Robbie remembered it well when we met up at the *Soccer Aid* charity event he organised in May 2006. He told me he really enjoyed visiting Norfolk, where he'd met lots of nice people and been able to relax. "Send my regards to all the folks back home," he said.

Robbie's visits offered a welcome release from his hectic schedule and profile with the band. Roger Kingsley also has fond memories of the time: he opened up his shop, Jonathan Trumbull, after hours a couple of times, especially for Robbie to pop in and do a quick designer clothes supermarket sweep.

The unsuspecting folk of Norwich never knew they had a pop superstar in their midst, but they all got to hear all about an episode involving our very own superstar, Chris Sutton. On the eve of his record-breaking move to Blackburn, a group of us, including Sutts' best mate Ruel Fox, went out on the town to send him off in style.

We had a few drinks in a couple of bars before finishing the night off with a visit to Hy's nightclub in the city centre. I didn't stop in the club long because it was the first day of pre-season training at Norwich the following morning. After one quick drink I said my farewells to the rest of the lads and headed home just before midnight. I grabbed a word with Chris before I left. "Watch what you get up to now," I told him. "You're in the big time now and it can be a big bad world out there. Be careful what you do, and who your friends are, because the papers will be looking for stories. Make sure you keep your nose clean." With that, I gave him a big hug and wished him all the best.

Little did I know, ten minutes earlier Chris had done something fairly stupid on his way to the nightclub. For some reason, he'd decided to mangle a windscreen wiper on an open-topped Mini parked outside the club. I knew nothing about it until the next morning when I turned on the radio to discover he'd spent part of the night in police cells. Someone had seen him damage the car and reported it to the police. So much for my advice.

The story made front-page headlines in the national press the next day – hardly surprising, given that it happened just a few hours before Chris became the country's most expensive player.

Obviously, a certain amount of public interest goes with the job, and I really enjoy being in the spotlight, so I'm not complaining about that, but as I told Chris, you have to be careful when in you're in the public eye. Not only do you have to behave yourself, but also watch out because there will always be blokes trying to have a pop at you just because you're a footballer. I remember going to Hy's once with Susan and some friends. It was quite near to closing time, but they let us in and let us buy a drink. We'd just sat down when this doorman appeared and abruptly told the girls to hurry up and finish their drinks or he'd have to chuck them out. I told him to calm down, that we'd only just got there and that we would finish our drinks as quickly as possible. The next thing I knew, he ran up to me and punched me in the face.

"Is that your best shot?" I said. He started pushing me, and I made to have a go back, but the girls got between us and pulled me away. They were very upset so we left. But even when we were out in the street he was still having a go. There was no logical reason for him to be so aggressive towards us. I can only suppose it was because I was a footballer. I bumped into him again a few years later. The head doorman from Time nightclub had invited us to come and see Luther Vandross, one of my all-time favourite artists, when he played at the club. When we got there, my old friend the bouncer from Hy's was on the door. My mate, the head doorman, was standing next to him, and I told him about the earlier incident.

"Oh, he'll be all right if you just apologise," he said.

"Apologise for what?" I exclaimed. I had done nothing wrong. I refused to say sorry for something that wasn't my fault and told Susan that we weren't going in. She wasn't best pleased as she had really been looking forward to the gig, but it was a point of principle.

Anyway, Sutts' move went through as planned – and then Robert Chase quietly forgot about his pledge to leave the club if Sutts did! Despite losing our star striker, the 1994/95 season didn't start badly. In fact, I kept five straight clean sheets before we beat Ipswich in the local derby at Portman Road. That was followed by a 2–1 victory over Leeds United, courtesy of a penalty save from Scotland's chief penalty-taker, Gary McAllister. Gary and I were good friends, and often ended up practising spot-kicks in training for Scotland. I saved my fair share and he put plenty past me. On this occasion I managed to outfox him, guessing correctly by diving to my left to keep his shot out.

By Christmas we were seventh and not really missing Mike Walker, Chris Sutton or Ruel Fox, who'd also left by then. Then it happened. We played Spurs at Carrow Road at 3pm on Boxing Day, losing 2–0. Straight after the game we travelled to the Belton Woods hotel near Grantham, ahead of our match at Nottingham Forest just over 24 hours later (players today don't know they're born). Keith Creamer, a part-time physio who'd travelled with us to help Tim Sheppard out, gave me a massage that night at the hotel. I never normally had a massage, it wasn't part of my usual routine but I thought it would be a good idea with two games in such quick succession. It certainly didn't bring me any luck.

We played Forest in an evening kick-off, live on Sky. Early in the first half, with the game still goalless, Ian Woan tried his luck from the edge of the box. I saved the shot with my outstretched leg, but as I fell back my studs stuck in the ground. My foot didn't move as I hit the deck, dislocating my ankle and breaking my leg in the process. It was a totally freak injury. The ball stayed in play as I lay on the floor watching helplessly as a shot flew over the bar. Suddenly Stuart Pearce was standing over me.

"What's wrong, Big Man?"

"I think I might have broken my leg."

I wasn't in particularly bad pain – more shock I guess – but I knew I'd done some damage. The fact my ankle was at right angles to my leg was a bit of a giveaway. As soon as Tim Sheppard saw my foot, he called for a stretcher and gently brought my legs together. As he did so, the ankle clicked back into place.

"Tim, it's all right. It's gone back in. Just strap it up and I'll be okay."

"No way," he replied. "You're coming off with me. You've got a broken leg and a dislocated ankle." Okay, I thought. Best I come off then.

As they carried me off I told the lads to get stuck in and make sure they got a result. I also asked the Sky touchline reporter to tell Susan I was all right. I knew she'd be watching the game on TV and be worried about me and getting a message to her via the TV would be quicker. The reporter told Richard Keys in the studio, who was good enough to pass on the news on air that I was all right. As soon as I'd asked the

reporter I could have kicked myself, if I'd been able to. I'd forgotten to say, "And please tell my mum, too!"

I was taken straight to the Queen's Medical Centre in Nottingham. They operated almost straightaway, inserting a pin into my ankle and putting my leg in plaster. But I woke up in the middle of the night in excruciating pain and started screaming for the nurses. There had been a reaction to the operation; my leg had swollen up and it felt as if it was about to explode as the plaster meant there was no way for the pressure to escape. It's one of the most painful things I've ever experienced; I felt sick with pain. The doctors told me I had compartment syndrome which happens when your muscle gets compressed by the plaster, and is fairly common after breaks. They said they would have to operate immediately as my leg was swelling up by the minute. They had to remove the plaster and cut my leg open to relieve the pressure. Having my muscles sliced open to reduce the pressure was painful, but nowhere near as agonising as it had been with the plaster on. Tim Sheppard told me they caught it just in time, an hour or so later and I could have lost part of my lower leg.

Danger over, I returned to the Norfolk and Norwich Hospital with a gaping wound a couple of days later. Robert Chase came to see me on New Year's Eve. He brought me a fantastic basket of fruit and a Radio Canary hat, with in-built radio, so I could listen to our match against Newcastle United at Carrow Road that afternoon.

Andy Marshall came into the side in my place. Funny really, I was the big Gunn with a Marshall as my deputy – I always said I played with a bunch of cowboys! Andy was a raw young keeper who still had lots to learn. He was capable of pulling off spectacular saves but also susceptible to making glaring errors, which would have defenders looking over their shoulders. When he came on for me at the City Ground, he had conceded a soft goal direct from a corner, gifting Forest a 1–0 win.

Andy made his full debut in the Newcastle match. Neil Adams and Ashley Ward scored in the first half and Ruel Fox pulled one back with a penalty, but according to the commentary on my new Radio Canary hat Andy saved everything they threw at him after that, pulling off stop after stop to play a big part in our 2–1 win. It seemed the club had an instant replacement for me. Andy was certainly sure that was the case.

He was confident enough to go on the radio afterwards and tell everyone he'd earned a win bonus for me that day. Lying flat on my back listening to him, I thought, "You cheeky sod!" I was pleased we'd won and pleased for him, but it wasn't exactly what I was expecting to hear from a rookie keeper after his first full game. There are ways and means of doing things – I just felt he was slightly arrogant.

Anyway, Andy was brought back down to earth just two days later when he and the lads got hammered 4–0 by Liverpool at Anfield. No win bonus that day then.

The club sent me and the family away to a resort in Lanzarote to continue my recuperation with a spot of sunshine. At first, the place seemed a bit like La Manga without the golf, but it soon became clear there were a few cracks under the surface. To begin with we were put in a room on the second floor, which wasn't too clever seeing as I was on crutches and they didn't have a lift. Then they switched us to a ground-floor room crawling with cockroaches, so I spent most of my time crushing them with my crutches before we moved to a third room. We finally settled down for a good night's sleep and a nice relaxing break, only to be woken up at 5 o'clock on the first morning by loud banging music. It turned out they were holding the World Aerobic Championships in the hotel. Bleary-eyed, we ventured down to breakfast, where we promptly bumped into Frank Bruno. He was in town with a huge entourage, preparing for a big fight. I felt really sorry for his sparring partners; they were being paid to train with Frank, which basically meant acting as his punchbag. I went along to watch them train one day and these poor guys had to stand there and take the best that Frank could deliver – an assortment of broken noses, cauliflower ears and black eyes. But he was more concerned about my injury than theirs.

"What have you done to your leg, Big Man?" he asked over breakfast one morning. I told him how the injury had happened, as he ladled another couple of steaks onto his plate.

He called me 'Mr Norwich' whenever we bumped into him after that. "Good mornin', Mr Norwich," he would say in his distinctive deep voice, followed by his trademark chuckle, "He he he he he."

There wasn't much to laugh about back home. After another defeat against Wimbledon, John Deehan decided he needed an experienced goalkeeper as cover and signed Simon Tracey on loan from Sheffield United. Simon replaced Andy Marshall for a midweek match at Carrow Road against Coventry City, who were struggling at the foot of the table. It was a game we really needed to win. I called the club from Lanzarote to find out the result. Dixie himself picked up the phone, much to my surprise.

"Hello, it's Gunny," I said. "How did we get on?"

"You won't believe it," he replied. "We brought in Simon Tracey to give us a bit of experience and what's he gone and done? F***ing made a right balls-up, that's what."

The gaffer explained that poor Simon had endured a nightmare debut, not least when he made a right hash of a backpass. He'd come out of his box to meet the ball, turned to take it back into his area and slipped over, allowing Peter Ndlovu to nip in and score. That slip proved costly. We drew 2–2 instead of winning the game and getting three crucial points. Andy Marshall was recalled for the next match, but the club went 11 games without a win in the Premiership, slipping from seventh in the table to 14th by the end of March. It was hugely frustrating to have to sit and watch it all being played out from the sidelines.

I went to all the home games during that time. Away trips were more difficult, although I did take in a match at Upton Park during a visit to London with the Fandabidozi Club. Two of our friends were celebrating their birthdays, and while they prepared for the party at the Ritz that evening, I headed to West Ham with Roger Kingsley. The game was five minutes old by the time we took our seats in the away section. The Norwich fans soon spotted me hobbling on my crutches and immediately launched into a spontaneous rendition of "Bryan Gunn, Bryan Gunn, Bryan, Bryan Gunn!" followed by "Gunny, Gunny, Give Us A Song!" It was really uplifting. I replied with, "Kick it off, throw it in . . ." the opening lines of 'On The Ball City', and there was a massive cheer from the fans, so much so that the players heard it and looked round to see what was happening.

We threw away a two-goal lead that afternoon. Darren Eadie and Rob Ullathorne gave us a great chance of recording a first league win since New Year's Eve, but the Hammers pulled one back. Then, at 2–1 up with only a couple of minutes to go, Andy Marshall threw the ball out quickly when he really should have taken his time. Tony Cottee pounced and ran through to equalise. Another two valuable points dropped.

By the time Ipswich came to Carrow Road for the return local derby the transfer deadline was looming. Dixie desperately wanted to bring in another experienced goalkeeper. Andy Marshall was still learning his trade, and the defence lacked confidence in him, which had a knock-on effect throughout the rest of the team. Despite that, the lads beat Ipswich 3–0 on the night, albeit it with a bit of luck when John Wark was sent off just before half-time when it was still 0-0. With eight games still to play it seemed we had a good enough buffer to avoid the drop, thanks to our good start to the season. Just another three or four points would see us safe.

In reality, the win over Ipswich was the worst possible thing that could have happened. With seemingly enough points in the bag to avoid relegation, the board felt we didn't need to splash out on an experienced goalkeeper, and the transfer deadline came and went.

As his most senior professional, John Deehan asked me to join the lads for the final away games of the season, hoping my presence and encouragement would spur them on. I duly made the trip to Arsenal where we were thrashed 5–1. It was painful to watch. The confidence was visibly draining out of the side. A few days later we were at Leicester, who were rock bottom of the table. It was a huge chance to take the pressure off. We had a couple of good penalty appeals turned down early on which was doubly disappointing, mainly because we needed the points, of course, but also because Carl Bradshaw was our penalty-taker and I had a few quid on him to score the first goal, at 33–1. We lost 1–0 at Filbert Street.

The pressure was really building on Dixie as we headed for Newcastle three days later. We travelled up to a hotel in Durham the day before the game. At the end of a light training session, our captain Jon Newsome called all the players together.

"Come on lads, this is getting serious. We really all need to pull together and we can get out of this," he said. You didn't argue with Newsome. He was a tough, committed leader, a vociferous voice out on the pitch who commanded total respect. Crooky agreed. "If we all get stuck in tomorrow we can get a result." Mark Bowen and Rob

Newman said a few words too and all the lads seemed really fired up.

I was so frustrated at being unable to play my part; all I could do was urge the guys to think positive and believe they could grind out the necessary results. We lost 3–0 at St James' Park. Peter Beardsley started the rout, spotting Andy slightly off his line and smashing a shot into the back of the net from the best part of 40 yards. It was a long, long trip home from the north-east. The bus was deathly quiet and we sat there grimly, not even brightening up when we stopped for the customary beer and fish and chips at Swineshead.

The next day, Sunday, I returned from a trip to the coast with Susan and Melissa to find a chap called Alan Smith in my driveway. He was a former policeman who'd become part of Robert Chase's backroom team.

"You should be more careful," he said, reverting to his previous life in the CID. "You left one of your kitchen windows open."

Needless to say, checking up on my home security precautions wasn't the real purpose of his visit.

"The old man would like to see you down at the ground. Now."

I could move my ankle by now as it was in a hinged walking brace, so I drove to Carrow Road, and was ushered into the chairman's room where the club directors were sitting behind a vast polished table. They smiled and thanked me for coming, but I could tell instantly why I'd been summoned. Pleasantries dispensed with, the mood was distinctly serious – ominous, even.

They wanted to know my views on John Deehan and whether I thought he should continue as manager. I liked Dixie a lot. I had held enormous respect for him right from the day he arrived at the club. He had brought a lot of good ideas and techniques to the training ground and played a key part in the success we had under Mike Walker. He'd also helped me a lot after Francesca's death, especially in that one-on-one training session right after we lost her. He handled that situation magnificently, for which I had, and still have, the utmost gratitude. I was unequivocal in my response.

"Yes, I think you should stick with John and see it through to the end of the season. He's a great man and the players had a meeting in

Durham when everyone seemed to be right behind him. We all feel we're in this together and we should stick together to get out of it." Then I left.

The next morning Gary Megson told us Dixie had been fired. To say I was surprised and disappointed is an understatement. I'd stood up for John, but I was clearly in a minority. I later discovered that some of the other senior professionals were also summoned for their views. I never spoke to any of the other lads about what they said to the board, not at the time, nor since. Dixie knew I'd spoken up for him. I think one of the directors, Jimmy Jones, would have probably told him. Dixie sent me a message via our chief scout, John Benson, to let me know how grateful he was. Sadly, it hadn't been enough.

Gary Megson took over for the remaining five games. I had played with Meggy and we enjoyed the occasional game of golf together. As a manager, he played the game from the touchline, hitting every pass and shot himself, encouraging, ranting and inspiring his players. He was a nice guy, with an almost impossible task. Successive defeats against Forest, Spurs and Liverpool meant we travelled to Leeds on the penultimate weekend of the season needing a win to avoid the drop.

We drove up to the Oulton Hall hotel, just outside Leeds, the day before the game. I tried not to think about what would happen if we went down. I was relying on others to do their jobs and I couldn't do anything to affect the outcome, so I had a couple of glasses of wine and drifted off into a fitful sleep.

I still shudder to recall what happened on Saturday 6th May, 1995. Ashley Ward put us 1–0 up before they got a really dubious penalty, which Gary McAllister rifled home. That really hammered home how badly I missed being out there on the pitch. I'd saved Gary's penalty earlier in the season, and felt I should have been there to face this one. I don't remember their second goal that put us 2–1 down; I do remember slumping on the bench with Gary Megson and Tim Sheppard as the ref blew the final whistle on our time in the Premiership. We were down.

I felt so empty. I couldn't stop the tears. After what seemed like an age, I dragged myself to my feet and limped over to where our players were – lying strewn on the ground, utterly exhausted and dejected. I went round, picking them up, patting them on the back and hugging them. "Come on, mate. We've got to go over and say thank you to the fans." Our supporters were once again magnificent. As we staggered over to them, Gary McAllister patted me on the back. "Hard luck, mate. You'll be back."

Thankfully, it was a sunny day and I was wearing sunglasses so nobody knew exactly what was going on behind them as I stood there applauding our fans, wondering where, and how, it had all gone so wrong. Only a few months earlier we had been one of the top teams in the country, having finished third in the Premiership and enjoyed some wonderful times in Europe. If only I hadn't suffered such a bad injury, or the club had invested in another experienced goalkeeper, we wouldn't have been in such a mess. It was an extraordinary fall from grace; one from which many supporters still feel Norwich City Football Club has never fully recovered.

CHAPTER TWENTY
Who's the Pride of Anglia?

With four defeats and a draw from his five games as our caretaker manager it was hardly a surprise Gary Megson wasn't offered the job on a permanent basis. The man charged with guiding us to an immediate return to the Premiership was another former Norwich City player. I didn't know too much about him but plenty of people told me he was a big favourite with many Canary supporters, having enjoyed two brief spells with the club during the 1980s.

Luring Martin O'Neill to Carrow Road was a real coup. The Irishman was a young, upcoming manager, who'd impressed a lot of people with what he had achieved at Wycombe Wanderers, where he'd won back-to-back promotions, taking them into the Football League and then winning the old Third Division play-off final. Martin was very much a man in demand. He'd rejected overtures from various other clubs, including Nottingham Forest where he'd made his name as a player under old Big 'Ead himself, Brian Clough.

Working with Cloughie had clearly rubbed off. Martin was a straight-talking disciplinarian, who made it clear from the start who was boss. I was on holiday in La Manga with Susan and Melissa, having recovered from my broken leg, when I got a call from Tim Sheppard.

"Martin wants you back. Right away," he said.

"Why?" I replied. "We don't start pre-season for a couple of weeks."

"He wants you to have a fitness test to make sure you're going to be ready for the start of the season."

"Tell him not to worry," I said. "I'm fit and raring to go. I'm training out here and I'm in good shape."

"I don't think he'll accept that," said Tim. "He wants you to prove your fitness before pre-season starts."

There were only a couple of days of our holiday left. I asked Tim if he'd settle for me reporting for the fitness test the moment I got back.

"A day or two isn't going to make a difference, surely?"

"Okay," said Tim. "I'll tell him you'll be back in a couple of days. Just make sure you're here."

I duly reported for training the morning after we returned from holiday. The club had just moved to its all-new training ground at Colney on the outskirts of Norwich. I was the first player to sample the state-of-the-art facilities as part of my rehabilitation under Tim Sheppard. The new training ground was first class. There was a swimming pool and a weights room with every bit of aerobic kit you could wish for, as well as a canteen and dining area which was a real bonus – we used to have to pop over the road to the pub or down to the local bakery when we were at the old training ground. Colney was Robert Chase's baby. He'd seen brilliant facilities at clubs like Bayern Munich and felt we should have the same. Can't knock him for that!

Maybe the facilities were part of the reason Martin O'Neill decided to join Norwich. I met him for the first time that day at Colney and was immediately struck by his charm. He's got that Celtic touch; the ability to engage you from the moment you meet him with a good strong handshake and warm demeanour. He's not a big person in stature but he has real charisma and personality – a really likeable bloke. Given what he'd achieved in his career with Nottingham Forest and Northern Ireland, I couldn't help but admire him as a player. After all, he'd won the European Cup with Forest and captained Billy Bingham's Northern Ireland team that beat Spain so famously in the 1982 World Cup finals.

Tim and club doctor Hugh Philips put me through a thorough fitness test. Martin then asked me to kick a few balls on the training pitch. I still had a slight pain in my ankle, nothing too bad, but a twinge all the same. Martin then asked for the doc's opinion. He assured us I would be okay come the start of the season, which was still some six weeks away. In the meantime, we were to embark on our pre-season trip to the gaffer's native Northern Ireland. Again, Dr Philips gave me the go-ahead, with a warning not to overdo things with my ankle.

No sooner had we arrived in Northern Ireland than we were given another early indication of the new gaffer's no-nonsense approach. Martin was happy for us to go out at night, but he imposed strict curfew times. If he told us to be in by eleven o'clock, that was it; one minute past eleven was simply not good enough, as a couple of the younger players discovered to their cost. Johnny Wright and Keith O'Neill were Irish lads, albeit from opposite sides of the border. One night they decided to pay a visit to Johnny's family who lived near Belfast, not far from our hotel. One of Johnny's folks offered to give them a lift back, but they arrived about two minutes late. They might have got away with it, had they not been late for training one morning earlier in the week. Two strikes and they were out. Martin sent them straight home to Norwich. It wasn't as if they'd been up to mischief. They hadn't even been to the pub. They apologised and desperately tried to explain that it was a genuine mistake, but Martin was having none of it. They'd broken the curfew and that was it; their tour was over.

My room-mate on the trip was Ashley Ward, the original GGTW, aka God's Gift To Women. Wardy was a good-looking bloke and a great centre-forward to boot. He was also a fitness fanatic, always working out and strong as an ox. He and I got on like a house on fire,

235

we had quite a lot in common. Aside from both being GGTW, obviously, we both loved golf, both had bad backs and both had links with the north-west, where Wardy hailed from. Oh yes, and we both enjoyed the odd beer.

Ashley and I joined some of the lads one evening for a couple of drinks, or 'pots' as Wardy called them in his Lancashire accent, at a local pub. We made sure we got back before the curfew and turned in for the night. Suddenly, a couple of team-mates burst into our room and ambushed us we lay in our beds. It was Carl Bradshaw and Jerry Goss – who else? Carl dived on Ashley and Gossy attacked me. They caught us unawares and gave us a few slaps, before we leapt out of bed and launched our retaliation. It was all a bit of fun and after a couple of manic minutes one bright spark – it must have been Gossy – suggested we rounded off the night with a stomach-punching contest. (Don't ask me why, it was just one of the little games we used to get up to from time to time, usually after a few beers.) There were no rules as such – just hit each other in the stomach until someone gave in. Carl challenged Wardy, while I took on God. After trading a few blows, I caught Gossy with a slightly misplaced uppercut and heard a crack. He winced: "You got me there, Big Man. You've done me." Game over. Jerry left the room, gingerly clutching his ribs.

We didn't realise the extent of the injury until the next morning at breakfast. Gossy was in real pain. To make matters worse, we had a game that day. It was a fair drive from our hotel and we stopped off en route for a snack. Gossy got off the bus, but instead of joining the rest of the lads he conducted an impromptu personal fitness test, running around the car park on his own. It was no good; Jerry was really struggling. He had little choice but to confront Martin O'Neill with the news.

"I'm sorry, boss," he said. "I can't play this afternoon."

"Why's that?" said Martin, with a puzzled look.

"I've hurt my ribs," replied Gossy.

"And when exactly did you do that?"

"It must have been in training yesterday," said Jerry.

Whether the gaffer believed him or not, I don't know, but it certainly wasn't the best of starts. Martin had his favourites and Gossy was never going to be among them from that moment. Sure enough, he never played a single game under Martin O'Neill.

Much the same applied to Mike Milligan who made the mistake of getting involved in a spot of verbal sparring with the new gaffer. Mike was a tough-tackling midfielder who prided himself on winning the ball and keeping things simple. There was nothing fancy about him: once he got the ball he'd invariably knock a short pass, backwards, sideways, whatever. But he seldom gave it away. One night on the tour we were all sat at dinner with Martin at one end of the table and Mike at the other.

"Hey, Milly," said the gaffer.

"Yes, Boss."

"Are you going to church on Sunday?"

"Why's that?" said Milly.

"Don't forget to pray for some ability!" said Martin.

We all roared with laughter. Milly muttered something under his breath.

"What was that, Mike?" said Martin. "Let's all hear it."

"Okay," said Mike, "Are you going to church on Sunday?"

"Of course," replied the boss.

"Well, you'd better pray for a personality."

There was an awkward lull: no one knew whether to laugh or not. We looked at Milly, staggered that he'd had the front to take on the boss. One of the lads quickly changed the subject and the conversation moved on. Mike, like Jerry, hardly got a look-in after that.

Martin wasn't everyone's cup of tea, but I got on well with him. He handled different players in different ways. He once strolled up to me during a training session, after I'd given someone an almighty bollocking. It was nothing new; I did it all the time as part of my normal game to keep players on their toes. Martin casually walked towards my goal, leant against a post and said, "Gunny, you are a c***, aren't you?" I looked round, not sure how to respond. "I was told a few stories about you," he continued. "It's right what they say; you are a bit of a c***."

With that, he turned and walked away. I took it as a compliment. At least I think it was. I assume he approved of the fact that I was hard on my defenders and demanded maximum effort at all times. Either that or he was playing some strange mind game.

Who's the Pride of Anglia?

Martin is incredibly knowledgeable about the game, but his philosophy at Norwich was simple: get the ball up the other end of the pitch, play in their half, get it into the box, score a goal. That's it. Equally, most of our training was basic. Nothing too technical, mainly plenty of running and a lot of fitness and strength work. Steve Walford and Paul Franklin did most of the tactical and set-piece sessions, although Martin was very much the man in charge. He liked to keep things interesting, setting little challenges to test you. At the end of training, for instance, he'd call over the losing team in a five-a-side. "See that tree over there?" he'd say. "Run there and back – in 30 seconds. Gunny, you've got 31 seconds."

That was his concession for me being a goalkeeper. It was all part of his competitive nature. He loved winners, whatever you did: five-a-sides, table tennis, keeping the ball up, whatever. If you lost, you paid a price. He wouldn't simply order a spot of sprinting as a punishment, there had to be more of a challenge to it than that, hence the 30 seconds there and back routine. It was uncanny; he had a knack of judging distances, knowing how quickly we could do it if we really pushed ourselves. The stopwatch would come out, and he wouldn't let us finish until we'd done it. There were one or two smiles on the way, but not many when it came to training or playing. Martin wanted to win. That's what really motivated him: winning.

There were other things that set Martin O'Neill apart. Every other manager I played for named his team the day before a game. Not Martin. He usually wouldn't announce his line-up until the day of the match, sometimes not until 45 minutes before kick-off. We weren't allowed to put our kit on until we were told we were playing. I think it was shades of Cloughie – a deliberate ploy to make sure we didn't take anything for granted. I certainly never assumed I was guaranteed my place and I was a regular. Before Martin's arrival the lads would get to the ground, change into their kit, have a plate of soup and then relax in the build-up to the game. Not any more. We couldn't even sort our match tickets for friends and family because we got four if we were playing, but only two if not.

Having said that, Martin had a knack of getting the best out of people. He's a great motivator. Somehow he managed to inspire everyone to give their all for him, even those who didn't appreciate his methods.

He'd get as nervous as anyone before a game, all hyperactive and really stirring us up, urging us to go out and play with passion and pride – for him and ourselves. He was a happy character, constantly building us up, never giving us the hairdryer treatment. If we weren't playing well, his half-time team talks would still be calm and focused on where we were going wrong: "We're not winning the tackles in midfield" or whatever. If we won, there would be no post-match analysis, simply a "Well done. I'll see you back for training on Wednesday." Normally players report back for training on the Monday, but Martin was rather erratic. He'd sometimes tell us not to come back until the Thursday after a win, which also acted as a great motivator. I've never played for anyone who gave us several days off together. And, as we never knew what our prize for winning would be, we were always eager to find out!

Martin wasn't an advocate of total football, he just wanted us to go out and win. His job was to get us back in the Premiership at the first time of asking, and that was what he was determined to do. If we nicked a win with a scrappy late goal it was every bit as good as a convincing 4–0 victory – and he'd celebrate the fourth goal as wildly as the first. Either way, he would come into the dressing room and hug and kiss you.

We kicked off the season with a 3–1 win at Luton, my first competitive game since the injury at Forest. I didn't have much to do, apart from picking the ball out of the net when Bontcho Guentchev scored after Danny Mills conceded a penalty on his debut. A couple of weeks later we played Oldham at Carrow Road. I tipped a shot over the bar with an acrobatic save in the last minute to help us to a 2–1 win. Martin came up to me in the dressing room and gave me a big cuddle.

"Ah, you're not a bad keeper," he said. "It's almost September and you've made your first save for me, at last." Things tended to be very personal with him.

Martin wasn't so impressed a fortnight later at Bramall Lane. We were leading 1–0, approaching half-time. The referee added on five minutes of injury time, during which they scored with what I thought was a blatantly offside goal. I was fuming as we walked off the pitch, shouting and swearing at the ref and his linesman, calling him a f***ing something or other. Mr A P Butler sent me off in the tunnel, joining D Elleray, D Gallacher and, of course, Mr J W D Gunn on the select list of referees who have given me my marching orders. I went into the dressing-room and told Martin.

"Gaffer, I think we've got a bit of a problem. I've been sent off." I said, explaining what had happened.

"Get back in there immediately and apologise," he snapped.

I knocked on the ref's door, went in and did my utmost to try and get out of it, apologising profusely. For a moment it seemed like Mr Butler was willing to reconsider. He looked towards his linesman as if to get a nod of approval. No doing; the lino shook his head. The ref had no option. "Sorry, you're off," he said.

I went back in and told Martin. He just ignored me and carried on with his team talk.

We didn't have a recognised keeper on the bench so Rob Newman took over in goal for the second half. We lost 2–1. Martin told me I was stupid and fined me a fortnight's wages.

East Anglian local derbies are something special. Forget Everton against Liverpool, Spurs versus Arsenal, or Manchester United against City; nowhere in Britain do passions run higher than games involving Norwich City and Ipswich Town. Okay, apart from Glasgow, granted. Ask anyone who's played in an East Anglian derby and they'll tell you – players like Mike Milligan who'd been there, done that in the Merseyside derby with Everton. You don't appreciate the fierce sense of rivalry between Norwich and Ipswich unless you've experienced it. In a way, it's strange: the two places are a good 40 miles apart. Nevertheless, the great geographic Norfolk-Suffolk divide, with all its historic prejudices and grudges, manifests itself every time the two clubs meet. It's all about regional pride. For 99 per cent of supporters it's the only result that matters, although this being East Anglia, where folk like to 'do different', there are a few fans in the vicinity of the border who have season tickets at both Carrow Road and Portman Road. Strange, but true.

The two derbies this season would, as ever, ooze drama and controversy. The first came at Carrow Road, where Ipswich Town's tormentor-in-chief returned to haunt them. Flecky's spell at Chelsea never really worked out and he was one of Martin O'Neill's first signings. It was an inspired move. After the trauma of relegation, bringing Robert back was a masterstroke. He's one of the most popular players ever to wear a Norwich City shirt – a huge favourite with fans. It was great to have him back, both from the supporters' point of view and for me personally. Robert was a close friend, even more so when he and his wife Jayne had been such towers of strength for Susan and me when Francesca was ill.

With a typical sense of occasion, Flecky scored with a spectacular half-volley from 20 yards out, mid-way through the second half to make it 2–0 after Jon Newsome had given us the lead. Everything was going well then, but Town staged a tremendous late rally and won a penalty. I've saved a few in my time, from great players like Ian Wright, Gary McAllister and Brian McClair, but never from John Wark. I'd say Warky was the most clinical penalty-taker I ever faced. I'd always wanted to stop one of his; I knew how good he was at taking them. We knew each other well because of Scotland trips and the East Anglian connection so I jokingly asked Warky where he was going to put it.

"To your right, Big Man," he growled, in his broad Glaswegian accent – so deep even I have trouble understanding it, especially through his big, bushy moustache. "But don't worry, you won't get anywhere near it."

Sure enough, he calmly stroked it to my right. And, sure enough, I didn't get anywhere near it.

Ipswich pushed forward for the equaliser. It was all hands to the pumps. With just four minutes left the game developed into chaos. Ashley Ward was back in the area helping defend, there was a frantic scuffle and Wardy appeared to pull Claus Thomsen to the ground. Referee Kevin Lynch pointed to the spot for another penalty. There was pandemonium as we protested against the decision. Our supporters were livid, their fans were delighted. But then I glanced over toward the linesman and noticed he wasn't up with play. He was standing level with the 18-yard box right in front of the Ipswich fans. He didn't have his flag up, but he seemed to want to catch the ref's attention so I decided to run over to see what he had to say. It was partly desperation, partly intuition, I guess.

The noise was deafening. There were about 2,000 Ipswich fans hurling all kinds of abuse at me as I stood right in front of them and asked the linesman what he'd seen. He told me it was offside. I raced back towards Mr Lynch with a big smile on my face. "Ref, you've got to have a word with your linesman," I said. "He reckons it was offside."

Mr Lynch went over and consulted his assistant. After what seemed like an eternity he blew his whistle, signalled for a free-kick and ran away from the Ipswich fans as quickly as he could. It was a very brave decision. We won 2–1.

The victory over the old enemy came in the middle of four straight wins and took us up to second in the table. Martin O'Neill was beginning to weave his magic. We were on course for an immediate return to the Premiership, or so we thought. December was about to change everything.

Our match at Filbert Street had been put back to the Sunday afternoon for live coverage on Anglia Television. Leicester City were without a manager. Among the candidates for the job was our old boss Mike Walker, whose time in charge at Everton had been short-lived. I bumped into Mike in the corridor just after the game. He was at Filbert Street to commentate on the match for Anglia. He had been interviewed by the Leicester board a few days earlier and was convinced he'd got the job. I said I'd keep my fingers crossed for him. Mike, like us, was in for a big shock.

Although we were going well, the relationship between Martin O'Neill and Robert Chase had become tense. The press had reported a difference of opinion over Martin's attempts to strengthen the squad. It was an all too familiar story. Martin wanted to buy a striker, Dean Windass, from Hull City and, according to reports, the club weren't prepared to match the asking price. It was shades of Mike Walker, all over again. None of the players realised things had reached crisis point until our pre-match meal at the hotel in Leicester, shortly before we left for the ground.

When we had all sat down, Steve Walford and Paul Franklin came in and told us they had something to say. They then hit us with the bombshell news: Martin had resigned. We couldn't believe what we were hearing. How could that possibly be the case? We were flying high, second in the league. Talk about timing, we didn't even get a chance to say goodbye – but that's football. Martin was a man of principle and obviously felt he was doing the right thing, so we just had to get on with it and lift ourselves for the match. Mind you, a couple of the senior pros weren't sorry to see the back of Martin and let out a few cheers.

At the ground, we were greeted by a media scrum with cameras thrust in our faces and reporters jostling to hear what we had to say about the shock announcement. Anglia's Stuart Jarrold shoved a microphone in my face. "No comment," I said and barged through, almost knocking him to the ground on my way to the players' entrance.

There was no time to answer, nor ask, questions about Martin. We had a game to play. "Come on lads, let's get off this beach," I urged, my favourite saying for when a job just needs doing – and quick.

Paul Franklin took over the pre-match preparations. He must have done a decent job because we got off to a flying start at Filbert Street. Darren Eadie scored after a minute, Robert Fleck made it 2–0, and it was very nearly three when Robert Ullathorne rattled the crossbar. We were dominating the game until about 10 minutes before half-time, when Mike Whitlow smashed a free-kick past me from the edge of the box to make it 2–1. That proved a turning point. Big Iwan Roberts, who was to become a big hero at Norwich a few years later, bundled an equaliser in from close range and Emile Heskey pounced on a bad backpass from Bob Ullathorne near the end to sink us with their third. It wouldn't be the last time the words 'Ullathorne' and 'backpass' would appear in the same sentence that season.

We left Filbert Street with no points, and no manager. It was a defining moment in the season. Within days Martin O'Neill was named manager of Leicester City. They went on to win promotion via the play-offs while our season fell apart. You don't have to be a genius to think what might have happened had Martin stayed. I'm convinced we would have been promoted, and you won't find many Norwich fans who disagree. It should have been us.

Four days later, we went to Bolton Wanderers for a Coca-Cola Cup tie. It was my first visit to Burnden Park since I'd had my picture taken there with Susan for the local paper, shortly after we announced our engagement. It was a scrappy affair – the game, not the photo shoot – and the tie went into extra time and then penalties. We lost the toss, which meant I would be in goal in front of the home fans. I saved kicks from Fabian de Freitas and Sasa Curcic. We also missed a couple to take the shoot-out into sudden death. Jon Newsome scored, which meant Mark Patterson stepped up to keep Bolton in the tie. He hit it hard and low to my right. I guessed correctly, threw myself at the ball and saved it. We were through, thanks to a hat-trick of penalty saves. Boy, did it feel good. I got the lads to sign the match ball, which I gave to Susan's brother Allan. Normally, Susan would have jumped at the chance of a trip back home, but by now she was heavily pregnant. Given the part I played in the thrilling climax to the match, it was probably a good thing she stayed at home.

The victory at Burnden Park was just what we needed after events at Leicester. Martin's sudden departure was a blow, but we were convinced we had the squad to go on and win promotion in the second half of the season. Who knows, we might even be on for a good cup run, too, after the win at Bolton. No such luck. Next up, in the quarter finals, it was Birmingham City. We drew 1–1 at Carrow Road, but lost the replay at St Andrews 2–1 after extra time.

Sandwiched between the two Birmingham matches I became a dad again. Angus Fraser James Gunn was born in the Norfolk and Norwich Hospital on Monday, 22nd January 1996. A son! He was a tiny baby but he had big hands and feet – all the attributes for a great goalkeeper already in place. It wasn't long before we were struck by how much he looked like Francesca. He was the spitting image, the same eyes, face, everything. If you look at pictures of Francesca and Angus as babies they look identical. I was the proud father of my very own 'Son of a Gunn', and a couple of weeks later I was also the proud captain of Norwich City.

Paul Franklin and Steve Walford followed Martin to Filbert Street, paving the way for Gary Megson to return for a second stint at Norwich. He promptly made me club skipper. I was delighted to get the armband, but it was to be a relatively brief and, in all honesty, not particularly enjoyable experience as, once again, poor old Meggy had a tough time of it. The results tailed off and we dropped to mid-table.

The supporters were far from happy with the way things appeared to be going and the protests inside and outside Carrow Road were getting more vociferous. It shouldn't be an excuse, but it definitely didn't help the players. I'm quite good at blocking stuff like that out, but not everyone is able to do that. Those dark days got even bleaker one morning in March when our skipper, Jon Newsome, and striker, Ashley Ward, were called away from training. They emerged from the manager's office with extraordinary news: they were both being sold. There and then.

We were shell-shocked. Fair enough, Jon had been linked with his former club Sheffield Wednesday, but news that a £1.5 million deal had been done still came as a big surprise, while Ashley's £1 million transfer to Derby County was a total bolt from the blue – for him and us. Both lads were stunned and really cut up. They loved Norwich and didn't want to leave. It quickly transpired the club was in such a bad way financially that the bank had pulled the plug. Jon and Ashley were fire sales. In other words, they had to go to keep the club afloat. Again, no one had seen it coming – apart from Martin O'Neill, perhaps.

Norwich City was a club in turmoil. Gordon Bennett, previously in charge of youth development at Carrow Road, was thrust into assuming control of the day-to-day affairs. He'd done a similar job at Bristol Rovers when they were in financial crisis. The supporters were becoming agitated, staging increasingly noisy protests after games, demanding Robert Chase's resignation.

We limped through the rest of the season, flirting dangerously with relegation. It was a tough time for the players, but if anything the crisis brought the dressing room together. We decided on a public show of unity ahead of the return local derby against Ipswich at Portman Road. During the week leading up to the game Carl Bradshaw and I took a set of clippers into training and shaved our heads. The rest of the boys followed suit, but one of the lads went one better on the day of the match. We were in the dressing-room, about to go out for our pre-match warm-up, when Jamie Cureton emerged from the toilet with his hair – what was left of it – sprayed bright green! We burst into howls of laughter.

"You're mad, you are," I said. "The fans are going to love you."

They did, chanting, "Green hair, Jamie's got green hair!" as we ran out. He then went even better, sparking wild celebrations after coming on as sub and promptly scoring to wipe out Ian Marshall's first-half goal. Jamie should have emerged from the match as a hero. In the event his goal, and his hair, were all but forgotten on the back of one of the most extraordinary episodes of my entire football career.

Portman Road was renowned for having one of the best playing surfaces in the land, going right back to when I went there with Aberdeen in the UEFA Cup more than a decade earlier. Not this time. It was in a terrible state; badly cut up. Having seen the condition of the pitch before the game, we specifically mentioned that we shouldn't take any chances with backpasses. "If you have to knock a ball back to me, make sure it's wide of my goal," I said.

At 1–1 we were bossing the game and pushing for the win, when Mike Milligan got the ball just inside our half. Instead of passing it forward, Milly knocked it back to Robert Ullathorne in the left-back position on the edge of the box. Robert turned and knocked the ball back to me. I must have seen it back hundreds of times since. As the backpass came towards me it hit a divot, took a couple of bobbles and jumped up to about knee height, just as I shaped up to meet it with a mighty clearance. The technique was good, the follow-through superb. Unfortunately, there was no connection. The ball went straight over my foot. I looked round in horror as it seemed to suddenly speed up. I was totally helpless as it rolled into the back of the net. I was gutted. Briefly, I remained rooted to the spot on one knee, head in my hand. Right back to my Aberdeen days, Bobby Clark, Jim Leighton and Teddy Scott had always taught me not to show my disappointment at conceding a goal – those keepers who thump the floor or kick the post in frustration never make it as they don't recover from their mistakes – so I quickly picked myself up, strolled into the back of the net and whacked the ball out to the halfway line as the Ipswich fans directed a barrage of taunts and gestures in my direction.

"Let's all do the Gunny," they chanted, gleefully, as they can-can danced their way up and down the aisles.

Poor Robert was totally bemused. He'd turned away after knocking the ball back, and was oblivious to what was happening until he heard the huge roar from the crowd. The camera focused on him as the ball nestled in the net. I'll never forget his face: a picture of total bewilderment. Mind you, I blame Mike Milligan, not him. I always wind Milly up about it. If he had passed the ball forward in the first place, like any good attacking midfielder, it would never have happened.

I went up for a couple of late corners to try to make up for my blunder as we threw caution to the wind in search of an equaliser in a frenetic last few minutes. But we couldn't score and they beat us 2–1. It was the worst moment of my career. Of all the games and all the grounds, there can't have been a worse place, or time, for me to concede the most embarrassing goal of my life. I played 477 matches for Norwich and that's the game everyone brings up, and not just Ipswich fans. It's always: "What about that dodgy goal you let in at Ipswich!" rather than: "What about that brilliant save you made in Munich!"

The local press had a bit of fun with it for a few days. I fronted up to the media the next day, happily doing interviews – well, there was no point in hiding or trying to pretend it hadn't happened. The television boys staged a reconstruction of the goal in a local park in Ipswich with the help of a few ready volunteers. Their local newspaper, the *Evening Star*, even made a badge featuring the picture of me on my knee in Bruce Forsyth pose. They turned it into a fundraiser, inviting fans to make a donation and sent the money to my leukaemia appeal, which was a nice touch. Ever since that day Ipswich fans have always given me a good reception, and I get looked after well whenever I go to Portman Road. Let's face it, there can't be many players who get a warm welcome in Norwich and Ipswich, so maybe it wasn't all bad. Bloody embarrassing, though.

CHAPTER TWENTY-ONE

Don't Call Me Fatty!

The financial crisis at Carrow Road reached a peak in the close season, when it was reported that the club was at least £5 million in debt and Robert Chase was forced out as chairman after 10 years in charge. It was the end of an era. It was also the end of Gary Megson, again, as his second stab as manager of Norwich City turned out to be just like the first – short and not so sweet.

Mike Walker took over again as manager. It was a smart move. The club had been in free-fall since his departure; there was a hostile atmosphere among the fans at Carrow Road and a sense the supporters wanted him back. Mike's return appeared to be good news for all parties. I was happy about it, having enjoyed working with him during his first stint in charge. His arrival was sure to inspire the fans and, hopefully, the playing squad, too. As I've already said, Mike is very cool, calm and collected in the way he speaks and does things – just what was needed to steady the ship.

I was entering my 10th year at Carrow Road as the 1996/97 campaign got under way and the club granted me a testimonial. We set up a committee, chaired by Keith Colman, to organise a variety of events, including my testimonial game. We approached Alex Ferguson to see if he would bring Manchester United to Carrow Road. Fergie said he would be delighted to, but only if it could be fitted in during the season. Easier said than done. Keith and I scoured the fixtures as soon as they were published. There was a gap at the beginning of November, a free weekend to cater for international matches. Keith was straight on the phone. Yes, United would come to Carrow Road on the evening of Monday, 4th November. Bingo! Better still, Fergie promised to bring a decent squad.

The season started well enough. Once again we lost only one of our first ten games in the league, including a 1–0 win over Oxford, who we played three times in the space of a fortnight after being drawn against them in the first round of the Coca-Cola Cup. We drew the first leg at the Manor Ground 1–1 and were confident going into the return at Carrow Road. It turned out to be an ill-tempered tie, to put it mildly. Neil Adams put us ahead but they equalised so it was also 1–1 at the end of 90 minutes at Carrow Road, by which time we were down to nine men. Robert Fleck was having an early bath by the time Darren Eadie got involved in a scuffle with their captain, Mike Ford. It was six of one, half a dozen of the other, but Ford was a mouthy sod and managed to talk the referee into sending Darren off. I wasn't impressed; it meant we'd have to play extra-time while being two men short.

It takes a lot to make me lose my cool on a football pitch, but Ford managed it. During the extra period, Oxford got a free-kick on the edge of our area. I grabbed the ball to give my defenders time to organise themselves. Ford ran up to me and shouted, "Get back in your goal, Fatty."

Now, I'd been called a few things in my time, but never fat. You can call me anything you like on a football pitch: a Scottish twat, lanky dickhead, whatever. But not fat. I lost it. I looked Ford in the eye and said: "I'm going to have you." He said it again: "Get back in your goal, Fatty." I was steaming. The sod went on to score and they ended up beating us 3–2. They really rubbed it in with their celebrations at the end of the game, right in our faces. I was absolutely livid as I walked off, as angry as I've ever been in my life. The boys on the bench saw how wound up I was and rushed over to try to calm me down. I tore off my gloves, turned to our reserve keeper Andy Marshall, threw them to him with my glove bag and said, "Here, hold these. I'm going to do that f***ing left-back."

I caught up with Ford in the tunnel.

"Oi! Who do you think you're calling fat?" I said.

"No, no, no," he said, clearly realising I meant business. "I didn't call you fat, I called you bald."

There were a few players in my way, but I started pushing my way through them, trying to get at Ford. John Faulkner, our assistant manager, tried to restrain me, holding my arms behind my back as I went to throw a punch. There was no stopping me though. I landed a head-butt right on Ford's nose. It wasn't a full-bloodied blow – I wasn't looking to hurt him seriously – but I did enough to let him know I wasn't going to let him get away with calling me fat. Big Matt Elliott, the massive Scottish centre-half, was standing next to us. For a moment I thought he was going to wade in to help his team-mate, but he just stood there and broke into a wry grin as if to say, "Well done, Big Man, I don't like him either." That was the end of the matter. Then again, nothing happened. No-one saw anything, because there was nothing to see, if you get my drift, partly because Mike Walker intervened when a TV crew attempted to follow us down the tunnel. Mike slapped his hands over the lens, stopping them in their tracks. Actually, Danny Casey, our ticket office manager, saw the lot and takes great delight in reminding me about it.

A month later we played Ipswich at Carrow Road, the first local derby since my infamous faux pas at Portman Road. Would the Town fans give me any stick? What do you think? I ran out for my warm-up and the Norwich supporters immediately started singing my song.

> *Bryan Gunn, Bryan Gunn,*
> *Bryan, Bryan Gunn,*
> *He's got no hair,*
> *But we don't care!*
> *Bryan, Bryan Gunn!*

Don't Call Me Fatty!

The Ipswich contingent immediately followed suit; suddenly my name was ringing out from every corner of the ground. Mind you, there were two slightly different versions. The Ipswich one ended: "He gets the ball, we score a goal, Bryan, Bryan Gunn!" Very funny. But we had the last laugh. Flecky was on fire that night. He didn't score, but he ran Town ragged, setting up Andy Johnson for the first of two goals. John Polston also scored as we beat them 3–1.

A few weeks later Alex Ferguson brought Manchester United to Norwich for my testimonial. And he brought a good squad, just as he'd promised, including Brian McClair, young Paul Scholes, Phil Neville and goalkeeper Raimond van der Gouw who'd played against us for Vitesse Arnhem before moving to Old Trafford. But, best of all, Eric Cantona agreed to come along. He was out of favour with the French team so wasn't on international duty, which was brilliant news for me. Cantona was *the* man at the time and the fact he'd promised to come was the major attraction. Steve Bruce, by now at Birmingham City, and Jerry Goss, playing up at Hearts, also agreed to make guest appearances. The tickets sold like hot cakes and the ground was absolutely packed on the night.

As part of the build-up to the United game, I was followed by a camera crew who were shooting a special feature for the TV show *Futbol Mundial*. On the day of the game I woke up on a real high. It was like Christmas only even better: it was going to be a special day, but I would be the only one getting the presents. I met a lovely old gentleman called John Mann in the morning. He was 90 years old and presented me with a painting of me in my Norwich City shirt with the Cathedral and Castle in the background. "Here we are," he said. "This is for you – you're a Norfolk boy now." I was truly touched.

My testimonial committee hired a couple of planes to bring all the United players down for the day and put them up in the Sprowston Manor hotel just outside Norwich so they could get a decent meal and a bit of kip before the game. I popped up to see the United lads that afternoon and took the painting with me.

"Look at this," I said to Stevie Bruce, in front of the *Futbol Mundial* cameras. "I bet you didn't get anything like this when you were here. It's me – Mr Norfolk!"

There was a terrific atmosphere as I walked out of the tunnel for the match, proudly holding hands with Melissa. She was just a few days' shy of her fifth birthday and looked cute, all dressed up in her little Norwich kit, with her hair in pig-tails. I got a wonderful reception as I strode out between the two teams who'd formed a guard of honour, with the City of Norwich pipe band playing 'Scotland the Brave' and 'Flower of Scotland'. My testimonial committee did a fantastic job organising the whole evening: we had circus performers, a dog display and stilt walkers, all complete with a commemorative brochure featuring a variety of touching tributes from family, friends and colleagues, past and present. I took Melissa into the centre circle, lifted her up onto my shoulders and we waved to all four sides of the ground. She absolutely loved it – her little face was covered in a big, big smile as she waved to Daddy's friends, all 21,055 of them!

Everything was going smoothly until we kicked off. The first time the ball fell to Eric Cantona a chorus of boos rang out from the fans. I couldn't work out what was going on. Then it dawned on me. Eric had been involved in a controversial challenge on our defender, John Polston, at Carrow Road a few years earlier. The fans clearly hadn't forgotten it. Even so, it was downright embarrassing to have the bloke give up his time for my benefit, only to be jeered whenever he got the ball. I felt like stopping the game, getting hold of a microphone and telling them to shut up. No need; Eric knew how to handle it. He immediately started turning on the style, entertaining the crowd with a dazzling array of back-heels and flicks. The crowd warmed to him in an instant, cheering every time he performed a trick from his marvellous repertoire. What a star.

It was a very entertaining game, but the closest anyone came to scoring against me was a Mike Milligan backpass, which I had to dive for and scramble out for a corner. I told you Milly didn't pass forward too much! I came off after 60 minutes so I'd have time to get showered and changed before making a thank-you appearance at the final whistle and was interviewed in the dressing room by the TV crew. "It's a wonderful night," I said. "All it needs now is a goal." Right on cue there was a big cheer, United had scored. They went on to win 3–0, for the record.

I went back out in time for the final whistle and shook everyone's hand as they came off. "Nice one mate. So, where's the present?" said Brian McClair. It's traditional to hand over a gift to all involved as a thank you for their time. "You'll find out soon enough, you cheeky sod!" I said. Eric Cantona made a point of coming up to me to give me a hug. "Très bien!" I said, "Top man." (I didn't know the French for that.) Then I grabbed a microphone to address the crowd from the centre circle.

"Thank you so much for your support over the past 10 great years," I said, genuinely struggling to hold back the tears. "I've really enjoyed my time at Norwich and I hope to be here for many more years."

The United players had to get back to Manchester that night, but they all came up to the players' lounge for a bit of a party first. I gave each of the players and officials a portable CD player as a thank-you gift (which Brian McClair seemed happy enough with – he gave me his shirt, which I got all the United players to sign). I had a more personal present for Fergie though, a special framed photograph of the moment I tripped him up in Gothenburg – the infamous shot which captures superbly the moment he fell into a puddle after leaping up in sheer delight at the end of the match. It's wonderful, if only for the look on the faces of everyone on the bench. Fergie seemed genuinely touched. I hope it's hanging in his snooker room at home. All in all, it was a truly amazing and hugely emotional night, but not quite perfect. There was, as Susan said in her TV interview with *Futbol Mundial*, one very important person missing – Francesca.

With the testimonial match out of the way, it was time to concentrate on Norwich City's promotion bid. Our bright start to the campaign had seen us move up to second place in the First Division table, hot on the heels of eventual champions Bolton, but things turned sour as we hit a nightmare run in December, which saw us concede 17 goals in just five games, including appalling back-to-back performances at West Brom and Port Vale. Only now do I feel able to come clean about what happened on the eve of that visit to the Hawthorns. I was working on my testimonial video, *Top Gunn*, at Anglia Television with producers Steve Aldous and Kevin Piper (my co-author on this project). We were up against a tight deadline to get it turned round in time for Christmas, just as we have been in writing this book. The plan was to knock out a few final links in a couple of hours, but it turned into an epic production, so much so that I didn't get away until nearly four o'clock in the morning – just a few hours before I was due to board the bus for the journey to the Midlands.

I had a kip on the team coach and went straight to bed when we arrived at the hotel for a few hours' sleep in the afternoon. Not the ideal preparation for an important league match. Paul Peschisolido gave us the runaround that night. At one stage he broke clean through on the edge of the box. I ran out and scythed him down in no uncertain fashion. Andy D'Urso, who'd been one of the linesmen at my testimonial a few weeks earlier, was the referee. He went straight for his pocket. I was sure I was about to receive the fifth red card of my career. But I raced up to him before he produced the card. "Hope you enjoyed the CD player I gave you for doing such a good job in my testimonial match, Andy," I said with a big smile on my face. He looked at me, paused for a moment, and produced a card. It was yellow. (I'm sure it's what he was planning, anyway.)

That was one of the few things that went well for us on the night. We had several injuries: Ian Crook ended up playing totally out of position at centre-half and we were hammered 5–1. It could have been worse; they also missed a penalty, which at least meant we didn't get hit for six. Three days later that's exactly what did happen as we lost 6–1 at Port Vale. The goals were flying past me; 11 in two games.

Mike Walker branded us all "a disgrace", and he wasn't far wrong. I said as much in the local paper, apologising to the travelling supporters for two diabolical performances in a shocking week. I went as far as to question the players' preparation in public, which was rich given what I was up to the night before the West Brom match. The players didn't give me any stick for the interview, though: they knew what I was like, shouting at them, day in, day out, in training, and they knew I would have just been trying to motivate everyone.

I was also beginning to question my own form, especially after I conceded a poor goal at Southend United when a routine shot went through my hands. We drew 1–1, so it cost us the win. The Norwich fans behind my goal groaned loudly and gave me some real stick. "Gunny, you're rubbish. Time to hang up the boots." It wasn't just one or two voices either, which you always get, it was quite a large section of the crowd.

It was horrible. It was the first time I'd ever heard them have a go at me. I'd enjoyed such a wonderful rapport with them over the years. Now they were turning on me. It hurt. So did Mike Walker's response to my performance at Roots Hall. He dropped me. I was devastated. I'd been Norwich City's number one for the best part of a decade. How could he possibly drop me?

This was a whole new experience. Okay, I'd had to make way for Jim Leighton when I was a youngster at Aberdeen and been in and out of the Scotland team a few times, but that was different. Now, I was being dropped to make way for my understudy. Mike was quick to say I still figured in his plans and that he was just withdrawing me from the firing line, but to say I was disappointed is a massive under-statement.

In hindsight, perhaps I took my eye off the ball after my testimonial. The Manchester United game was the climax of months of preparation and maybe subconsciously I rested on my laurels a bit after the success of the night. It goes to prove you can never afford to take your foot off the pedal when you're playing top-class sport for a living. Mind you, it wasn't just me, the rest of the team were struggling for confidence and form as well.

Having suffered the ignominy of being dropped, I was determined to regain my place – and my form. I worked harder than ever in training, which was just as well. Andy only played three games before he suffered a pelvic injury, and I was recalled for the trip to Crystal Palace where we lost 2–0, with a certain precocious youngster by the name of Craig Bellamy making his debut as substitute. I kept my place for five games in all, the last being a 3–2 defeat at Molineux where I damaged my shoulder. The injury ruled me out of the next game, by which time Andy was fit enough to return. He kept the jersey until the end of the season. The writing was on the wall.

CHAPTER TWENTY-TWO

Son of a Gunn 2

Heard the one about the professional footballer who turned up for his medical with a broken leg and still passed?

A week or so before the start of the 1997/98 season I received a phone call. It was a chap called Murdo Mackay, an agent from north of the border. "Bryan, how would you fancy a move to Celtic?" he said. The Hoops had qualified for the UEFA Cup and were looking to mount a serious challenge to arch rivals Rangers for the Scottish Premier League title. Murdo told me they were looking for an experienced goalkeeper as cover for Gordon Marshall. I thought about it for half a second and told him I would walk to Glasgow if I had to. It was a brilliant opportunity, provided Norwich were prepared to let me go. And if I wasn't going to start the season, I could see no reason why they would want to keep me.

I went to the Colney training ground and headed straight to the manager's office to see Mike Walker and ask him if I could go. He said he wouldn't stand in my way. I was delighted. It seemed like everything would be sorted fairly quickly.

I was like a big kid in training that morning. At the end of the session I grabbed a handful of green luminous bibs and handed them out for the five-a-sides, playing outfield and pretending I was Paulo di Canio, Celtic's star signing at the time.

The lads were off to Peterborough that night for a pre-season friendly. As far as I was concerned, I would soon be off to Glasgow. After almost 11 happy years at Carrow Road it was time to move on.

An hour later, towards the end of training, Mike came out to name his team. I was expecting him to tell me he'd put the wheels in motion for my transfer. Far from it: "Gunny, you're starting at Peterborough tonight," he said.

"You sure, Gaffer?" I said. "I thought you were happy for me to go."

"No, Big Man, you're still very much part of my plans."

I was baffled. Not an hour before, he'd given me his blessing to go. Now he was saying the opposite. I called Murdo Mackay and he confirmed Mike had told him he didn't want to let me go. What was going on? Oh well, at least it looked like I was going to be first choice at Norwich after all.

A week later Mike announced his line-up for the first league match of the season against Wolves. Andy would be starting – not me. It was another hammer blow.

"What do you mean – I thought I was still a big part of your plans?" I asked.

"I'm thinking of the future. Andy's done well enough to get a chance and I need you as cover. I'm sorry."

I was disappointed, but I suppose I could understand Mike's point of view and maybe I wouldn't have been Celtic's first choice, anyway. For all I knew they'd been offered three or four goalkeepers and I was second or third on the list. Managers are always being offered players. There was paper talk that Terry Venables wanted me at Tottenham at one stage, but no one ever contacted me about it. In fact, the only time I had a direct offer to leave Carrow Road was when Bernt Killat, the German agent who set up my deal with Uhlsport, phoned up. "I know the manager at Monaco," he said, "and I could put in a good word for you, if you like." I turned him down: I was happy at Norwich and so was my wife. We were settling in Norfolk and enjoying life. "Monte Carlo?" said Susan when I told her. "You turned down a move to Monte Carlo!"

Just to rub it in, Celtic signed Jonathan Gould. Gordon Marshall then picked up an injury in the first match of the season and Jonathan played the rest of the campaign, winning the league in the process. I always used to buy the Scottish *Sunday Mail*, turning instantly to the results page to check how Aberdeen, then Celtic, then Ross County had got on. There are several Scots in the village where we live, so I had to be up early to make sure I nabbed a copy. As the weeks went by and Celtic's points tally grew, my trips to the paper shop on a Sunday morning got later and later.

It was a difficult time for me. On match days I prepared for the game as per usual, gearing myself up in case I was involved, but after 11 years as an automatic choice, it was tough. I'm a great believer in fate, though, and a very positive person, and although the Celtic move didn't come off and I was still out of favour at Norwich, at least it gave me plenty of opportunity to hone my broadcasting skills. I joined the Radio Norfolk commentary team for home games. While I wasn't sure I wanted to be a pundit when I hung up my boots for good, it was all useful experience and gave me something else to focus on on a match day. I wasn't daft enough to think I could go on for ever, especially after suffering a broken leg and back problems. I'd had a great career and a brilliant testimonial, so I did what I've always done in my career – just move on, looking to the next opportunity.

I did play a handful of games for Norwich that season though – four to be precise – after Andy Marshall was sidelined with a thigh strain. The first was a thumping 5–0 defeat at Molineux. I came into the dressing after the game and said, "Sorry lads, the fifth goal was my fault. The first four weren't, though!"

A week later I played a blinder at Carrow Road, earning rave reviews for a Man of the Match performance in a 1–0 win over the league leaders Nottingham Forest. It was just like the old days as I produced a series of spectacular saves, including one of my all-time favourites, tipping a deflected free-kick over the bar from Pierre Van Hooijdonk. He was renowned for his swerving free-kicks and I set up a three-man wall to protect the right-hand side of my goal. I was fairly central, and the kick looked like it was heading straight for me until it took a wicked deflection off the wall and veered towards the top right-hand corner. I managed to move my feet quickly and scurry across, flicked up my hand and scooped it up and over the bar. As I told the press at the time, it goes down as one of my top-ten displays for Norwich. It was the first time Angus had come to watch me play, dressed in a replica of my bright orange keeper's top with 'Gunn 1' on the back, shortly before his second birthday. A few days later we beat Sunderland 2–1, which turned out to be my last ever match at Carrow Road.

Then I played my final match for Norwich City at Crewe's Gresty Road. It was an inauspicious way to end my Norwich career, losing to an own goal by our Norwegian defender Erik Fuglestad who gave me no chance as he sliced an attempted clearance into the net. Andy recovered from his injury and was recalled for the next game.

I got another call from Scotland a few days later. This time it was Alex McLeish, my former Aberdeen team-mate, now manager at Hibernian. The Hibees were really struggling, rooted to the bottom of the SPL. Their Icelandic goalkeeper Ole Gottskalksson was having a torrid time and Alex was looking for an experienced pair of hands to help him out. It was an opportunity to prolong my playing days and they were going to match my Norwich wages.

This time Mike didn't stand in my way; I was allowed to go to Easter Road – on loan for the rest of the season. I packed my bags, booked a flight from Norwich to Edinburgh, and headed north. No sooner had I arrived in Scotland than Hibs discovered a cock-up on the administration side. They'd already filled their quota of loan players. But Alex McLeish was desperate for me to sign and, rather than let the deal fall through, he asked me if I would consider making the move on a permanent basis. "This is really embarrassing, Big Man," he said, "It's the only way we can make it happen. If not, we'll have to send you back."

I wanted to go. Now it was down to Norwich City. They were prepared to let me go, but wanted an 'undisclosed' transfer fee for me, which I believe was around £25,000. I thought it was unreasonable. My contract was up at the end of the season, and Norwich weren't likely to renew it. The club were in dire financial straits, but Hibs didn't have a lot of money to play with either.

I suggested we met halfway. Chief Executive Gordon Bennett wasn't going to budge: it was £25,000 or the move was off. After much to-ing and fro-ing, Hibs paid up and that was it, I was no longer a Norwich City player, but I had become Hibernian's number one keeper.

I signed for Hibs until the end of the season. I didn't think much further forward than that. It was February 1998. All I wanted to do was help out an old mate, to do my bit in Hibs' fight against the drop. If things went well, there might be a contract at the end of it, but that could wait for now. Fortunately, there was a daily flight from Norwich to Edinburgh, so I commuted for a couple of months. I flew back when I could; Susan came up every fortnight and also brought Melissa and Angus up during the school holidays.

I played 12 games for Hibernian, including an Edinburgh derby against Hearts in which my former Scottish team-mate, John Robertson, scored a free-kick against me. It was a record 50th Edinburgh derby goal. The game was played in blizzard conditions, and I remember barely being able to see the ball as it came through the snow. We went on to win 2–1 and the Hibs fans were going mad. It's a great memory from my short time at Easter Road, and felt almost as good as beating Ipswich in the East Anglian derby.

There was also a memorable match towards the end of the season at Celtic where, of course, I might have been playing regularly if things had turned out differently at the start of the campaign. It was a daunting place to go at the best of times, especially for a club struggling against relegation and even more so knowing that Celtic could clinch the title with a victory against us. It was top versus bottom. The champagne was on ice at Celtic Park and everyone was expecting it to be cracked open come the final whistle.

Everybody except Alex McLeish. He had a plan. As part of their pre-match routine, the Celtic players would gather in the middle of the pitch before kick-off for a team-bonding huddle. It really got the crowd going, and the sound of 60,000 manic Celtic fans roaring their team on can be pretty intimidating, believe me. We needed to shut them up, and Alex suggested we do a Haka, just like the New Zealand rugby team.

As the Celtic lads went into their pre-match huddle a massive roar rang out around Celtic Park. Our captain John Hughes, a former Celtic player, called us together: "Come on lads, it's Haka time!"

We made our way to the halfway line, faced our opponents and started shouting and screaming in their direction, jumping up and down, stamping, punching the air and generally making all sorts of noises and silly movements. It worked. The crowd suddenly went quiet and the Celtic players looked at us as if to say, "What the bloody hell is going on here?" We could see our little stunt had really unnerved them. We followed it up with an outstanding defensive performance and held Celtic, Henrik Larsson and all, to a goalless draw. The champagne would have to remain on ice a bit longer.

It was a tremendous result given Hibs' plight at the time, and gave us an outside chance of beating the drop with two games to play. Defeat against Dundee United the following week sealed our fate though; we were destined for the First Division.

Despite relegation, I'd enjoyed the dozen games I played for Hibs. I struck up an immediate rapport with the fans and was delighted when Alex McLeish offered me a new contract. The problem was, Alex wasn't in the position to offer me any more than a year. I needed more security than that to justify moving the family, lock, stock and barrel, from Norfolk to Scotland. It was a major commitment.

I took the issue up with Hibs' managing director, Rob Petrie, who was renowned, like all good Scotsmen, for keeping a tight rein on the purse strings. The negotiations went on until the night before I was due to report for pre-season training.

"Look Rob," I said. "This is a massive move for me. I'm prepared to sell my house and move my family to Edinburgh. Give me a two-year contract and I'll be up there on the first flight out of Norwich tomorrow. I tell you what, I'll even pay my own air fare." He must have admired my commitment because then, and only then, did Rob agree. I could have two years.

I kept my part of the bargain and bought the first flight out of Norwich the next morning, but moving away from Norfolk wasn't going to be as easy. It was home. Our children were born there and, of course, Francesca is buried there. But it was time to start the next chapter in our lives, to move on. I signed a contract, subject to a medical. (In the rush to get things sorted with the initial move, we hadn't got round to such trivial things as medicals.)

We sorted out a school for Melissa and I took her up to Edinburgh for the start of the new term. She lived in a flat with me in Stockbridge while Susan stayed in Norfolk with Angus to take care of things like selling the house. It worked out nicely because I was able to drop Melissa off at school in the morning before I went to training and pick her up again in the afternoon.

My medical was booked for the end of the first week of pre-season. On the morning of 7th July I went into training as normal. After some running and general fitness work we played a game, during which I came out to punch a cross clear and collided with Peter Guggi and Paul Tosh. We landed in a heap, falling on top of each other. I went to get up, but my leg promptly collapsed underneath me and I fell back to the ground. It was the same leg I'd broken at Nottingham Forest.

Alex McLeish drove me straight to the local BUPA hospital, where I was due to have my medical. Strange as it may seem, they went ahead with the examination. I had X-rays on my hands, knees, back and legs. Guess what? They confirmed I'd broken my leg, but the doctor said it wasn't as serious as the first break. Apart from that, I was in good shape – I actually passed the medical in plaster!

I called Susan from the hospital. She had to run in from the driveway to answer the phone because she had been outside supervising the loading of our furniture into the removal van.

"You'll never believe what's happened. I've only gone and broken my leg!"

Susan thought I was joking. I assured her I wasn't.

"Should I stop the furniture van?" she asked.

"Don't be stupid, I've got a two-year contract and we're moving to Edinburgh whatever happens."

So Susan and Angus finally joined Melissa and me in Edinburgh. I missed the start of the season, obviously, but it wasn't too long before I was able to return to light training. When I got to the stage of kicking a ball again something wasn't quite right, however. There was a pain in my leg. I assumed it would improve, but it didn't. I worked as hard as I could to regain full fitness, but it was no good, my leg just didn't feel right.

Aside from my injury, we were enjoying life in Edinburgh. Angus started nursery school at Edinburgh Academy while Susan got a job in a designer clothes shop and began to make new friends. All was going well, then we hit a problem with the house sale back in Norfolk. Having agreed a price, the prospective buyer started to muck us about, claiming the survey had shown a problem and trying to get us to reduce the price. We weren't going to be messed around. We pulled out of the sale and put the house up for rent. Perhaps it was fate. With my broken leg and the house sale falling through, we started to wonder if the move to Scotland was meant to be. We had planned to buy a house in Edinburgh, but now we were having second thoughts. Perhaps someone, somewhere, was trying to tell us something.

I continued to have problems whenever I kicked a ball. The surgeon told me my leg had effectively healed and couldn't guarantee when, or if, the pain would disappear. Still, it just didn't feel right. The club and I came to a gentlemen's agreement whereby they were prepared to sign me off and pay up the first year of my contract provided I didn't claim the second year's money, which I thought was fair. I was 35. After two broken legs and with an arthritic back, my body was telling me it was time to quit. The game had been good to me; I'd played more than 500 matches in total for Aberdeen, Norwich and Hibs, and picked up some wonderful memories along the way. And I'd achieved my childhood dream of going to a World Cup with Scotland. I'd enjoyed a great career and had absolutely no regrets.

Gordon Bennett had always told me there would be something for me at Carrow Road if ever I decided to return. I'm not sure he had the manager's job in mind, but that's exactly what I applied for while I was considering my future at Hibs. Mike Walker had been sacked at the end of the 1997/98 season, much to the surprise of many people, including me. I decided I had nothing to lose, so sent off an application. Fair enough, I didn't have any managerial experience, but that wasn't a problem as far as I was concerned; I would appoint an assistant to help me on that score.

I received a letter from the club politely informing me I hadn't got the job. They were looking for someone with more experience to guide them through somewhat troubled times. Steve Bruce was in the running for the job. I rang him and told him I would love to be his assistant, and he agreed to take me on if he got the job. After weeks of speculation it eventually went to another Bruce – Rioch.

That summer I also got a call from Mel Henderson, a sports reporter in East Anglia, suggesting I might like to throw my hat into the ring for the vacancy at Colchester United. I spoke to one of the Colchester directors, who suggested I approach the club's chairman, "Peter Hird". I made a point of checking how to spell his surname, as a matter of courtesy, and sent off a fax to say I was interested in the job at Layer Road.

Again, I received a reply thanking me for my interest, but pointing out that they too were looking for someone with experience. At the end of the letter the chairman added a line saying: "Please note the spelling of my name – Heard." His fellow director had misinformed me. Who knows, I might at least have got an interview if I'd spelt his name right.

After those two polite rejections, I contacted Gordon Bennett. Good as his word, he said there was an opening in the commercial department at Carrow Road and they were looking for a new business manager, someone to attract new sponsors. Gordon and Andrew Cullen, director of sales and marketing, decided to offer me the job. I'd already been offered a similar role at Hibs. Edinburgh is a great place, but Norwich is home, and the chance to move back to Carrow Road was too good an opportunity to miss. It was a big change of direction, but I relished the prospect of getting out and about among local businesses and the community.

It was wonderful to be back in Norfolk. Everything fell nicely into place. Melissa returned to her previous school and Angus started there too. We'd put his name down in case we decided to move back, which was just as well. It worked out a treat with the house too. We'd let it to Michael Watt, a young goalkeeper who joined Norwich after I left. He played a few games but his contract wasn't extended after the first year, so he moved on at the same time as we were returning to Norfolk. It was obviously meant to be.

As for Hibs, Ole Gottskalksson returned to form and helped them win the First Division and promotion back to the Premiership at the first attempt under Alex McLeish, which I was delighted about.

I miss playing football, of course I do, but not nearly as much as I had thought I would. I'm incredibly proud to be part of what's been happening at Norwich City Football Club over the past few years. We celebrated the club's centenary in 2002, and two years later won the First Division title and promotion back to the Premiership at last: all great occasions which I've been lucky enough to be involved in.

Delia Smith and her husband Michael Wynn-Jones saved the club from financial disaster, becoming the major shareholders in 1997, and they have done a fantastic job, transforming Carrow Road into a modern, fashionable stadium. As well as investing millions of pounds into the playing side, they've spent a lot of their own money creating a variety of outstanding facilities, including no fewer than five top-class restaurants, which are routinely full to capacity on match days.

The club paid me a huge compliment when they refurbished the old players' lounge, turning it into a members' club for supporters to enjoy before and after each match. Delia invited me to a meeting just before it was due to re-open. "Bryan, we've been talking about what we should call the new members' club. Would you mind if we named it after you?"

"What do you mean?" I asked.

"We would like to call it the Gunn Club. We think it's a great idea," said Delia.

I felt honoured by the gesture and very, very chuffed. Part of my role on match day would be to interview the Man of the Match on the stage after the game, and host presentations and photographs with our sponsors. We've had all kinds of people in the Gunn Club, including the actor Stephen Fry and former Home Secretary Charles Clarke, who are both big Norwich fans. We've even had visits from Curly Watts from *Coronation Street*, who's a Manchester City fan, and Tony Blair's former right-hand man Alistair Campbell, who supports Burnley. We also had Mylene Klass, from the band Hear'say, who's a local girl. She was a guest on BBC Radio Norfolk. Her mini-skirt was so short that when she climbed into the radio commentary position we had to wrap a blanket round her waist to retain her modesty.

I was promoted from new business to sponsorship manager, a position I held for seven years, but in the spring of 2006 I took up a new post as the club's community ambassador. It means getting out and about as the face of Norwich City at all manner of events, from school presentations and community projects to corporate functions, promoting the club and all it stands for in the area – oh, and playing the odd round of golf! I just love meeting people and the job suits me – and the club – down to the ground.

I got plenty of practice for the job when I spent a year as Sheriff of Norwich in 2002, the club's centenary season and also the 10th anniversary of the Bryan Gunn Leukaemia Appeal. I had a busy year dressing up in the civic chains and robes, representing the city at a variety of events, around 350 altogether. I reckon I had more Christmas dinners that year than some people have in a lifetime. The Sheriff is the understudy to the Lord Mayor. But while he went off to places like our twin city of Rouen, Rome and the Vatican, I seldom ventured beyond the old city walls. Mind you, I did get to meet the Queen when she visited the Norwich City centenary exhibition at Norwich Castle. I waited in line at the castle, reminding myself of the correct etiquette by repeating to myself, "Hello Ma'am, which rhymes with spam."

I told the Queen I would be attending her garden party at Sandringham that evening and then pointed to part of the exhibition featuring me during our European cup run. Her Majesty was more interested in my robes and chains, which I have to admit were pretty spectacular: purple robes edged with fake ermine and lined with fur and a Napoleonic hat and white gloves. Beats anything that Charlie Nicholas used to wear!

"Wear them again tonight at Sandringham," she said. "Then I'll be able to spot you." The fact I was 6'4" with a goatee beard and bald head clearly hadn't registered. I didn't see her at the party, but maybe she didn't spot me after all, as the entire Norfolk 'chain gang', as we mayor-types called ourselves, were there.

I was also invited to a garden party at Buckingham Palace as Sheriff. Like many people I brought home a souvenir of my visit. Nothing fancy, just a couple of plasters. I had bought a new pair of shoes for the occasion and had to visit the medical tent because my feet were in agony from blisters.

Being Sheriff was a wonderful opportunity to see a wide spectrum of life. During my year of office the club was awarded the freedom of the city and I was also immensely proud to be involved in the subsequent civic ceremony at St Andrew's Hall. As I tell people, I did everything from opening a skateboard park to meeting the Queen – and she only fell off twice!

It was an immense honour to spend a year as Sheriff. My mum and dad had come to the inauguration ceremony in May 2002, and were obviously proud as punch to see me in all the regalia. Sadly, Dad died at Christmas that year. He was always there for me when I was young, doing everything he could, running me around from one game to another – just like me with Angus now. Being a parent has also helped me appreciate just how proud Dad was of what I had achieved, something I didn't realise at the time. Although he always said he thought my brother Alan was the better goalkeeper, I know he was very proud of me, as I am of my own family.

Nothing my incredible wife does surprises me any more, but she continues to constantly impress me. She is determined and ambitious, warm and compassionate, a fantastic wife and mother. She resumed her art studies again in 2000 and eventually graduated from the esteemed Norwich School of Art and Design with a first class BA Hons in Fine Art. Since then she's gone from strength to strength, winning the Bishop's Art prize in 2003 and, I'm proud to say, the prestigious European Sovereign Art Prize in 2006. If she spent years as Mrs Bryan Gunn while I was in the spotlight, I reckon I am now officially Mr Susan Gunn, as my in-demand wife jets off to art exhibitions in Venice and high-powered Arts Council meetings. I've been to the Venice Biennale and many art events with her, but occasionally I have to be at home to look after the kids as the 'primary parent'. And I love it.

Melissa and Angus are blossoming into wonderful people. Melissa is 14, and showing signs of following in her mum's footsteps. She's grown into a very pretty, six-foot-tall teenager, and has already appeared on the catwalk and featured in the London finals of a national hair competition. She's very down to earth and has a job waitressing in a local restaurant to earn a bit of extra pocket money. She's also a bright girl, very adventurous and has an artistic streak, although we reckon she's more likely to become a cracking defence lawyer because, like most teenagers, she's very good at arguing!

Melissa's sporty and plays in goal for Framingham Earl High School. She's very brave and happily dives at strikers' feet to save a goal. As does Angus, now 10. He's a goalkeeper as well, just coming up to his third year at the Norwich City Academy. Funny that both of them should follow in Dad's footsteps, but all the more inevitable, I guess, when you consider that Susan also used to play in goal for her school hockey team.

Angus went to his first trial with Norwich as an outfield player but Colin Watts, the youth development officer, suggested he gave it a try between the posts. He took to it like a duck to water. Can't think why. I tend to give him a few hints and tips on a match day, nothing heavy, just a little advice here and there which I'm pleased to say usually sinks in. He's in good hands at the academy. I'd love to see him go on to play for Norwich and, ultimately, become an international. There could be a few arguments on that score, though, as he's determined to represent England rather than Scotland. Perhaps we could get lawyer Melissa in to settle the debate.

Angus is one of those people who seems to have the golden touch with any sport – cricket, basketball, tennis, golf, you name it – but he's also great at drama (given that his dad loves any excuse to dress up I suppose that's inevitable too!), and has had major parts in school plays. He's a lovely lad, with a great set of friends. I'm so proud of them both.

My job as Norwich City FC's Community Ambassador gives me more time to spend with my family and it's wonderful to be able to take a back seat and watch them all blossom.

Francesca, of course, will always be in our thoughts, and we will continue to raise funds in memory of our lovely daughter. We took things onto another level in 2006 when we launched the Gunn Appeal Parent Support line, GAPS (www.gaps.uk.com), nationally, at the House of Commons. We had identified a need for a specialist helpline for anyone connected with the suffering caused by child cancer or leukaemia. It was originally launched in the Norwich and Eastern region in 2004. We were delighted to roll it out to the rest of the country, with assistance from Dr Ian Gibson who's been a big supporter from the beginning. It's due to expand to Scotland in the near future.

Back in 1995, I took special pride in being awarded an Honorary Fellowship from the University of East Anglia, in recognition of our fundraising efforts in the region and the setting up of the Francesca Gunn Laboratory at the university. Whilst I received the award personally, I feel strongly that I accepted it on behalf of absolutely everyone who has supported the appeal in whatever shape or form.

We started the Bryan Gunn Leukaemia Appeal with the aim of raising a few thousand pounds in memory of Francesca. At the time of writing, the fund stands at somewhere in the region of £800,000, which hopefully will be boosted by sales of this book. It would certainly be great to reach the £1 million mark. It would be even better to find a cure for all forms of childhood leukaemia and wipe the disease out for good.

That would be the greatest legacy to Francesca.

MY ALL-TIME
TOP TEN SAVES

1. v Adolfo Valencia – Bayern Munich 1 Norwich City 2 (1993)
2. v Terry Hurlock – Millwall 2 Norwich City 3 (1989)
3. v Pierre Van Hooijdonk – Norwich City 1 Nottingham Forest 0 (1998)
4. v Ian Wright – Arsenal 1 Norwich City 1 (1993)
5. v Tony Cottee – Everton 0 Norwich City 1 (1993)
6. v Willie Miller (deflection) – Aberdeen 3 Hibs 0 (1986)
7. v Dean Saunders – Derby County 0 Norwich City 0 (1991)
8. v Tim Breaker – Norwich City 2 West Ham 1 (1991)
9. v Gary McAllister – Norwich City 2 Leeds 1 (1994)
10. v Mark Walters – Norwich City 2 Liverpool 2 (1994)

MY TOP TEN
PENALTY SAVES

1. v Brian McClair – Manchester Utd 2 Norwich City 1 (17th October 1987)
2. v Brian McClair – Manchester Utd 1 Norwich City 2 (26th October 1988)
3. v David Platt – Aston Villa 3 Norwich City 1 (3rd December 1988)
4. v Dean Saunders – Derby County 0 Norwich City 0 (23rd February 1991)
5. v Brian Burrows – Norwich City 1 Coventry 1 (16th January 1993)
6. v Ian Wright – Norwich City 1 Arsenal 1 (3rd March 1993)
7. v Peter Beagrie – Man City 2 City 0 (24th September 1994)
8. v Gary McAllister – Norwich City 2 Leeds Utd 1 (8th October 1994)
9. v Andy Hunt — WBA 1 Norwich City 4 (21st November 1995)
10. v Jonathan Hunt – Norwich City 1 Birmingham City 1 (10th January 1996)